Who Owns Native Culture?

WHO OWNS NATIVE CULTURE?

Michael F. Brown

HARVARD UNIVERSITY PRESS

Cambridge, Massachusetts
London, England

Library of Congress Cataloging-in-Publication Data

Brown, Michael F. (Michael Fobes), 1950–
Who owns native culture? / Michael F. Brown.
p.   cm.
Includes bibliographical references and index.
ISBN 0-674-01171-6 (alk. paper)
1. Indigenous peoples—Legal status, laws, etc. 2. Intellectual property. 3. Cultural property—Protection of. I. Title.

K1401.B79 2003
346.04′8—dc21   2003044978

Contents

Illustrations

Illustrations

Preface

In the late 1980s, ownership of knowledge and artistic creations traceable to the world's indigenous societies emerged, seemingly out of nowhere, as a major social issue. Before then, museum curators, archivists, and anthropologists had rarely worried about whether the information they collected and managed should be treated as someone else's property. Today the situation is radically different. Scarcely a month passes without a conference examining the ethical and economic questions raised by the worldwide circulation of indigenous art, music, and biological knowledge.

In 1997 I set out to learn how these questions were being addressed in specific places. I went to Australia, and later to the American West, to interview participants in disputes, examine official documents, and gauge local sentiment in less formal ways. My research eventually expanded to include debates over the legal status of sacred sites on public lands. The parallels between sacred sites and intellectual property proved illuminating. Both involve competing claims to a public resource and diverging visions of how that resource should be treated. Both raise challenging questions about the legal standing of native societies within pluralist democracies. Under close scrutiny, these conflicts are more complex than they seem at first glance—and in a world of short attention spans and media sound bites, a first glance is all that most citizens get.

My interest in moral and economic claims on culture grew out of a range of research projects in Latin America and the United States. The earliest dates to 1976, when I began conventional ethnographic fieldwork among the Aguaruna, a native people of the Peruvian Amazon. My two years in Aguaruna villages were a life-changing apprenticeship. I felt privileged to live with Indians who retained pride in their identity even as they modified tradition to meet the challenges of Amazonian colonization. During those years, I crossed paths with several spiritually inclined travelers who had come to the Upper Amazon to consult Aguaruna shamans, widely known for their knowledge of sorcery and healing. The sometimes bemused shamans were happy to receive the fees paid by these affluent tourists, even changing their ritual practices slightly to accommodate outsiders' expectations. Only later did I see that these chance encounters were the leading edge of an intensifying global interest in indigenous spirituality and healing arts.

In the 1990s, turning to research opportunities closer to home, I spent several years studying facets of the New Age movement. It was impossible to track the New Age without noticing announcements for weekend workshops led by self-identified shamans, some claiming to be teachers of Native American spirituality. When reading polemical essays that denounced these New Age Indians as poseurs, blasphemers, and "plastic medicine men," I was struck by the complexity of the ethical issues raised by cultural imitation. After all, it is hard to think of a religion that hasn't adopted elements from other faiths. Why should the incorporation of native symbols into new religious forms be condemned as theft when native peoples themselves have selectively appropriated Christian symbols and ritual practices? Curiosity about cultural flows in the sphere of religion drew me to debates about movements of knowledge in other fields, including art, music, and medicine. This book is my attempt to bring these diverse strands together in a unified analysis.

As an anthropologist, I may be suspected of special pleading when I offer a partial defense of information gathered under circumstances that fail to meet today's ethical standards. The chapters that follow confront troubling moments in the history of my own profession and others, with special emphasis on insensitive use of texts, photographs, and sound recordings that never should have been subject to wide circulation. Today native nations properly insist on their right to determine who conducts research among them and to what end, a principle that is fully acknowledged and embraced by working anthropologists. At the same time, it is important to call attention to the difficulty—the near-impossibility, in some cases—of recapturing information that has entered the public domain and determining its proper owner. Sorting out the unhappy legacies of the past will require years of discussion and pragmatic compromise.

Because my project involved multiple research sites and contacts with people in various parts of the world, I was unusually dependent on the kindness of strangers. In the Acknowledgments, I thank those who guided me through their social or occupational worlds and provided other valuable assistance. Some debts have special standing. My wife, Sylvia Kennick Brown, and our daughter, Emily, put up with my research-related absences, collaborated cheerfully in a sabbatical relocation, and continually reminded me, each in her own way, that life consists of more than the single-minded pursuit of scholarship. I also wish to honor the memory of a friend and former teacher, Alfonso Ortiz (1939–1997). A Tewa Indian from San Juan Pueblo, New Mexico, Ortiz introduced me to the Southwest thirty years ago and strongly influenced my decision to become an anthropologist. His pride in the achievements of Pueblo peoples was inspiring, as was the almost visceral pleasure he took in the beauty of their religious life. He fought tirelessly for the rights of American Indians throughout his career in anthropology, a commitment that might have led him to disagree with my attempt to weigh indigenous claims of cultural ownership against the broader society's need for open communication. I like to think that we would have settled the matter as we had resolved differences in the past, over bowls of fiery New Mexican food—a duel from which, as always, he would have emerged flushed, perspiring, and victorious.

Williamstown, Massachusetts
January 2003

Author's Note

The terms "native," "indigenous," and "aboriginal" are used interchangeably throughout this work. In some countries one may be strongly preferred over the others; conventions about their capitalization differ as well. Rather than impose artificial consistency, I have followed local usage when discussing specific countries and American usage everywhere else. In deference to the everyday speech of native people in the United States, "Indian" and "American Indian" are used more frequently than "Native American," although the latter has the advantage of inclusivity, encompassing Inuit and Aleut peoples of Alaska as well as the aboriginal population of the lower forty-eight states.

Who Owns Native Culture?

Introduction

Route 2, the state highway that links the northern half of Berkshire County, Massachusetts, to the Connecticut River Valley and Boston, is known for scenic views of the Berkshire Hills and Vermont's Green Mountains. The westernmost leg of Route 2, between Greenfield and Williamstown, where I live, is called the Mohawk Trail. It is said to follow the path used by Mohawks and other Indian peoples, and later by European settlers, as they moved between central Massachusetts and New York's Hudson Valley. Scattered along the highway are several "Indian trading posts," rambling places stocked with moccasins, beaded belts, dream-catchers, Indian princess dolls, and an occasional work of serious Native American art. The shops' exteriors are time capsules from an earlier era of automotive tourism. Crudely painted tipis, totem poles, thunderbirds, bison, and statues of Indian chiefs embellish the parking lots. The anachronism is charming as long as one ignores the jumbling together of distinct traditions and the casual stereotyping of American Indians.

To the best of my knowledge, the Mohawk Trail's trading posts have yet to feel the sting of public denunciation. Elsewhere, however, native leaders and indigenous-advocacy organizations have embarked on a global campaign to assert control over elements of culture that they consider part of their patrimony: art, music, folklore, even landscapes regarded as sacred. A sense of the scale and rhetorical tone of this process of cultural recuperation is conveyed by the following events, all of which took place in 2002:

• In Australia, Aboriginal militants removed the coat of arms from the Old Parliament House in Canberra, declaring that images of the kangaroo and the emu on this national symbol were the cultural property of Aboriginal people. "We have now reclaimed our sacred emu and kangaroo from the Coat of Arms of the colonizers," the group announced. In a related incident, an Aboriginal activist demanded that the national airline, Qantas, should no longer be allowed to use the kangaroo as its logo because this animal is the intellectual property of Aboriginal Australians.

• In Peru, a group of Andean farmers publicly denounced two U.S. patents issued to an American firm that processes and markets extracts of a traditional Andean crop plant, *maca* (*Lepidium meyenii*, a member of the mustard family). The firm's preparation based on *maca*, a species that has been used in the Andes for centuries to increase the fertility of livestock, is being sold as a natural product that enhances human sexual performance.

• In India, the government inaugurated an electronic database that provides comprehensive inventories of traditional Indian healing methods and plant medicines. An example of "defensive publishing," the database is intended to make it more difficult for researchers in the developed world to register patent claims that exploit traditional Indian medical knowledge.

- In the online world, fans of the "Bionicle" line of toys sold by the Danish firm Lego found their website repeatedly disrupted by a hacker claiming to be Maori. In a message posted before the disruptions, the hacker denounced the use of Maori words to name individual figures in the Bionicle line.

- In New York, the Rockefeller Foundation announced a funding initiative to promote greater concern for the intellectual property interests of "marginal constituencies," including indigenous peoples. As part of the new program, the foundation invited a score of indigenous experts to its conference center in Bellagio, Italy, to refine strategies for defending the intellectual property rights of native communities around the world.[1]

It is hard to identify a single moment when this social movement arose. For decades particular groups had quietly sought the return of religious objects acquired by museums under dubious circumstances. Here and there, the publication of formerly secret information about important rituals evoked complaints—and in a few cases, legal action—by affected communities. In the 1980s these disparate efforts gathered strength around the idea that heritage, both tangible and intangible, is a form of group property that must be returned to its place of origin, much as the excavated physical remains of Aboriginal Australians or Native Americans are repatriated from the museums and laboratories in which they have been held.

As the movement gained momentum, its rhetoric intensified. The expressions used to describe the flow of cultural elements from indigenous societies to the larger world progressed from the clinical "cultural appropriation" to "biopiracy" and "ethnocide," and then to "cultural genocide" and "the new vampires." In a book provocatively entitled *Cannibal Culture,* the art historian Deborah Root likens

Western society to a devouring beast with a heart of ice, perpetually hungry for cultural difference with which it can feed its imperial fantasies: "It is possible to consume somebody's spirit, somebody's past or history, or somebody's arts . . . The sites where this consumption takes place can be some of the most cherished institutions in Western culture: art galleries, libraries, museums, universities." Such strong language suggests a full-blown moral panic, to which the only adequate response is the imposition of formally defined, legally enforced safeguards for indigenous heritage.[2]

A common thread in these debates and denunciations is the concept of culture, which anthropologists long ago defined as the unique mix of beliefs, practices, values, and institutions shared by members of a society. Culture was an abstraction distilled from behavior and shared understandings. It served as a shorthand way to talk about the habits and attitudes that give each society a distinctive signature. It was, in other words, a useful analytical device and nothing more. But in promoting the concept of culture anthropologists inadvertently spawned a creature that now has a life of its own. In public discourse, culture and such related concepts as "tradition" and "heritage" have become resources that groups own and defend from competing interests.

Meanwhile, science and technology created a situation in which culture arguably *is* a commodity. The market's restless search for novelty turned unfamiliar folktales, art, and music into exploitable commercial resources. Beginning in the 1980s, pharmaceutical and agrotechnology firms began to search more aggressively for medicinal plants and crop varieties whose useful qualities could be privatized, at least temporarily, via the developed world's patent system. Even religion has proved vulnerable to commercial influences, as middle-class spiritual seekers in North America, Europe, and Japan enroll in workshops promising to introduce them to the religious understandings of aboriginal peoples.

Growing disquiet about the unauthorized use of elements of native cultures implicitly challenges influential academic work that celebrates the creative mixing of cultures, a process referred to as "hybridity" or "creolization." Scholars interested in hybridity call attention to the ways in which people in the developing world grab ideas, objects, and technologies from the industrial West and reshape them to suit local needs. No longer is this mixing of traditions seen as evidence of cultural decline or acculturation. Ironically, many of the peoples whose hybridity has been so enthusiastically documented become upset when it is their own culture that begins to flow elsewhere. Sometimes the objections are economic: rarely are indigenous peoples compensated for knowledge that has commercial value. More often, however, anger is fueled by fear that elemental understandings are coming under the control of others, so that native people are no longer masters of their own traditions, their own identities.

In a discussion about what it means to have an intellectual commons, the legal scholar Lawrence Lessig argues that the resources of the public domain should be considered "nonrivalrous" because they are inherently inexhaustible. We do not compete with one another when we use them. Lessig uses Einstein's Theory of Relativity as an example: one person's invocation of the theory sets no limits on anyone else's. Many elements of the world's cultural commons would appear to be similarly nonrivalrous. The adoption of religious practices by members of one community does not prevent other communities from following suit. In fact, widespread emulation of the practices only strengthens the religion's influence.[3]

Yet indigenous leaders argue strongly that the same is not true of their most hallowed ideas and rituals, which cannot diffuse to others without suffering harm. Consider the case of the sweat lodge, a rite of purification and spiritual renewal for many American Indians. Some Indians are offended when middle-class Anglo-Americans adopt the sweat lodge ritual as part of their quest for authentic spirituality. Native critics insist that practitioners who fail to observe proper sweat-lodge rules are guilty of blasphemy and cultural aggression. From the perspective of social science, the diffusion of the sweat lodge into Anglo society is threatening to Indians because it blurs the boundaries between native and non-native.

Although Internet prophets express enthusiasm about the anticipated arrival of a computer-mediated intellectual commons in which, as the journalist Charles Mann puts it, "every scrap of human culture transcribed, no matter how obscure or commercially unsuccessful, will be available to all," the stewards of indigenous cultures find this prospect unsettling, even horrifying. As a man from Oregon's Klamath Tribe told an audience of archivists and records-management professionals at a 1999 meeting in Phoenix, Arizona: "All this information gets shared, gets into people's private lives. It's upsetting that the songs of my relatives can be on the Internet. These spiritual songs live in my heart and shouldn't be available to just anyone. It disturbs me very much." The uncontrolled replication of ceremony, music, and graphic arts, which is facilitated by new electronic media, threatens to strip cultural elements of their history and undermine their authenticity.[4]

Many advocates for native rights would like to see the integrity of indigenous cultures ensured by laws that treat heritage as an inalienable resource. Proposals for new forms of cultural protection build on arguments that justify the sovereignty of native nations. Those who argue such positions hold that political sovereignty is meaningless without cultural sovereignty. The practical effect of this ferment has thus far been modest, but new forms of regulation are being considered in many parts of the world. Several countries, including New Zealand, Australia, and Panama, have implemented laws designed to protect the intangible heritage of native populations—everything from art and dance to the vocabulary of indigenous languages—and further legislation appears likely. Various branches of the United Nations have floated far-reaching heritage-protection schemes. Those who traffic in cultural information—historians, folklorists, anthropologists, museum curators, archivists—are learning to live with restrictions on access to cultural records formerly available for public use.

In this book I seek answers to questions raised by efforts to protect native heritage from commercial and non-commercial use by outsiders. To what extent can law control the movement of ideas? Does it make sense for ethnic groups to define their cultural practices as property that cannot be studied, imitated, or modified by others without permission? How far can democratic states go to provide indigenous peoples with cultural protections without violating the rights of the general public? What is the future of the public domain, which is squeezed on one side by the privatizing logic of the world's corporations and on the other by native-rights activists promoting novel forms of collective copyright? Unlike questions of monetary reparations or the return of indigenous lands, struggles over intangible resources lead to vexing questions of origins and boundaries that are commonly swept under the rug in public discussions, which tend to treat art, stories, music, and botanical knowledge as self-evidently the property of identifiable groups.

The more I learned about the current trend in intellectual property law—the drive by large media and biotechnology companies to expand copyright, trademark, and patent protections far beyond their historic scope—the more it became obvious that novel forms of cultural copyright come with substantial risks. If we turn culture into property, its uses will be defined and directed by law, the instrument by which states impose order on an untidy world. Culture stands to become the focus of litigation, legislation, and other forms of bureaucratic control. The readiness of some social critics to champion new forms of silencing and surveillance in the name of cultural protection should trouble anyone committed to the free exchange of ideas.

One lesson taught by the twentieth century and surely applicable to the twenty-first is that there is reason to be wary of totalizing solutions to complex social problems. The historian Robert Conquest has noted that our times are littered with the ruins of failed utopias that caused untold human misery. The alternative is an approach that Conquest calls imaginative realism, a willingness to accept a degree of imperfection in the interest of balance "between the individual and the community, between the desirable and the possible, between our knowledge and our imagination."[5]

A half-century ago the literary critic Lionel Trilling voiced similar opinions in *The Liberal Imagination*. Commenting on the tendency of progressive social policies to simplify and bureaucratize, Trilling worried about the loss of a "lively sense of contingency and possibility, and of those exceptions to the rule which may be the beginning of the end of the rule—this sense does not suit well with the impulse to organization." For him, the liberal imagination requires "awareness of complexity and difficulty." Recast in the idioms of contemporary debate on political pluralism, it demands a commitment to civil societies defined by distributed power and dynamic internal diversity.[6]

My account emphasizes the virtue of striking a balance between the interests of indigenous groups and the requirements of liberal democracy. This often leads to the awkward middle ground that Isaiah Berlin once described as a "notoriously exposed, dangerous, and ungrateful position." My centrist stance is inspired by what I found in many of the places I visited: thoughtful people coming together to negotiate workable solutions, however provisional and inelegant. Their successes, achieved one at a time, convinced me that grandiose, one-size-fits-all models of heritage protection are likely to hinder rather than encourage improved relations between native peoples and the nation-states in which they find themselves citizens.[7]

The general strategy that I follow in this book is to immerse readers in the moral and legal complexity of situations often portrayed as simple miscarriages of justice. The first chapter plunges directly into controversies surrounding photographs of Hopi Indian religious observances taken by a missionary early in the twentieth century. This is followed in subsequent chapters by case studies of the alleged infringement of indigenous art, religious symbols, and botanical knowledge. Then I shift the focus to conflicts over the protection and use of sites defined as sacred by indigenous communities, or at least some members of them. Sacred places, unlike intangible expressions of heritage, are rivalrous resources: one group's use of them limits their use by others. Yet the management of sacred sites raises similar questions about how the state should weigh conflicting moral and political claims on public space.

The concluding chapters step back from case studies to consider how contesting views about the proper use of information and public space can be resolved in democratic societies. In particular, I question two key doctrines of the heritage-protection movement. The first, promoted by the United Nations, holds that indigenous cultures, as distinct from indigenous *peoples,* may be readily identified and sheltered by law. The second is that principles of indigenous sovereignty and self-determination, so central to political negotiations with the state, should set the terms of debate in struggles over music, art, and access to sacred places.

My reading of the situation leads to different conclusions. One is that the crux of this problem does not lie in irreconcilable views of ownership, even where these exist. It is instead a fundamental matter of dignity. Reframed as a question, we should be asking not "Who owns native culture?" but "How can we promote respectful treatment of native cultures and indigenous forms of self-expression within mass societies?" The cases documented here suggest that the quest for dignity in the expressive life of indigenous communities will best be advanced through approaches that affirm the inherently relational nature of the problem. These include judicious modification of intellectual property law, development of workable policies for the protection of cultural privacy, and greater reliance on the moral resources of civil society. All of us—native and non-native alike—have a stake in decisions about the control of culture, for those decisions will determine the future health of our imperiled intellectual and artistic commons.

1. The Missionary's Photographs

Anyone who has read about the Hopi Indians, a small Arizona tribe famous for multi-story dwellings and a resolute commitment to traditional religious practices, is likely to have seen photographs taken by the Reverend Heinrich (Henry) R. Voth. The years that have passed since Voth's death in 1931 have done little to stem the controversy surrounding his activities as missionary and anthropologist. Contemporary anthropologists, even those who respect his ethnographic work, are uncomfortable with Voth's religious zeal and with the oppressive Indian policies in force during the years that he worked at Hopi. Among Hopis, anger at Voth's publication of sensitive information about their religion continues to smolder as if his alleged misdeeds had taken place only yesterday.

H. R. Voth was raised by German Anabaptists who emigrated to Kansas from southern Russia in 1874. He trained as a Mennonite missionary and took his first assignment among the Arapaho, in what was later to become the state of Oklahoma. In the early 1890s the Mennonite Mission Board invited him to evaluate prospects for a mission among the Hopi, then considered one of the most religiously intractable tribes in North America. He and his growing family eventually settled in Orayvi (Oraibi), the largest Hopi village and one increasingly torn by disputes over how the community should respond to government intrusions, which included the forced removal of Hopi children to boarding schools. Other tensions in the region—notably, government efforts to limit the spread of Mormonism, then considered a dangerous cult—had produced what amounted to a low-intensity war of conflicting religious and cultural ideologies, hardly what one would expect in such a remote place.

After two years of hard work, Voth apparently had a working knowledge of the Hopi language. But the seeds of Christianity fell on stony soil. The Mennonite mission at Orayvi produced only about forty converts in its first thirty years. Meanwhile, Voth's detailed study of Hopi religion, initially undertaken to help him understand the beliefs he was trying to supplant, began to absorb more of his energy. Eventually it became his principal means of financial support. He was hired to produce major displays, including facsimiles of Hopi altars, for museums and southwestern tourist sites, such as Grand Canyon National Park.[1]

Biographical accounts describe Voth as steadfast in his Mennonite faith but also fascinated by Hopi ritual. Although committed to the young discipline of anthropology, Voth proved unwilling to distance himself from the Mennonite community; he refused a position at Chicago's Field Museum of Natural History that he was offered on several occasions. Yet his passion for the systematic study of Hopi religion sometimes put him at odds with Mennonite authorities.

Voth's relations with Hopis were complex. Cathy Ann Trotta, one of the few historians who have examined the journals of Voth and his wife, Martha Moser Voth, concludes that over the nine years of their ministry their day-to-day dealings with Indians were mostly cordial.

Voth also seems to have worked closely with several Hopi priests, who gave him access to ceremonies from which outsiders were usually excluded. Community feelings about Voth took a strongly negative turn after Hopis became aware that he was publishing detailed information about their religion. Voth captured at least 2,000 photographic images during his years at Hopi. Most document everyday household and agricultural activities. But he also photographed religious rituals, images that are disproportionately reproduced in magazines and books to the present day. So detailed are his photographs and written descriptions of Hopi ritual practices that they are said to be consulted occasionally by the tribe's religious authorities.[2]

With the passage of time, Voth's knowledge of Hopi religion came to be portrayed as the fruit of intimidation. Don Talayesva, a Hopi whose autobiography, *Sun Chief,* was first published in 1942, presents an unremittingly harsh view of Voth's activities: "When he had worked here in my boyhood, the Hopi were afraid of him and dared not lay their hands on him or any other missionary, lest they be jailed by the Whites. During the ceremonies this wicked man would force his way into the kiva [an underground structure used for ritual activities] and write down everything that he saw. He wore shoes with solid heels, and when the Hopi tried to put him out of the kiva he would kick them." The hostility conspicuous in this recollection contrasts sharply with the spirit of tolerance and good humor that characterizes the rest of Talayesva's autobiography.[3]

Voth's publication of the details of important rituals offended Hopi sensibilities about the proper circulation of knowledge. To outsiders, contemporary Hopis seem almost fanatically committed to secrecy. They forbid the use of cameras, audio recorders, and sketchpads by visitors, a policy that annoys Anglo tourists accustomed to photographing whatever they like. Within Hopi society, religious knowledge is rigorously compartmentalized among a range of spe-

H. R. Voth preaching at Hopi, Winter 1901.

cialized organizations. Community values discourage curiosity about the details of rituals in which one is not a direct participant. Hopis understand this to reflect their tribal history, which has been marked by the continual incorporation of new groups into a greater social whole. Everyone depends on the efforts of other clans and specialized religious societies to complete the annual cycle of rituals that keep the world functioning properly.[4]

In common with a growing number of Indian nations, the Hopi Tribe now maintains a cultural protection office that systematically monitors publicly available information about Hopi culture and, in particular, Hopi religion. It was in this spirit of cultural protection that in 1994 Vernon Masayesva, then tribal chairman, sent a letter to museums and repositories whose holdings include information about the Hopi. Among these are the Mennonite Library and Archives at Bethel College in North Newton, Kansas, which houses many of H. R. Voth's photographs. Chairman Masayesva requested that all repositories declare a moratorium on use of materials relating to the Hopi people and their ancestors, including field notes, photographs, and drawings, particularly those containing "esoteric, ritual and privileged information on religious and ceremonial practices and customs." The letter asserted the Hopis' ownership interest in all materials relating to their culture and the expectation that these materials will eventually be returned to the Hopi Tribe as part of a comprehensive process of repatriation.[5]

Hopi anxiety about use of their traditional images in the world beyond their isolated mesas is a local expression of global concern about the disposition of cultural heritage. This uneasiness is by no means limited to indigenous communities; people in the cultural majority worry about it, too. Various emotions drive what the geographer David Lowenthal has called the "heritage crusade": a search for meaning amid the moral emptiness of materialism, a desire for rootedness, and a fear of the unanticipated effects of technological change.

Settler societies such as the United States and Australia have long used monuments and other material expressions of heritage to unify their ethnically diverse populations. Without symbols of shared heritage, it would be difficult to mobilize citizens for national defense and other collective tasks. In the developed world, the latter half of the twentieth century and the dawn of the twenty-first have seen this nationalist myth-making challenged by ethnic minorities who demand their own monuments and historical sites. Through such memorials they express collective pride and celebrate their resistance to the state's efforts to assimilate them.

The cultural heritage and sacred places of indigenous peoples have become the focus of special attention, and laws designed to safeguard the cultural resources of indigenous communities have been implemented in a number of countries. This campaign is motivated by concern about endangered environments in which some indigenous peoples live, popular fascination with exotic ways of life, and collective guilt about the acts of genocide that stain colonial histories. Few would judge the rise of native-heritage legislation to be anything other than a hopeful sign. In most places where such laws have come into effect, native peoples already enjoy basic human rights. Secure in their relative physical safety, they are now free to focus on defense of their language, religion, and right of self-governance. These issues are central to a law passed by Australia in 1984, the Aboriginal and Torres Strait Islander Heritage Protection Act, the goal of which is the "preservation and protection from injury or desecrations of areas and objects in Australia" when these can be shown to be significant to the country's Aboriginal population. In the United States, heritage protection is effected through a network of laws, including the National Historic Preservation Act of 1966, the American Indian Religious Freedom Act (AIRFA) of 1978, and the Native American Graves Protection and Repatriation Act (NAGPRA) of 1990.

Paralleling national heritage-protection initiatives are declarations issued by the United Nations and its various arms, including UNESCO and the Working Group on Indigenous Populations. The Draft U.N. Declaration of the Rights of Indigenous Peoples, for example, stipulates that native peoples "have the right to practice and revitalize their cultural traditions and customs." This mandate encompasses "the right to maintain, protect and develop the past, present and future manifestations of their cultures, such as archaeological and historical sites, artifacts, designs, ceremonies, technologies and visual and performing arts and literature, as well as the right to restitution of cultural, intellectual, religious and spiritual property taken without their free and informed consent or in violation of their laws, traditions, and customs."

When the Hopi Tribe proposes that culturally sensitive information be "repatriated," it clearly builds on the language and political success of NAGPRA. This law provides a framework for the return of human remains, burial goods, and religious objects to tribes that can substantiate claims of descent or prior ownership. NAGPRA requires every repository receiving federal funds to inventory its Native American holdings and notify tribes with a potential interest in them. Tribes can then, if they choose, request that cultural objects falling within the law's purview be repatriated to them.

Many museum professionals were understandably reluctant to embrace NAGPRA at first. They faced the prospect of returning their priceless collections to tribes that often lacked resources to preserve them. A few tribes, including the Hopi, made clear their intention to put religious objects back into use until worn out and discarded, a disheartening prospect for curators who dedicate their working lives to such objects' conservation. Physical anthropologists, whose collections were significantly affected by the law, were convinced that pure emotionalism had drowned out serious discussion of the scientific value of human remains that might eventually offer up genetic information crucial to the future health of Native Americans.

Most of these fears proved groundless. Tribes are often content to allow contested objects to remain in the possession of museums until proper tribal facilities can be constructed. In other cases, tribal officials feel that the power of specific ritual items exceeds the ability of today's religious experts to control them. Better, then, that they remain in storage elsewhere. NAGPRA forced museums and Indian tribes to open discussions that have led to rewarding partnerships. The law does not specify what is supposed to happen to museum artifacts; it demands only that a serious conversation take place. Although grumbling continues in some quarters, many curators today hail NAGPRA as one of the best things ever to have happened to American museums.[6]

The law is equally popular with the public. The press represents NAGPRA as legislation that rights historical wrongs typified by the removal and storage of the brain of Ishi, the California Indian often described as "the last Yahi," after his death in 1916. (Researchers searching for the brain located it in the collection of the Smithsonian Institution, which promptly repatriated it to the Pit River tribe of Redding Rancheria, California. It was buried in a secret location in 2000.)[7] In other cases, sacred artifacts looted from Indian shrines have been returned to their proper owners. As with almost every manifestation of public interest in Indian issues, however, impressions of NAGPRA are colored by a diffuse sentimentality that blinds outsiders to the law's unanticipated effects.

The Hopi Cultural Preservation Office (HCPO), an arm of Hopi tribal government, is located in Kykotsmovi, Arizona, on the edge of Third Mesa. When I visited the HCPO in 1997, two employees, Lee Wayne Lomayestewa and Clyde Qotswisiuma, struggled to make room for me among the stacks of NAGPRA reports that lined their cubicle. Lee, a gregarious man who appeared to be in his twenties, wore his hair long in traditional Hopi style. Clyde, older and with a gray military cut and glasses, was more reserved. Conversation eventually angled toward the tribe's policies regarding NAGPRA. Far from praising this supposedly progressive law, Lee and Clyde offered a withering critique. Clyde expressed anger that NAGPRA was written to cover all Indian tribes. The Hopi, he said, deserve a law tailored to their specific circumstances. When pressed for details, he mentioned that members of the Navajo Nation, which surrounds the small Hopi reservation like a great sea embracing a tiny island, are now producing kachinas for sale. (Kachinas, often called "kachina dolls" by outsiders, are small carved and painted images of Pueblo spirit-beings.) This threatens the income of Hopi artists. Navajos, Clyde continued, are also claiming Hopi sacred places and beliefs for themselves: "The Navajos are taking Hopi qualities, saying that they came into the fourth world and that they have four sacred colors for the directions. But those ideas came from us. Now they are involved in eagle gathering, which is a Hopi practice. We Hopis don't talk first in public gatherings anymore. Now we're afraid that if we say something, the Navajos will say that it's theirs too."[8]

Hopi suspicion of the Navajo must be seen within the context of a long-running, acrimonious land dispute between the two tribes. But the issues run deeper than land and natural resources. In a video documentary released in 1998 by the Museum of Indian Arts and Culture in Santa Fe, representatives of other Pueblo tribes assert that NAGPRA has caused "stress, conflict, and confusion," largely between peoples of Pueblo ancestry and their Athabascan neighbors, the Apache and Navajo. For some purposes, the law places the religious beliefs and oral histories of Indian tribes on the same footing as science, leaving policymakers with little choice but to respond to political pressure. Most archaeologists, for example, hold that Athabascan peoples are relative latecomers to the American Southwest. The current scientific consensus is that the ancestors of the Navajo and the Apache came into the region in the fourteenth or fifteenth century A.D., long after ancestral Pueblo peoples. But according to Tim Begay, a Navajo spokesperson, "We've always been here."

Simmering conflict over ancestry came to a head in 1999 when the National Park Service concluded that Navajos have a legitimate "cultural affiliation" with the Anasazi culture of Chaco Canyon National Monument in northwestern New Mexico. The Anasazi—a name now rejected by Pueblo tribes in favor of "Ancestral Puebloans"—constructed magnificent cliff dwellings and multi-storied stone structures that draw thousands of tourists to Chaco Canyon, Mesa Verde, and other national parks in the Southwest. Ancestral Puebloans are said to have vanished in the thirteenth century A.D., but the preponderance of scientific evidence, which in this case generally agrees with Pueblo oral history, supports the view that the cliff dwellers scattered throughout the region to found the communities today identified as Pueblo. Contemporary Pueblo people react to the assertion that Navajos have a "cultural affiliation" with the Anasazi about the same way the Irish would respond to an English claim of affiliation with pre-sixteenth-century cultural remains in Ireland. The question is more than academic. Within the boundaries of the immense Navajo reservation lie scores, perhaps hundreds, of unexcavated Ancestral Puebloan sites whose future will apparently be determined by the Navajo Nation.[9]

Evidence, both documentary and testimonial, plays an important part in NAGPRA negotiations. These disclosure requirements make sense from the perspective of Anglo-American law, but they trouble Indians who are put in the unhappy position of violating their tribe's canons of secrecy in order to substantiate claims that particular objects are sacred. Resistance to public disclosure of religious information has led the Hopi Tribe to request repatriation of all Hopi artifacts on the grounds that anything made by Hopis is sacred by definition. When challenged to show how utilitarian household objects could be considered sacred, Clyde Qotswisiuma of the HCPO replied, "Even something like a digging stick could have a ritual use, but we're not about to say what it is."

NAGPRA has sometimes contributed to strife within tribes as well as between them. The law is weighted strongly toward the notion that material held by museums is the cultural patrimony of entire tribes rather than the property of the individuals or families from whom it may have been acquired. Among tribes of the northwest coast, certain repatriated items are displayed in community museums over the objections of older members of the tribe who feel that public access to them is inappropriate. Some protest because, as long-time Christians, they are uncomfortable with the display of powerful objects from the group's pre-Christian past. Others argue that according to traditional rules of ownership the items belong to specific individuals or families. These views pit them against some younger members of the community who are committed to a reconstruction of their cultural history in a communitarian mold.[10]

From a distance, the debate touched off by the implementation of NAGPRA occasionally looks as if it were taken from the pages of an instruction manual in postmodern politics. Both Indians and government officials cite science when it suits their purposes. Pueblo officials, for instance, insist that there is no archaeological evidence linking Navajos to Ancestral Puebloans. When scientific perspectives deviate from native ones, however, science is denounced as ethnocentric. Such contradictions do not vitiate NAGPRA's positive impact, but they illustrate how well-meaning laws inadvertently contribute to a muddying of truth-standards that sometimes undermines the interests of indigenous communities.

Beginning in the early 1980s, native peoples concerned about the flow of information from their societies to outsiders acquired a new adversary, the New Age movement, threatening because its adherents put knowledge of traditional religions into practice. Faux medicine wheels and sweat lodges are now used by religious seekers on at least three continents. At American Indian sacred sites on public lands, New Age devotees sometimes compete with native people for space, prompting demands from activists that the government close the sites to non-Indians. Aboriginal Australians have not been immune to this kind of attention. In her book *Mutant Message Down Under,* Marlo Morgan claims to describe her initiation into the secrets of Aboriginal spirituality. Originally self-published, the book was later picked up by the publisher HarperCollins, reportedly for $1.8 million, and became an international bestseller. It provoked a major public relations campaign by Aboriginal leaders, who denounced it as "soul destroying" and equivalent to "cultural genocide." Morgan eventually confessed that the account was entirely fictional, a revelation that only heightened Aboriginal anger.[11]

Among American practitioners of New Age spirituality, the Hopi receive disproportionate and largely unwanted attention. Their reputation for peacefulness, their ability to provision themselves despite the unforgiving climate of their mesas, the age of their villages, which are among the oldest continuously occupied communities in the New World, their spell-binding dances and tradition of prophecy—all exert a force irresistible to moderns searching for primal authenticity. A few Hopi elders have been willing to share their knowledge with outsiders, but most simply want to be left alone. The relative remoteness of their reservation affords scant protection today. New Age "offerings"—in at least one case consisting of cremated human remains—regularly turn up at Hopi religious sites in the backcountry. In 1993 a delegation of twenty Hopis traveled to Tucson to protest a workshop on Native American spirituality given by Thomas Mails, a former Lutheran minister who has published books with titles like *The Hopi Survival Kit* and *Hotevilla: Hopi Shrine of the Covenant.* Hopi spokespersons argued that the workshop trafficked in ideas that are "the birthrights of the Hopis, to be shared only under strict religious standards by those vested with that religious authority to do so." The situation is richly veined with irony. Indigenous peoples now perceive themselves as more threatened by outsiders who claim to love their religion than by missionaries dedicated to its overthrow, with whom they have usually managed to achieve a modus vivendi.[12]

NAGPRA has had no direct impact on New Age activities, but its implementation has helped to define information as the next frontier, raising questions about the future of the countless ethnographic photographs, field notebooks, diaries, and audio tapes held by the world's libraries and museums. Here the Hopi exercise a leadership role that belies their small numbers. The tribe's 1994 letter to museums and archives was followed a year later by a conference for researchers at the Heard Museum in Phoenix. At the conference Hopi leaders declared their determination to protect Hopi culture from the theft of knowledge that they consider proprietary. As an example of the violation of Hopi cultural resources, one speaker, Marilyn Masayesva, singled out the work of H. R. Voth. "According to oral Hopi stories," she said, "Voth was physically ejected from the Hopi kivas on many occasions. In spite of clearly expressed objections by Hopi, judged by the Hopi conventions of the time period, Voth continually trespassed into the very private spaces of the Hopis . . . Why is there one law for the Hopi and yet another for the non-Hopi? This concept of public domain requires re-examination."[13]

Another speaker, Wallace Youvella Sr., mentioned a case that caused great unhappiness among Hopi elders. In 1992 Marvel Comics published an issue of its forgettable series *NFL Superpro* (the protagonist being a former professional football player turned superhero) entitled "The Kachinas Sing of Doom," in which chain-saw-wielding thugs disguised as Hopi spirit-beings try to assassinate a Hopi figure skater. Among Hopis, the emotional impact of this abuse of religious symbolism was similar to the effect on devout Christians of Andres Serrano's controversial work *Piss Christ* (1987). Especially upsetting was the comic book's appeal to young readers. According to Youvella, this incident led to the closing of some Hopi dances formerly open to the public. The freedom of outsiders to use traditional religious symbols in disrespectful ways increases Hopis' frustration with Anglo-American legal norms, which offer their culture what they see as inadequate protection from abuse. From this perspective, the photographs Voth took at Hopi should never have been available in the first place. That they continue to be archived and circulated against Hopi wishes—practices justified by high-minded appeals to free speech and the importance of the public domain—serves as a constant reminder of Hopi subordination.[14]

The Hopi are hardly alone in harboring resentment about anthropological work conducted in the past. Among tribes of the northern Midwest, a focus of attention has been audio recordings, especially those made by the pioneering ethnomusicologist Frances Densmore (1867–1957). Born in Redwing, Minnesota, Densmore studied music at the Oberlin College Conservatory and pursued formal training as a pianist. After returning to Minnesota to live with her middle-class parents and sister, she became interested in the music of American Indians. The origin of this interest is hard to divine from her education and austere upbringing, although it would appear to have been motivated by a mix of genuine curiosity and a desire to become an acknowledged expert in something unusual. Even before her studies had progressed beyond superficial encounters with Indians at the 1893 Columbian Exposition in Chicago, Densmore began to lecture widely on Native American music. In 1905 she set off with her sister on what was an adventurous expedition for the time: a trip to record music among the Ojibwe (Ojibwa) of northern Minnesota. Her diaries and letters indicate that Densmore alternately charmed, badgered, and bribed Ojibwe informants to perform songs that were in some cases sacred and secret. By 1907 she was using an Edison recording machine to preserve music on wax cylinders. For the rest of her life she doggedly pursued her mission of collecting indigenous music, primarily among Indians of the Plains and Southwest but also in places as disparate as Washington State, Florida, and Panama. The fruits of her labors include three thousand cylinder recordings, now housed in the Library of Congress, and more than twenty books, several regarded as classics of ethnomusicology.

Present-day ambivalence about Densmore and her work illustrates the difficulty of assessing the moral status of information collected in other eras. Some anthropologists lionize her as a female pioneer who fought her way to a prominent place in the history of the Smithsonian Institution's male-dominated Bureau of American Ethnology. Others see her as the savior of American Indian musical traditions then considered worthless by Anglo-American society. Indian activists denounce her as a butterfly collector, preserving traditions in museum cabinets while doing little to help Indian people survive in a hostile world. The latter view informs the historical play *SongCatcher,* a drama about Densmore written by Marcie Rendon, a White Earth Anishinabe playwright from Minneapolis. In Rendon's play, Densmore's recording of a particularly potent song leads to the singer's banishment from the lodge and the death of his wife. Confronting Densmore, the man laments, "I let you take my songs and now the spirits have taken my wife. My songs, my wife, my religion. You took them all."[15]

Although sympathetic biographers insist that Densmore respected

Frances Densmore and Mountain Chief (Blackfeet) listening to a cylinder recording (possibly of songs gathered in Montana in 1898 by Walter McClintock), ca. 1914. Mountain Chief is apparently interpreting a song in sign language.

the Indians with whom she worked, others hold that to the end of her life she remained primly Victorian in her attitude toward social fraternization with her subjects. Her research methods, she insisted, did not involve "pretending to be one of them and eating out of the same dishes." Nor did she show great concern for their political and economic situation. "I never let them criticize the government nor the white race, nor come across with any sob-stuff about the way they had been treated as a race," she wrote to an acquaintance in 1945. The anthropology of Densmore's time assumed that Indian cultures would die and Indian peoples be assimilated into the general population. Densmore shared this view, and much of her drive to record Indian songs came from a conviction that they would soon be lost to humanity. Happily, things did not turn out that way. Today some Indians resent Densmore's compulsion to collect. Others express gratitude. In an interview on National Public Radio, Earl Bullhead, a Sioux resident of the Standing Rock Reservation, described Densmore's recordings as "kind of like a seed, and that seed now is starting to flourish among a lot of people my age and older and the young ones coming up because you got to remember a lot of this was almost lost."[16]

When indigenous activists demand new controls on the kind of cultural information gathered by H. R. Voth and Frances Densmore, they often struggle to identify an appropriate rationale. Their rhetoric moves restlessly from references to copyright and intellectual property to ideas of blasphemy and misrepresentation. Also common in recent years are allusions to a principle known as the "right of cultural privacy."[17]

The concept of cultural privacy seems to have emerged more or less spontaneously from the spirit of the moment to make its way into the literature of the policy world. A Canadian research paper about the introduction of telecommunications services to the country's Inuit communities, for instance, refers to their "rights of refusal, their right to cultural privacy." In the United States, a policy document about the disposition of archaeological materials on army bases discusses the need to balance "Native American concerns for cultural privacy" against prevailing standards of public disclosure. These sources suggest that cultural privacy is defined as the right of possessors of a culture—especially possessors of a native culture—to shield themselves from unwanted scrutiny. A right to cultural privacy is presented as self-evident and morally unassailable, even if its scope remains unspecified.[18]

From the perspective of anthropology, cultural privacy flirts with self-contradiction. The salient features of culture are, by definition, shared and therefore public. Yet the collective nature of culture does not mean that its elements are uniformly distributed. Information is nearly everywhere held differentially along lines of age, gender, social class, kinship, and occupation. It may be acquired through interactions with other peoples. Through selective borrowing, cultures come closer together; through dialectical contrast, they mark themselves as different. We are left with interweaving and to some extent paradoxical visions of culture: as shared yet differentiated, as segmented yet intrinsically free-flowing, as something that exists unto itself yet which is also defined by opposition. At first glance, this intricate bundle of dichotomies is hard to reconcile with a concept as deceptively simple as privacy.

Legal textbooks find the cornerstone of modern American ideas of privacy in the essay "The Right to Privacy," published by Samuel Warren and Louis Brandeis in 1890. Warren and Brandeis assert that people have a "right to be let alone" and, more important, to an "inviolate personality." They see this right as emerging from the advance of civilization, which progressed from concern with life and property to a "recognition of man's spiritual nature, of his feelings and his intellect . . . [and] recognition of the legal value of sensations." Restrictions on the unwanted flow of certain kinds of personal information are essential to the preservation of human dignity, they argue. As in most rights-based thinking in the United States, privacy is construed in individual terms (the "right to be let *alone*") rather than as something that applies to groups or communities. A bestselling book on privacy makes no mention of group privacy and goes so far as to declare that "privacy is by definition a personal right." The private and the personal, in other words, are assumed to be identical. This is consistent with the view, long advocated by therapeutically inclined commentators, that personal privacy is essential for the normal development of the "true self," which contrasts with the necessary, and necessarily artificial, "social self" created through engagement with others.[19]

Nevertheless, there are situations in which privacy rights extend to groups. Law and popular sentiment protect the confidentiality of exchanges between doctors and patients, attorneys and clients, priests and parishioners. Within limits, we recognize that families, businesses, fraternal organizations, and government bodies have a legitimate need for confidentiality. In a review of the history of collective privacy, the legal scholar Edward Bloustein concludes that the right of association offers at least modest protection for groups that seek to avoid intrusion into their affairs. "The right to associate with others in confidence—the right to privacy in one's associations—assures the success and integrity of the group purpose," he insists. From a communitarian perspective, associational privacy creates the conditions that make personal freedom possible.[20]

Application of contemporary Western notions of privacy to indigenous societies raises perplexing questions. It is often observed that life in premodern societies offered scant opportunities for privacy. Living together in close quarters, people had no choice but to witness actions and events that today virtually define the sphere of personal privacy. Even among indigenous peoples fully incorporated into modernity—which is to say, all indigenous peoples known to exist—the circumstances of everyday life may make middle-class standards of privacy impossible to introduce even if people were inclined to adopt them.

Yet if we define privacy as freedom from unwanted or inappropriate attention, there is little doubt that many indigenous communities depend on collective privacy for the successful completion of important cultural activities. In the accounts of anthropologists, group privacy tends to come under the rubric of secrecy, especially secrecy about rituals. Theorists of liberal democracy are strongly inclined to treat secrecy as inherently corrosive, a practice that is rarely necessary and frequently abused. Hence the ubiquity of "sunshine laws" that require public entities to bring their deliberations out of the shadows into the bright light of public scrutiny. Anthropologists see secrecy in more explicitly structural terms. It may be associated with antisocial forces such as sorcery, but it also creates and maintains fundamental social distinctions. When young men and women are introduced to secret knowledge during rites of passage, they emerge from seclusion utterly changed in their self-perception. Everyone else in the community sees them differently, too. Secrecy generates social hierarchy, distinctions between those who know and those who don't. Within societies that lack significant economic stratification, the social ranking fostered by ritual secrecy may anchor existing patterns of leadership. Conversely, a breakdown of secrecy threatens traditional patterns of political and religious life.[21]

Indigenous attitudes toward revelation and discretion have also been affected by colonial realities. Pueblo Indians are known for the rigorous way that they shield religious knowledge from those whose interest they deem illegitimate. One anthropological assessment of privacy practices among the Zuni of New Mexico, a group with strong cultural affinities to the Hopi, describes them as having a "safehold" system in which religious understandings are "defended against penetration by foreigners, unauthorized Zunis, and criminals, i.e., witches." The survival of traditional religious practices at Zuni depends at least partly on security strategies not unlike those of underground organizations or top-secret government agencies.[22]

Another group noted for reticence is the Tarahumara, who live in the rugged canyon country of Chihuahua, Mexico. So difficult is it to convince them to talk about their culture that some early ethnographers expressed doubt that the Tarahumara possessed any folklore at all. Tarahumaras keep their own counsel for several reasons: well-founded fear of outsiders, a lack of self-consciousness about their cultural practices, and a belief that words harbor inherent power and should be used with great care.[23]

With the intensification of identity politics since the 1970s, access to ritual secrets has become a key marker of indigenousness. In colonial Australia, for example, Aboriginals felt they had no choice but to reveal ritual secrets in response to European demands. Today Aboriginal people are free to make a choice, so revelation is considered a greater betrayal than it once was.[24] Secrecy continues to be a double-edged sword that defends powerful knowledge but also imperils the reliable transmission of cultural information. When esoteric knowledge is held by only a handful of anointed experts, entire bodies of tradition may be lost through a few unexpected deaths. In a surprising number of cases, information "stolen" by inquisitive missionaries or anthropologists has saved indigenous communities from tragic cultural losses.

Calls for institutions to honor indigenous rules of secrecy have already affected everyday practices in cultural repositories. Many archives entrusted with Native American materials have implemented policies that urge and sometimes require patrons to contact relevant tribes before using collections. Some archivists confess privately that they have relocated sensitive records to storage areas that casual visitors are unlikely to find. In following these procedures, the managers of documents walk a tightrope. Their profession pledges them to fairness in dealing with the public, which means that they must respond to every reasonable request for information. At the same time, they are obliged to "respect the privacy of individuals who created, or are the subjects of, documentary materials of long-term value, especially those who had no voice in the disposition of the materials," according to the ethics code of the Society of American Archivists. Reconciling these conflicting goals requires finely tuned judgment.

In Australia, museum curators have sometimes acceded to Aboriginal requests that female staff be barred from handling Aboriginal religious artifacts. (Similar requests in the United States have been denied in deference to state and federal laws that prohibit discrimination by gender.) Surprisingly, representatives of some Aboriginal groups have aimed their most vigorous complaints at museums that allow ritual objects to be seen by Aboriginal people belonging to different societies or clans. In these cases, they prefer that the materials be handled by non-Aboriginal staff.[25]

The types of information that concern native peoples vary greatly from place to place. Although birth and death records are considered quintessentially public in Anglo-American society, North American Indian tribes may treat them as confidential when parentage is regarded as a private family matter. Where genealogies are the sine qua non of tribal membership, genealogical information is a valuable and often hotly contested resource.

One might think that archival collections managed by Indian nations would be liberated from ethical dilemmas that now face archivists elsewhere, since native archives are presumably free to manage information according to their own rules. But during a 1999 meeting of Native American archivists at the Newberry Library in Chicago, it became clear that they, too, are forced to wrestle with difficult ethical questions. An archivist for an eastern tribe told of having been pressured to release a collection of medical records to tribal attorneys seeking to substantiate the tribe's claim that its members had been injured by pollution from off-reservation factories. She had refused to cooperate, citing the small size of the community, which made it easy to associate records with specific individuals. An archivist from a western tribe reported that her institution allows information on cultural practices to be seen only by enrolled members of the tribe. Even these are denied access to religious documents until they can show that they were raised in local communities. The elders, she explained, feel that the most powerful religious knowledge can be used wisely only by persons of traditional upbringing. Although most of these Native American professionals are committed to the principle that, as one put it, "we have to control the documents to control our history," privacy is not something readily governed by a set of shared standards even within their own tribes.

Thus far there have been few legal actions dealing with alleged violations of indigenous secrecy standards by outside researchers. A rare exception is *Foster v. Mountford,* an Australian case dating to 1976. The defendant was the distinguished anthropologist Charles Mountford, author of numerous works on Aboriginal art and religion. Upon publication of what some consider his masterwork, *Nomads of the Australian Desert* (1976), members of the Pitjantjatjara people, whose religious iconography, myths, and rituals are featured in the book, came forward to seek a permanent injunction to stop distribution of the book within Australia's Northern Territory, where the Pitjantjatjara and related groups live.

The circumstances of the lawsuit are straightforward. Mountford interviewed and traveled with Pitjantjatjara people in the 1930s and early 1940s, a time when their contacts with outsiders were limited. The anthropologist and his assistants were obliged to travel by camel through the Pitjantjatjaras' difficult desert country. Like any good ethnographer, Mountford took detailed notes, drew charts, and photographed rituals and sacred sites. The Pitjantjatjara plaintiffs declared that religious information had been shared with the understanding that it would never be made available to inappropriate persons, which in the Pitjantjatjara case meant children, women, and uninitiated Aboriginal men. They were therefore dismayed when, thirty-five years later, copies of Mountford's massive tome, complete with photographic plates and drawings, were put on sale in Alice Springs and other towns in the Northern Territory. Legal representatives of the Pitjantjatjara argued to a justice of the Northern Territory's Supreme Court that Mountford had committed a "breach of confidence" by reneging on his implicit promise of discretion.

In agreeing to impose the injunction, the judge acknowledged that Mountford's was "a magnificent publication" that "highlights much that was earlier not recognized of the traditional dignity and wisdom" of the Pitjantjatjara. At the same time, he said, the plaintiffs had made a convincing case that "revelation of the secrets to their women, children, and uninitiated men may undermine the social and religious stability of their hard-pressed community." On that basis, he concluded that "continuance of such publication in the Northern Territory and of course perhaps elsewhere, may cause damage of a serious nature." In a related case several years later, the Pitjantjatjara were allowed to review Mountford's photographs, which had been put up for sale after his death, and to remove images that they identified as sensitive.[26]

Although the decision was a victory for the Pitjantjatjara and a wake-up call to anthropologists whose notes contain secret information on native religions, its legal scope was limited. Mountford's monograph remained available elsewhere in Australia, and copies of it can be found on library shelves throughout the world. (The controversy surrounding *Nomads of the Australian Desert* has only increased its value on the used-book market.) The logic of the judicial decision pushed cultural privacy to the background in favor of a contractual approach emphasizing good faith.

I n their landmark 1890 essay on privacy, Warren and Brandeis acknowledge that private information is bound to circulate in the form of gossip. The crux of legal measures to protect privacy, they argue, lies not in limiting gossip but in preventing it from being "proclaimed from the house-tops" by newspapers. The implication is that mass media convert the petty aggravation of gossip into something far more harmful. Warren and Brandeis were critical of irresponsible, hurtful reporting by the newspapers of their time. In the intervening century, the pervasiveness of mass media has become substantially greater. From the indigenous perspective, it is one thing for cultural records to lie mostly unused in archives and on library shelves, quite another for the information contained in them to appear on television, in bestselling books, and on the Internet.

In this sense native anxieties converge with broader public concern about the alarming possibilities of new information technologies. Vast amounts of personal information, ranging from the assessed value of private homes to divorce proceedings, have been available to the public for decades. In practice, however, only trained professionals could readily locate information contained in widely scattered paper records. Such logistical obstacles decline dramatically once records are digitized. Now any persistent teenager with a modem may gain access to public documents, a situation that is not helped by the tendency of public agencies to sell their information to the highest bidder. Meanwhile, the same technologies that enable easy publication of data by corporations have made it possible for individuals of modest means to distribute information to millions via the World Wide Web. The Web's ability to provide everyone with a global audience has been celebrated as a triumph of information democracy. It transforms the process of publication from one dominated by well-ordered institutions into an unruly bazaar that has thus far proved difficult for governments to control, raising questions about whether a right to cultural privacy can be comprehensively enforced even if it were to be universally recognized.[27]

Active protection of cultural privacy inevitably raises the specter of censorship, although the indigenous-rights literature typically steers away from the term. Among the few commentators to abandon euphemism is the anthropologist George E. Marcus, who bravely offers a defense of indigenous censorship rights that would extend beyond the boundaries of native communities to encompass control over the circulation of sensitive cultural information in the wider society. The principal justification is that regulation of the flow of information is essential for the survival of many (perhaps most) native political systems. If democratic societies intend to honor their commitments to indigenous peoples, they are obliged to guarantee the minimal conditions in which survival of indigenous cultures is possible even if this requires new regimes of censorship. Marcus acknowledges that this poses a serious challenge to fundamental liberal values.[28]

A different rationale for censorship is advanced by those who insist that colonial and post-colonial settings are so inherently coercive that all cultural records, however obtained, are ethically tainted. A senior curator of a major American museum once told me that, in his view, the ethnographic documents in his care are as morally compromised as the concentration-camp medical records amassed by the Third Reich, documents so repugnant that they remain sealed despite their potential value for medical research. The extravagance of his assertion should perhaps be dismissed as the rhetorical excess that arises in spontaneous private discussion. Nevertheless, it captures sentiments that are by no means rare among anthropologists and indigenous-rights activists.

The case for censorship in support of indigenous interests would be more persuasive if the boundaries of native cultures could be defined precisely. In the United States, Canada, Australia, and New Zealand, hundreds of thousands of citizens claim native identities while participating only marginally in the everyday life of indigenous communities. How would a democratic society respond to their new right of censorship? Might not a formally articulated regime of censorship on behalf of native peoples provoke widespread public resistance or, worse still, demands that non-indigenous groups be granted an equivalent right?

In another of the ironies that mark these debates, efforts to grant broad legal controls over information originating in native societies are encumbered by the idiom of sovereignty favored by native-rights activists. Independent nations are not thought to possess a right of collective privacy that prevents outsiders from investigating or making assertions about how governments or individual citizens behave. The argument that a French "right to cultural privacy" made it improper for Americans to study the way French people live would be dismissed out of hand by legal experts and ordinary citizens alike. International law derives what little power it has from the principle that nationhood cannot exempt the internal affairs of states from external accountability. Self-governing native nations have sometimes abused the rights of their citizens and imposed forms of rule that in other contexts would be labeled corrupt and oppressive. Policies of cultural privacy could easily be used to shield a governing faction from much-needed scrutiny.[29]

U.S. law has been shaped by the conviction, articulated by Warren and Brandeis more than a century ago, that privacy is inseparable from questions of human dignity. Today's legal scholars find it harder to disentangle dignity from an individual's economic interests. When personal information (or for that matter, information associated with clearly defined groups) is appropriated by others for their benefit, the victims suffer both emotional distress and economic deprivation, at least relative to the economic gain enjoyed by the appropriators. The right of privacy envisioned by Warren and Brandeis differs from property rights in various ways. Privacy rights, for example, cannot be transferred to others, and they end when an individual dies. Property rights, in contrast, can be transferred to third parties and passed to succeeding generations. Nevertheless, a tidy separation of property and privacy is impossible within a market system that turns identity into a commodity. When persons or groups choose to commercialize their identity for economic gain, courts are less likely to accept the argument that unauthorized use of that identity undermines their dignity. Identity (in the sense of moral integrity and worth) and personality (in the sense of a social marker with commercial potential) coexist in a highly unstable relationship.[30]

This volatility helps to explain why indigenous peoples' complaints about the appropriation of elements of their cultures often jump from the abstract language of human rights to narrowly framed demands for monetary compensation. The difficulty of keeping the two issues separate is often misinterpreted as evidence that what indigenous peoples really care about is the economic value of their cultures. Even when grievances are presented entirely in terms of a group's desire for dignity and self-respect, capitalism imbues them with a mercantile logic that is difficult to suppress.

Despite the challenge of articulating a vision of cultural privacy that recognizes the dangers of censorship and the difficulty of separating questions of dignity from matters of financial interest, a principle of group privacy offers distinct advantages over other ways of framing demands for control of sensitive cultural information. Copyrights and patents are state-issued licenses that grant a limited monopoly. As such, they have an economic and utilitarian character that is hard to reconcile with the moral content of indigenous concerns. Appeals to concepts of blasphemy draw on the links between a people and their gods. This may provide powerful moral leverage for members of a faith community, but it leaves little room for outsiders who harbor different beliefs. Cultural privacy, in contrast, places emphasis squarely on the nature of the relationship between two parties, which is the nub of the issue. It foregrounds the way one individual or group deals with another, and how each can preserve moral integrity in their encounters. So what would a code of cultural privacy look like, and how might it be implemented?

One answer is provided by the ethics codes of professional societies and by existing cultural-protection policies enforced by native nations themselves. On the researcher's side of the equation are guidelines for the treatment of human subjects that require scholars to "do everything in their power to protect the physical, social, and psychological welfare and to honor the dignity and privacy of those studied," to quote from the American Anthropological Association's Statements on Ethics. When conflicts of interest arise, the needs of research subjects have first priority. Fieldworkers are also obliged to consider the potential impact that publications arising from the research may have on host communities. Skeptics insist that such guidelines are toothless, given the reluctance of professional guilds to police their members. Fortunately, indigenous peoples themselves are now able to set the terms under which outsiders work in their communities. In these situations, the protection of cultural privacy has become a familiar element of contemporary research protocols. This emerging norm may be bolstered by legal contracts that specify precisely what an investigator will be allowed to study as well as how information collected during the project will be distributed or archived.

Tighter community control over the activities of outside researchers, however, does not mean the end of ethical dilemmas. Restrictive codes create new ones. Researchers may stumble upon morally questionable activities that require a painful choice between honoring cultural privacy and calling attention to abuses of individual rights. (Familiar examples from the ethnographic literature include obligatory clitoridectomy—also known as "female genital mutilation"—and denial of basic education to girls.) A community's power to edit research results may produce conflict between the truth-standards of scholarship and a group's desire to see its culture presented in a favorable light. Anthropologists, folklorists, and others who work in native communities may face restrictions so constraining that they are reduced to trafficking in the public relations statements of indigenous political elites or serving as compliant puppets in new forms of cultural ventriloquism.

Unfortunately, ethics codes and community-controlled research protocols can do little to shelter native peoples from the curiosity of individuals unburdened by a professional identity. New Agers who insist on imitating Native American rituals are a case in point. Within the constraints of liberal democracy, it is hard to imagine a convincing legal argument for restricting the imitation of one group's religious practices by another unless the purpose of the imitation is to incite violence. In the United States, at least, religion is arguably the final frontier of unregulated creativity. If a New Age group were legally enjoined from identifying its rites as "authentically" Hopi, it could easily modify the practices slightly so that they qualified for constitutional protection. The only solution is moral education that sensitizes outsiders to the destructive impact of their misguided religious enthusiasms. Given those realities, appeals to shared notions of privacy and dignity are likely to be more effective than claims justified in terms of the novel proposition that a community "owns" its religious symbols and rituals.[31]

Cultural information collected in the past, material such as H. R.

Voth's Hopi photographs or the cylinder recordings of Frances Densmore, presents two distinct but interrelated problems. One is whether the circumstances under which the material was gathered meet the ethical standards of the researcher's own time. Densmore's work probably qualifies as ethical given the norms of her era, though not of our own. Voth's legacy is more disquieting, especially if Hopi leaders can substantiate allegations that he forced his way into rituals despite community opposition.

But the matter cannot end with judgments of behavior that took place decades ago. Equally important is whether the information's availability causes continuing harm. Critics of Densmore's work insist that wide circulation of certain songs documented on her wax cylinders is genuinely hurtful to members of tribes who have revived local traditions of secrecy or who believe they are the sole legitimate heirs of songs recorded by their lineal ancestors. Against this criticism must be weighed the useful role that the recordings may play in the revitalization of Native American religious traditions, as well as the near-impossibility of recapturing control of music that has long been available on mass-produced records, tapes, and compact discs. Here, as so often when cultures collide, we are denied the comfort of absolutes. What remains is the exercise of judgment on a case-by-case basis.

As for Voth's controversial photographs, concern for cultural privacy dictates that institutions show sensitivity to the use of images of Hopi rituals. What this means in practice is that anthropologists, folklorists, and historians should not publish Voth's contested religious pictures without prior approval by Hopi authorities. Such strictures are already in place in some archives, where researchers are actively discouraged and in some cases explicitly prevented from publishing Voth's religious images. His photographs of everyday life at Hopi are another matter. Although Hopi tribal authorities insist that everything in their world is sacred by definition, in the absence of convincing evidence that use of these images causes real harm, the photographs should remain accessible and reproducible. (Human images in themselves do not seem to offend Hopis, among whom are several accomplished professional photographers and filmmakers.) Harder to resolve is the fate of photographs already circulating in countless books and magazines. Short of large-scale book burning, Voth's Hopi images will continue to be available in library holdings for decades. Aggressive suppression of them, even when justified as a measure to protect native culture, arguably would cross the line into outright censorship. It would establish a precedent for more alarming efforts to edit history, and it might even backfire by encouraging unhealthy interest in Hopi rituals made more intriguing because of their increased secrecy.

The sociologist Edward Shils once declared that, to call itself civil and humane, a society must accept that complete openness cannot be achieved without violating an individual's sense of belonging to a unique community in possession of its own history. Where mass societies intersect with indigenous ones, all parties must define boundaries beyond which public scrutiny is deemed disruptive and improper. There may be a place for tightly framed legislation that would oblige cultural repositories to respond to requests from native nations that specific images, music, or texts be placed in long-term quarantine. But the administrative costs of such a measure would be high and its beneficial impact limited: there is simply too much of this information available to the world at large, far beyond the control of any institution. Imaginative realism favors less formal approaches—programs of public education, stricter ethics codes, institutional policies that sensitize staff members to the impact of specific kinds of field data—even as it recognizes that no effort to cleanse the world of hurtful information will ever enjoy complete success.[32]

2. Cultures and Copyrights

In September 1997 a cluster of lawyers, gowned and bewigged, gathered in a small courtroom in the city of Darwin, the capital of Australia's Northern Territory, about 2,500 miles northwest of Sydney. Their sober attire contrasted with the immoderate vegetation outside, in which galahs, lorikeets, and magpies chattered in the bright light of a tropical morning. Not far from the courthouse, in the shadow of the Northern Territory's gleaming Parliament House, lay coastal installations that had been bombed during World War II by Japanese planes that crossed the Timor Sea from New Guinea. Little else in Darwin predates 1974, when the city was leveled by Cyclone Tracy. The locals like to say that Darwin is closer to Singapore and Bali than to Sydney. It is the place, they say, where Australia is most conspicuously multicultural, where the city rebuilt after the cyclone incubates a new and better Australian society.

A small but important piece of the new Australia was being contested in a lawsuit that brought together legal talent from as far away as Melbourne and Canberra. The case, formally known as *Bulun*

Bulun and Milpurrurru v. R & T Textiles Pty Ltd, was the latest in a series of copyright-infringement suits brought by Aboriginal artists against Australian manufacturers and retailers. The first plaintiff in the Darwin trial was Johnny Bulun Bulun, whose clan community, the Ganalbingu people, occupies lands located around the Arafura Swamp near the center of Arnhem Land, a section of the Northern Territory larger than the state of Maine. By all accounts Bulun Bulun is committed to Aboriginal law and to his clan territory or "country," as Australians call it. But there is no longer anything provincial about Johnny Bulun Bulun's boldly designed paintings, which are coveted by buyers in a global market that generates more than US$135 million in annual sales for Aboriginal artists and the dealers who represent them.[1]

Beginning in the late 1980s, Bulun Bulun and several other painters from Arnhem Land successfully sued firms that trafficked in textiles featuring unauthorized images of the artists' works. Earlier in the twentieth century the art of Australian Aboriginals and other native peoples was often regarded as uncopyrightable on the grounds that as a "folkloric" form it automatically failed to demonstrate the originality that copyright requires. Jurists assumed that native stories and visual art lacked the spark of individual genius that informed Western high culture. But by the 1990s courts were sympathetic to the claim that Aboriginal paintings deserved the same copyright protection as the work of white artists. Earlier cases left unsettled a question that evidently troubled Johnny Bulun Bulun and others concerned with Aboriginal rights. Much Aboriginal art depicts themes central to a local group's religion and mythic charter. In fact, according to Bulun Bulun, creation of these images is a sacred duty entrusted to him by his clan. Regardless of whether his art eventually hangs in a museum or graces the wall of a penthouse in Miami, the act of creating it honors the beings who gave the clan its territory.

Misuse of those images, especially their illicit reproduction, endangers the clan's relationship to the spirits who animate the land. The communal significance of Bulun Bulun's work implies that his designs belong not only to him but to his clan. Put in more legalistic terms, the paintings are a physical manifestation of the fiduciary relationship between artist and community. Although there is no question that Bulun Bulun's specific expression of mythic figures reflects his personal talent, ownership of the work, at least from the Aboriginal perspective, resides in clan and community as much as in the artist.[2]

The case argued in Darwin in 1997 resembled earlier ones in certain respects. The principal defendant was a Brisbane-based textile company that had imported fabric imprinted with images taken from one of Bulun Bulun's best-known paintings, *Magpie Geese and Waterlilies at the Waterhole,* a work now in the permanent collection of the Museum and Art Gallery of the Northern Territory. The company never sought Bulun Bulun's permission for use of his work, nor had he been paid royalties. From the Aboriginal perspective, this infringement harmed not just Bulun Bulun but also his community; hence the inclusion of a second plaintiff, George Milpurrurru, identified as a senior clan official.

Representing the plaintiffs at trial were two attorneys, Colin Golvan, a Melbourne-based expert on intellectual property, and Martin Hardie, a Darwin solicitor then working for the North Australian Aboriginal Legal Aid Service. In their submission to Federal Court, Golvan and Hardie developed several interrelated strands of logic to assert the rights of Bulun Bulun's community in his art. They said, for example, that local custom determines whether an artist may depict certain themes or images. Johnny Bulun Bulun "is authorised or permitted by the traditional [clan] owners to depict the matters contained in the artistic work, and he does so for the benefit of those traditional owners and under their overall direction." This element of control is akin to community copyright although it does not undermine the validity of the painter's recognized copyright in the work. Instead, the artist works as "custodian or trustee on behalf of the traditional owners."

Here the arguments took a turn that moved the case from the dark corners of intellectual property litigation into the harsh light of national politics. From the Aboriginal perspective, clan rights to sacred knowledge cannot be separated from rights in land. A clan's local stories and rituals are focused on a specific piece of country and are seen as essential to its continued well-being. Therefore, community rights in traditional art must be approached as one element or reflection of "native title," a term that in the Australian context refers to Aboriginal land rights.

Any legal reference to native title was a red flag for the state and federal governments, which were grappling with a revolution in legal thinking about Aboriginal land rights. The principal spark for that revolution was a 1992 decision of Australia's High Court in *Mabo and Others v. Queensland,* which reversed more than a century of legal precedent. The primary plaintiff in the suit was Eddie Mabo (1936–1992), who lived on Murray Island, part of an island chain lying in the Torres Strait, off Australia's northeast corner. Mabo had reportedly been shocked to discover that his family's traditional lands were officially regarded as belonging to the Crown. This meant that despite the family's long occupation of the land, it remained under the formal control of the government of Queensland, the state in which the Torres Strait Islands are located. After Mabo filed a title claim, the Queensland government passed a law that summarily extinguished all native land titles in the Torres Strait Islands. This law was overturned by the High Court on the grounds that Eddie Mabo and his fellow plaintiffs clearly had a compelling common-law claim to their land by right of ancestral occupation. The decision reversed prior thinking in Australia, which assumed that lands were unoccupied and therefore under the power of the Crown except in cases where the native population could establish traditional ownership. With *Mabo,* the burden of proof shifted to the government, which was obliged to show that there were no prior occupants or that traditional owners had voluntarily abandoned their lands.

The effect of *Mabo* on Australian Aboriginal rights rivaled the impact of *Brown v. Board of Education* on African Americans in the United States. Suddenly a taken-for-granted part of national life was completely redefined. Almost overnight, Aboriginals became a force to be reckoned with in decisions about forestry, mining, and fishing rights. A 1996 court decision known as *Wik* acknowledged Aboriginal claims to grazing districts estimated to encompass more than 40 percent of Australia's land area. The government also faced the prospect of compensating native titleholders for lands taken without due process. Unfortunately, Eddie Mabo died before the court issued the ruling that made his name a household word in Australia.[3]

By the time *Bulun Bulun and Milpurrurru v. R & T Textiles* was ready to be heard in Darwin, federal and state governments in Australia had become exquisitely sensitive to issues of indigenous land rights and hostile toward the accumulation of new legal precedent that could further roil the turbulent waters of native title. The *Bulun Bulun* lawsuit, as well as an emerging strain of expert opinion, stressed the supposedly unbreakable link between land tenure and traditional art. Frank Brennan, a legal scholar, echoes the opinions of other lawyers and activists when he insists that Aboriginal art has become for its creators "a way of sharing the land through understanding and respect." "The painting," he continues, "both tells the story and evokes it; it is the text and the visual aid; it is the map, the code and the very terrain under which lies buried a world of meaning."

The art historian Geoff Bardon suggests that the work of an Aboriginal artist from the Western Desert, Tim Leurah, symbolically recovers land now owned by whites. Through the painting *Napperby Death Spirit Dreaming*, says Bardon, the artist "appropriates Napperby to himself as his own Dreaming, and by implication takes it away from its white owners."[4]

Because *Mabo* established that one criterion for determining native title is ongoing connection to the land, the *Bulun Bulun* case threatened to usher in a new era in which traditional painting was used as evidence in land-claims litigation. The plaintiffs in *Bulun Bulun* did little to discourage these fears. The heart of the case, after all, was the claim by the second plaintiff, George Milpurrurru, that the Ganalbingu people as a whole had rights in traditional designs that were inextricably tied to rights in land. Although an early submission in the case sought monetary damages for the community, this demand was dropped when the principal defendant, R & T Textiles, reached a financial settlement with Bulun Bulun and filed for protection under Australian bankruptcy laws. The company was excused from appearing at trial, so the nominal defendant was not even present in the courtroom. The case was pursued to make a point, and that point, however uncertain its implications, was perceived as threatening by various branches of Australian government. This accounts for the curious fact that the defense was mounted by the Minister for Aboriginal and Torres Strait Islander Affairs, the agency ostensibly responsible for protecting the interests of the plaintiffs.

The arguments in *Bulun Bulun* were heard on what was the trial's second day, September 23. On September 22, the attorneys and the presiding judge, Justice John von Doussa, surveyed Ganalbingu clan territory from the air and then landed to take testimony from community leaders who could not attend the courtroom phase of the trial. In court the next day, Justice von Doussa allowed the Attorney General for the Northern Territory to make a brief statement related to the territory's request for *amicus curiae* ("friend of the court") status. For the Northern Territory, as for the federal government, the plaintiffs' insistence that this case concerned land as well as copyright threw into doubt the federal court's jurisdiction. Disputes involving Aboriginal land are obliged to follow procedures specified in Australia's Native Title Act. With other Aboriginal peoples, the Ganalbingu share a large trust territory controlled by the Northern Land Council, a semi-autonomous Aboriginal organization. The implication of the Attorney General's statement, then, was that any court ruling that addressed Ganalbingu land title claims could undermine the legitimacy of existing trust arrangements. Justice von Doussa cheerfully acknowledged these objections while making it clear that he saw them as having little merit, especially because pre-trial changes in the plaintiffs' submissions had backed away from the native-title question in favor of a focus on the collective nature of Aboriginal rights in traditional art. When the barrister for the federal government raised similar jurisdictional objections, the judge declared that he intended to move the proceedings forward nevertheless.

After these opening salvos from the government, the plaintiffs' barrister, Colin Golvan, presented his case. A curator from the local museum arrived with *Magpie Geese and Waterlilies at the Waterhole* in tow, and samples of the infringing textile were entered as evidence. Once Golvan got to the heart of his argument, Justice von Doussa launched a series of questions from the bench. If an artist's clan and community jointly hold rights in traditional designs, the judge asked, what does that mean for any party that wants to license the work for reproduction? Can a company enter into licensing arrangements with an artist without first communicating with the artist's clan leadership? And how are we to define the artist's community? Does it consist only of those who reside around a specific waterhole, or might it include all Aboriginal people in Arnhem Land?

Behind these questions was a concern that recognition of community rights in art might have the perverse effect of making it more difficult to honor the copyright of indigenous artists. Let us say that a manufacturer offers reasonable royalties to an Aboriginal artist in exchange for a license to reproduce a given work. Must the manufacturer worry that clan leaders will later demand that they be paid royalties too? Beyond this lies a broader legal question: Are non-Aboriginal Australians to be held accountable for legal principles that apply within Aboriginal society alone?[5]

The trial, which ended late in the afternoon, provided an unusual introduction to Australian society for a visiting American. Despite the energy and good will that the judge and the plaintiffs' counsel brought to the encounter, it was discomfiting to witness Aboriginal attitudes toward land, religion, and law under discussion in such a formal setting and in the absence of any Aboriginal people themselves. The earnestness with which the debate took place lent credence to claims that the *Mabo* decision had sparked a crisis of identity among Australians of European ancestry, whose sense of their own society—its history, values, and goals—was thrown into disarray. In this courtroom white Australians were talking as much about themselves as about financial or moral injuries inflicted on an Aboriginal community.

With surprising frequency, these discussions touch upon the status and meaning of Aboriginal art. Aboriginal art is ubiquitous in Australia, part of the visual backdrop of everyday life. Most Australians claim to know something about it. Aboriginal paintings have become significant export commodities that when exhibited draw

Johnny Bulun Bulun, *Magpie Geese and Waterlilies at the Waterhole,* 1980. Natural pigments on bark.

sophisticated crowds in New York, Paris, and London. Aboriginal design shares totemic status with the Sydney Opera House as a symbol of the Australian nation.

An earlier generation of art critics represented the pointillist works of the Central and Western Desert as harbingers of Western modernism. This view is now dismissed as superficial and ethnocentric. Aboriginal art, today's critics declare, must be "understood on its own terms," meaning, apparently, that it should be interpreted through the lens of Aboriginal worldview, religion, and social relations. These have long been the province of social anthropology. But anthropology will no longer do, according to the next wave of politically aware commentators (among whom must be counted some anthropologists), because anthropology promotes "ethnocide," culture-killing, through its implicit promotion of Western categories of knowledge ("epistemic hegemony"). What is called for is hard-headed criticism attuned to the political economy of Aboriginal art production. Critics taking this approach suggest that market pressures are undermining the integrity of Aboriginal society as tradition is "reconfigured according to the relative success or failure of the commodity."[6]

Yet another wave of critics, claiming even greater political awareness than the last, reject any suggestion that Aboriginal society is harmed by the art market. Aboriginal cultures, they insist, are dynamic entities that must change to survive. Their art, even at its most commercial, is a form of cultural resistance, an assertion of presence, an object lesson in the mystical union of land and religion. So what if Aboriginal women have usurped traditional male prerogatives by producing dazzling art that fetches high prices in the global marketplace? That is not a corruption of Aboriginal law but a creative redefinition of it. Who cares if several well-known Aboriginal painters are found to have signed works actually completed by others? This simply reflects Aboriginal notions of collective ownership or foregrounds similarities between the workshops of Aboriginal paint-ers and the *ateliers* of famous European painters. In the world of aca-demic art criticism, this week's decoding of Aboriginal painting is next week's expression of disreputable tendencies, each one worse than the last: romanticism, ethnocentrism, essentialism, paternalism, neocolonialism, racism.

One thing about which the most recent critics agree is that Ab-original art is infused with significance that outsiders can approach only with difficulty, if at all. Aboriginal painters themselves have far less to say about their art, either because they are denied access to channels of mass communication or, as seems more likely, because they are observing rules of discretion that limit how much explana-tion they can provide. This reticence, of course, helps to create a spe-cial aura around their work, which in turn fuels demand. It is one thing to buy a garden-variety painting, quite another to purchase a work redolent of vast, timeless, impenetrable spiritual meaning. An odd contradiction permeating the current interpretive literature, then, is that even as it subjects romantic fascination with Aboriginal religion to withering criticism, it often ends on a note of submission to the mystical otherness of the Aboriginal mind, which is said to compress spirituality, politics, and love for the land into visually compelling works.[7]

Debate about the meaning of Aboriginal art parallels public dis-cussion about land and its newly recognized sacredness. The injec-tion of the sacred into copyright litigation is especially jarring be-cause intellectual property is an area of law historically characterized by pragmatism and an explicit balancing of multiple, conflicting rights. Compared to criminal law, which inevitably confronts deep-seated notions of revenge and purification of the social body, intel-lectual property law is the apotheosis of reason, which is why it has, at least until recently, been considered obscure and dull, even by many lawyers. It may have its own metaphysics, but that typically has less to do with religion or morality than with the nature of authorship.[8]

The pre-trial depositions of Johnny Bulun Bulun and George Milpurrurru emphasized the spiritual harm caused by copyright infringement. "It is the ultimate act of destruction under our law and custom—it upsets the whole religious, political and legal balance underpinning Yolngu society," Johnny Bulun Bulun declared. *At the Waterhole,* he said, "has all the inside [secret] meaning of our ceremony, law and custom encoded in it . . . To produce [the painting] without strict observance of the law governing its production diminishes its importance and interferes adversely with the relationship and trust established between myself, my ancestors, and Barnda [the long-neck tortoise, a creator being]."

Johnny Bulun Bulun's statement leaves important questions unanswered. Why, for instance, is reproduction of *At the Waterhole* in newspapers and books (including this one) theologically acceptable to the artist and his community while the reproduction of the same design on cloth was not? By allowing the work to be exhibited in public forums and mass media, the artist cedes control over who may see the image and how they behave in its presence. One may reasonably wonder whether the claim of grievous spiritual harm is exaggerated. A more sympathetic interpretation is that any unauthorized reproduction of art generates anxiety for Aboriginals precisely because it demonstrates their inability to control the circulation of images that tell important stories about the sacred.

Although the *Bulun Bulun* lawsuit has unique qualities, it exemplifies the high profile that intellectual property—an arena encompassing copyright, trademarks, patents, and trade secrets—has attained in global discussions about indigenous rights. Many lawyers and activists believe that intellectual property law holds the key to heritage protection. To understand this position, we must first trace the history of copyright and trademark in industrial societies.[9]

The European concept of copyright—literally, the right to make copies—arose at the intersection of several historical currents, including the spread of literacy, the decline of guilds, growing separation of private and public spheres, and the emerging conviction that individuals had innate rights worthy of protection. None of these may have been as important as the advent of the printing press. As historians of copyright explain, the printing press made it possible for one publisher to exploit the work of another by producing a low-cost version of any popular book. The pirate could sell his works for a lower price because he was not burdened by the fees that the original printer had paid to the author, nor did the pirate have to bear the cost of unpopular works that failed to turn a profit. In England, this problem was solved by the granting of royal licenses administered by a monopolistic stationers' guild. Early in the 1700s royal licenses were superseded by the Statute of Anne, which created formal copyrights that lasted for twenty-eight years, after which copyrighted material reverted to what we now call the public domain.[10]

The notion of copyright emerged as an untidy, negotiated arrangement that weighed principle against a calculus of utility. Copyright acknowledges the legitimacy of an author's desire to be rewarded for inventiveness and intellectual labor. At the same time, lawmakers recognized that permanent copyright could stunt creativity by throwing up walls around ideas. So from the time that formal copyright laws were drafted in England and the United States, copyright has always been designed to expire. Although copyright resembles real property, it differs from other forms of property in its impermanence. The term of copyright protection has tended to lengthen with each revision of copyright law—U.S. law currently protects works for seventy years after an author's death—but the conviction that it should not be perpetual has thus far managed to prevail.

The time-limited quality of copyright has always prompted objections. Those who favor perpetual copyright ask: Is *Moby-Dick* any less Herman Melville's creation fifty or a hundred years after Melville's death? If literary works are a form of personal property, why should they be any less permanent than land or a family business, which can be passed down from generation to generation? This approach to copyright has strongly influenced intellectual property law in Europe, where the rights of authors, according to one copyright expert, are "often invested with a sacred character . . . tied into natural law." In contrast, copyright in England and the United States has been viewed as a pragmatic compromise in which the author's right of control is balanced by society's need to have ready access to new and useful ideas. Lord Mansfield, an English judge who played an influential role in eighteenth-century debate about perpetual copyright, saw this balance as critical. "We must take care to guard against two extremes equally prejudicial," he wrote. "The one, that men of ability who have employed their time for the service of the community, may not be deprived of their just merits, and the reward of their ingenuity and labour; the other, that the world may not be deprived of improvements, nor the progress of the arts be retarded."[11]

Modern copyright experts frame the issue differently. For the legal scholar David Lange, copyright is an implicit contract that gives an author "the limited monopoly of copyright for a limited time, but only in exchange for an eventual dedication of the work to the public domain." Using a similar contractual framework, James Boyle, also a legal scholar, argues that the author "stands between the public and private realms, giving new ideas to the society at large and being granted in return a limited right of private property in the artifact he or she has created—or at least assembled from the parts provided by our common store of ideas, language, and genre."[12]

Copyrights are also constrained by what has come to be called the "fair use doctrine." Fair use says that anyone may quote from copyrighted material as long as the borrowed text does not harm the financial interests of the copyright holder. Thanks to this principle, I can selectively reproduce the copyrighted material of others in this book; they, of course, are free to do the same with my work, even in ways that I might find misleading or offensive. The pliable standards of fair use leave room for disagreement. Its limits are contested by corporate copyright holders who want to restrict its scale as much as possible. Nevertheless, the persistence of fair use represents one of the core compromises of copyright: the need to balance the rights of authors against the social benefits that flow from open public discourse.

American copyright law allows the private use of copyrighted material that receives more stringent protection when the use is public. Take the example of "Happy Birthday," a song some readers will be surprised to learn is under copyright until 2019. (It was among many copyrighted works affected by the 1998 extension of copyright terms authorized by the U.S. Congress.) Given the formal logic of copyright, singing the song to one's child infringes the copyrights of composer and lyricist. But fair use permits private performance of copyrighted music, largely because enforcement of the law in such situations would be intrusive and, perhaps more to the point, impractical. This principle has been put to stringent test in cases involving the photocopying or videotaping of copyrighted material for personal use. In each case, the Supreme Court has narrowly supported private reproduction over the claims of copyright holders. Majority opinions turned on such issues as the right to privacy, the hazards of criminalizing the behavior of millions of citizens, and the absence of compelling evidence that private copying causes significant economic harm to authors. These questions came to broad (and for copyright holders, regrettable) public attention in 1996, when it was widely reported that ASCAP, the American Society of Composers, Authors and Publishers, had demanded that Girl Scout camps begin to pay royalties for copyrighted campfire songs because their use qualified as "public performances." The policy proved to be such a public relations fiasco that the organization soon abandoned it and reimbursed fees to the few camps that had paid them.[13]

There is ample precedent for favoring free speech over the rights of authors when the two collide. The most heralded recent example is the "Pretty Woman" case (formally known as *Acuff-Rose Music, Inc. v. Campbell*, 1994), in which the Supreme Court ruled that the rap group 2 Live Crew's recording of the song "Oh, Pretty Woman" fell within fair use limits because the performers used the song for parodic purposes. An element in arguments against 2 Live Crew was that their musical parody was undertaken for commercial gain. This was relevant because American copyright law conceives fair use more broadly when users pursue not-for-profit ends rather than commercial ones. The Supreme Court's majority opinion downplayed the commercial dimension of the parody, but references to the different status of for-profit and not-for-profit uses of copyrighted material illustrate the extent to which copyright laws try to strike a balance between economic gain and society's need for open communication.

A frequently misunderstood aspect of intellectual property law is its role in protecting unpublished works. Under current U.S. law, personal documents, from private letters to random notes scratched on the back of an envelope, are automatically protected by copyright. This means that the author retains control over first publication of that material. This little-used aspect of copyright has attracted attention in recent years because of controversial decisions that blocked biographers from quoting from unpublished letters written by their subjects. Although an author's control of unpublished documents follows from the logic of copyright, it distorts copyright's broader intent, which is to encourage and facilitate the *dissemination* of creative work, not its suppression. Some experts believe that the use of copyright law to protect personal privacy is a dangerous trend. "Copyright law's constitutional mission is . . . neither to protect privacy nor to give authors total artistic control," concludes Diane Conley, an attorney and legal scholar. "It is, rather, to increase public knowledge." People who write or compose or invent are naturally drawn to the view that creative genius imbues their work with a quasi-sacred status. As many commentators point out, however, the originality of most copyrighted works is low. Copyright law equally protects the brilliantly innovative novelist and the commercial hack. However modest the creativity that a given author demonstrates, copyright allows the creator to profit from his or her work and to exercise some control over its use. At the same time, copyright law recognizes that this creativity draws from and depends on an intellectual commons to which authors eventually add the fruits of their labor.[14]

Several features of modern copyright systems have worked against native peoples. A foundational principle of copyright is that a work can be protected only when it has been translated to a "tangible medium." That means that ideas must be fixed in some way by being committed to paper or canvas or clay or photographic film. I may believe that my brilliant idea for the plot of a novel is mine alone. Until the book is actually written, however, the plot can be used freely by anyone with whom I am rash enough to share it over drinks. The reasons for this are both philosophical and practical. Ideas are, or should be, a shared human birthright, much like the air we breathe. On a practical level, it is impossible to police pure ideas, which are by definition volatile and insubstantial. Hence the maxim "You can't copyright an idea; you can only copyright the expression of an idea."

It should be obvious that the distinction between ideas and their material expression places traditional communities at a disadvantage. Prior to the introduction of writing, photography, and audio-recording technologies, many indigenous societies had only graphic design and architecture with which to "fix" traditional knowledge in the sense understood by copyright law. Most information was conveyed orally or through physical action. Even the availability of more permanent media might not have made a difference. Given the low standards of originality that characterize copyright, the existence of a written (and therefore automatically copyrighted) body of folktales or religious songs would do little to prevent someone else from copyrighting a different version of the same material. For example, if a pioneering Hopi photographer had managed to document her community's rituals before H. R. Voth came on the scene, copyright protections afforded these earlier photographs would not have prevented Voth from publishing pictures of his own provided that they differed slightly from those of his predecessor.

This point is often misunderstood by leaders of indigenous groups, some of whom seem to believe that copyrighting a text or an image preempts the use of anything that even vaguely resembles it. David Dinwoodie, an anthropological linguist on the faculty of the University of New Mexico, studies an Athabascan-speaking people of British Columbia called the Chilcotin. During his months of fieldwork in Chilcotin communities, he learned that tribal officials had installed a large and imposing safe in their modest office. They were close-mouthed about its contents. Dinwoodie tells of a day when one of the officials, to demonstrate the community's growing trust of the visiting anthropologist, offered to give him a tour of the safe. The heavy door was unlocked and ceremoniously pulled back. Inside lay a single document. His host explained that the document was a transcription of a Chilcotin myth. Chilcotin leaders, it seems, had heard that a folklorist living among a neighboring band of Indians had recorded the group's mythology and then published the stories in a copyrighted book. Now the folklorist "owned" the myths. To prevent this from happening to them, the Chilcotin were determined to record their own myths and secure them from theft.[15]

A folklorist or anthropologist could, of course, copyright a specific body of native texts. Given the vagaries of translation and the likelihood that any given story has multiple variations, other versions of the same texts would equally qualify for protection. One senses that beneath Chilcotin fears lies a different way of looking at stories. Perhaps in their society certain stories belong to specific categories of people—members of a particular clan or a specialized religious society, for example. But their anxiety also expresses broader concern about an alien intellectual property system that seems mysterious and exploitative.

Critics of the status quo cite instances in which unprincipled outsiders have taken advantage of indigenous artists. Some of the cases, like Johnny Bulun Bulun's, represent blatant infringement motivated by a belief that the illegal use will never be noticed. Others are less direct, exploiting recorded material now separated in time and space from its original performers. One such case is documented in fascinating detail by Steve Feld, an anthropologist and ethnomusicologist. Feld tracks the history of Pygmy music—more accurately, the flute music and distinctive yodeling of the egalitarian forest-dwelling peoples of Central Africa who collectively have been known to the West as Pygmies. First recorded systematically in the 1950s, the distinctive intervals and timbre of Pygmy music soon worked their way into the Afrocentric jazz of the 1970s (Herbie Hancock's *Headhunters* album), then into the emerging genres of world music and electro-acoustic music of the 1970s (the work of Egberto Gismonti and Brian Eno, among others), then, perhaps inevitably, into the pop diva Madonna's album *Bedtime Stories* in the 1990s. The most significant recent appearance of Pygmy music is a cameo role in the bestselling album *Deep Forest,* ostensibly created by French musicians but based heavily on material taken from field recordings of indigenous music. *Deep Forest* sold more than two million copies, and its music has been featured in advertisements for products ranging from skin cream to sports cars. Although the CD's producers claim that some of the proceeds from the album find their way back to the tribal people whose voices and instruments figure in it, Feld could find no evidence that Pygmy populations benefited financially from the album's success.[16]

The days when native artists could have their work pirated with impunity are coming to an end. Contemporary native performers, writers, and artists in countries like the United States, Canada, and Australia usually understand the basics of copyright law, and they know that their work is protected even if it has not been formally registered. Still, protection of economic interests touches only the surface of indigenous concerns. The fair use doctrine allows copyrighted works to be fragmented, quoted by others as part of their own creative efforts. In the case of a song, the entire work can be re-arranged and performed in radically different ways, provided that the arranger pays the pertinent fees. This violates what some see as the right of an artist to protect works from dismemberment or misuse, a principle usually referred to as the "right of integrity."

Equally problematic is the time-limited nature of copyright. It is one thing to accept that an artist's rights in creative work end at some point after death, quite another to countenance the idea that a group's sacred art or stories will eventually become detached from the community where they arose. The images painted by Johnny Bulun Bulun will not lose their spiritual potency seventy years after his death. Much of the current ferment over the intellectual property of indigenous peoples involves attempts to work around this fundamental limitation. Advocates for indigenous rights use the idioms of intellectual property to make a case for the creation of impermeable boundaries between native and non-native societies—or, more accurately, the imposition of a screen that allows selected external information to flow into indigenous communities while controlling what flows out.

Critics tend to see the creolization of art—the improvisational blending of the indigenous themes and motifs with other traditions—in two different lights. One is positive: the interweaving of two distinct cultures expresses a genuine effort to bring together natives and settlers in a bi-cultural society based on mutual respect. The pessimistic view is that native styles can move to the mainstream only when natives themselves have been neutralized and pushed to the margins. The theft of musical and artistic genres becomes the final assault after colonialism has taken away everything else. At present, the darker view prevails in the critical literature.[17]

Almost a year passed before Justice von Doussa handed down a decision in *Bulun Bulun*. On the face of it, his ruling went against the plaintiffs. He rejected the assertion that the case involved issues of native land title, a claim from which the plaintiffs had already backed away in their revised submission. He acknowledged that rights in land and the right to produce specific images are closely tied in Aboriginal thought. But the procedures associated with land claims are independent of Australian copyright law and therefore had to be removed from consideration. Because Johnny Bulun Bulun had already arrived at a satisfactory settlement with the infringing textile company, the issue remaining undecided was whether Mr. Milpurrurru, the clan leader, possessed an "equitable" (that is, equal) interest in Bulun Bulun's painting *At the Waterhole*. Justice von Doussa concluded that he did not. According to Australian copyright law, an equitable interest is associated only with joint authorship, defined as a collaboration "in which the contribution of each author is not separate from the contribution of the other author." No evidence suggested that anyone other than Bulun Bulun had created the painting. Nor was the judge persuaded that the artist had created the work as part of an implied legal trust that would make his community equal partners in the disposition of the work. The preponderance of evidence, Justice von Doussa observed, showed that "on many occasions paintings which incorporate to a greater or lesser degree parts of the ritual knowledge of the Ganalbingu people are produced by Ganalbingu artists for commercial sale for the benefit of the artist concerned."[18]

Within the negative decision lay a larger victory. Revealing the same thoughtfulness he had shown during the trial, Justice von Doussa concluded that although the artist and his community did not share an equal interest in *At the Waterhole*, they did share a fiduciary interest—in other words, bonds of trust and mutual responsibility. The judge reasoned that "an artist is entitled to consider and pursue his own interests, for example by selling the artwork, but the artist is not permitted to shed the overriding obligation to act to preserve the integrity of the Ganalbingu culture where action for that purpose is required." What this means in practical terms is that the community may expect the artist to defend his work from infringement or other abuse. Should the artist fail to do so, reasoned Justice von Doussa, the community is allowed to initiate its own legal action against an infringing party. Johnny Bulun Bulun had vigorously defended his copyright in this case, leaving the community with no need for remedy. "However, in other circumstances," concluded the judge, "if the copyright owner of an artistic work which embodies ritual knowledge of an Aboriginal clan is being used inappropriately, and the copyright owner fails or refuses to take appropriate action to enforce the copyright, the Australian legal system will permit remedial action through the courts by the clan."

It was this important final point—that communities or clans have defensible rights in traditional art—which evoked approving comments from Aboriginal advocacy organizations. In a radio interview, Martin Hardie, the solicitor who helped Colin Golvan prepare the case, concluded that "where a third party has somehow appropriated an image or an aspect of that corpus of ritual knowledge without permission . . . it may be possible for the clan now to bring an action based in equity—I would presume, to restrain that use." The interviewer was quick to see other possible implications of the *Bulun Bulun* decision. "Could it be used as a precedent for other non-indigenous, non-Aboriginal groups?" she asked. "Say for instance there's some small Eastern European tribal group that still has vestiges in Australia. They have their own unique story and language, and part of that story and language is turned into a very popular children's series. Could this case be relied upon to say that the community, notwithstanding that the individual artist is long gone, could step in and run a case on behalf of that communal knowledge?" Hardie acknowledged that the decision could set the stage for such claims.[19]

Beyond enthusiasm for the recognition of communal rights in art, then, lie unexplored legal paths, some of which hint at troubling possibilities. Can the emergent notion of communal intellectual property be limited to Aboriginal communities, or will it inevitably spill over, as the radio interviewer quickly saw, to other self-defined "tribal" or ethnic groups? And what of urban Aboriginals? Will claims be made against the work of Aboriginal artists living in urban areas, who may not identify at all with a particular clan or community? The current trajectory of policy and legal decisions may leave urban Aboriginals even more marginal than they are at present: denied access to political and economic resources yet regarded as somehow less authentic than their rural counterparts, who stand to benefit from the social changes put into play by the *Mabo* decision.[20]

Although it would be unfair to underestimate the genuine sympathy that many Australians feel for the country's original occupants, one also senses in the Australian situation the unconscious appeal of disrupting secular and impersonal legal processes by inserting the sacred into copyright law. It is satisfying to subvert bureaucratic rationality by insisting that intellectual property is about something more important than money. Of course, this valorization of the sacred must be at a certain remove from one's own life. Most of the whites who struggle for the legal recognition of Aboriginal religious concepts would fight just as hard to oppose mandatory public observance of the Sabbath or introduction of Creation Science into the biology curriculum of their neighborhood schools. They express commitment to the persistence of a social world in which religion is undifferentiated from education, law, science, and art, so long as the burdens of that mystical oneness are borne by others.

Similar sentiment animates public discussion about the communal nature of the Aboriginal economy. The *Bulun Bulun* case is at least partly about a perceived contrast between the individualism characteristic of capitalism and the collective work, real or imagined, of Aboriginal artists. No matter that today most works granted copyright or patent protection are the product of corporate laboratories, design studios, software teams, and research-and-development facilities, forms of communalism built on impersonal contracts and financial power rather than shared values and group solidarity. Today, white Australia needs Aboriginal Australia to keep alive the dream that there exist, somewhere not impossibly far away, forms of lived experience that retain the magical holism shattered by modernity.

The heavy burden that intellectual property law is being asked to carry becomes apparent in the curious case of the Aboriginal flag, whose bright yellow sun-disk, straddling bars of black and red, was much in evidence during the 2000 Sydney Olympics. In 1997 an Australian court determined that the flag is a copyrighted work and that its copyright is held by Harold Thomas, an Aboriginal artist who designed it in the early 1970s as the Aboriginal rights movement was gathering momentum. As a child Thomas was removed from his parents' home in Alice Springs and taken to an orphanage in Adelaide. From there he was adopted by a white family, about whom he speaks fondly even while helping to publicize the misguided policies that created a "lost generation" of Aboriginal adoptees. Thomas received a good education, and his subsequent career as an artist and designer has been successful enough for the *Sydney Morning Herald* to include him on its list of the hundred most influential Australians of the last century.

Thomas's statements about his much-publicized copyright case are somewhat contradictory. He has never denied that he benefits financially from the flag copyright. But his principal interest in pursuing the case seems to have been political. In court testimony, he said that he had been moved to assert his copyright after the Australian government officially declared his creation "a flag of significance to the Australian people generally." Rather than being gratified by official embrace of the flag, Thomas was angered. The proclamation was, he said, "a usurpation of something which properly belonged to the Aboriginal people." In statements after the court decision,

Thomas declared that he has no objection to the flag being reproduced freely by Aboriginal people themselves. What he wanted was to control its use by others, who must ask him for permission and, if permission is granted, purchase it from a licensed manufacturer.[21]

A national flag is by definition a public symbol, one of the most potent that a group possesses. Its power ensures that it will be used for many purposes, some of which may not be pleasing to the group's members. Hence the persistent quest of American conservatives for a constitutional amendment to criminalize desecration of the U.S. flag. The case of the Aboriginal flag is an unusually frank expression of broader indigenous efforts to use copyright law to control key symbols of native identity. Copyright stands little chance of dismantling the master's house, but it is already offering native peoples modest protection for their own dwellings.

3. Sign Wars

Members of the North American Vexillological Association, an organization dedicated to the systematic study of flags, recently voted the state flag of New Mexico the best in the United States. It is certainly one of the most memorable: against a field of brilliant yellow, a red circle radiates four lines in each of the cardinal directions. The design was officially adopted in 1925 at the behest of the Daughters of the American Revolution, who five years earlier had sponsored a competition for a flag symbolizing New Mexico's unique landscape and history. The winning proposal was submitted by Harry Mera, a physician and avocational archaeologist from Santa Fe. Mera's sun symbol was inspired by the central design element of a nineteenth-century ceramic pot crafted by an anonymous potter from Zia Pueblo, an Indian community located thirty-three miles northwest of Albuquerque. According to state documents, the Zia sun symbol "reflects the pueblo's tribal philosophy, with its wealth of pantheistic spiritualism teaching the basic harmony of all things in the universe." In 1963 these sentiments were formalized in the official salute to the flag: "I salute the flag of the State of New Mexico and the Zia symbol of perfect friendship among united cultures." A Spanish translation of the salute was officially recognized a decade later.[1]

In 1994 the people of Zia challenged this perfect friendship by formally demanding reparations for the state's use of the sun symbol. By 2001 the monetary demand had risen to $76 million, one million for each year that the symbol had been used on the state's flag and letterhead. When a bill responsive to the tribe's demand was first considered by the New Mexico legislature, it provoked expressions of skepticism and anger in the regional press. The Associated Press listed it among unusual legislative resolutions and bills reported under the headline "Lawmakers Tackle Asparagus-Bashing, State Dinosaur, Square-Dancing Lobby." The article implied that the sun-symbol bill was in the same league as a South Carolina measure making it illegal to lick hallucinogenic toads. In a letter to the *Arizona Republican,* a citizen named Shirley Kinney complained that "something is very wrong" when the Zia tribe demands compensation for use of its symbol. "The Zia Pueblo," she wrote, "should be proud to be American and have the tribe's symbol used on the state flag. We are one people, not separate, in this great country."[2]

The Zia demands proved anything but frivolous. They were precipitated by a trademark application submitted by American Frontier Motorcycle Tours, a Santa Fe–based company specializing in travel on Harley-Davidson motorcycles. The company's logo prominently displayed a stylized version of the sun symbol. Nothing was especially unusual about the application. New Mexicans are accustomed to seeing the sun symbol affixed to everything from automobile license plates to convenience-store signs. But the trademark of the motorcycle touring company pushed the Zia into action after decades of muted grumbling. The religiously powerful version of the sun symbol, which has clusters of three rays pointing in each direction rather than the four found on the state flag, is used by the Zia, and possibly by other Pueblo peoples, in rituals ranging from the ceremonies that welcome new babies into this world to the funerals that usher the dead into the next. Aside from their concern about the inappropriate use of a powerful religious symbol, residents of Zia were angry because no one had asked their permission before adopting the symbol for the state flag.[3]

In the face of unfavorable publicity and intervention by one of the state's U.S. senators, Jeff Bingaman, the touring company withdrew its trademark application. In a newspaper interview, Zia's tribal administrator, Peter Pino, noted that the Zia routinely approve the use of the symbol by businesses that seek the tribe's permission and declare in writing that it belongs to the pueblo. His comments imply that the issue is less one of religious desecration than of basic respect. There is little question, though, that some Zia residents object to the idea that businesses might profit from the use of a symbol strongly identified with the community's religious practices.

The dispute over the sun symbol secured a prominent place in public hearings mandated by Public Law 105–330, which called on the U.S. Patent and Trademark Office (USPTO) to examine its policies relating to the official insignia of Indian tribes. Central to the hearings was the question of whether tribal insignia—the scope of which, as will become clear, is difficult to define—should be granted the protections conferred on the insignias of local, state, and federal agencies. A related issue was whether marks already registered by commercial firms are disparaging of Native American cultures.

Interest in the protection of signs and symbols is an expression of the continuing search for ways to shore up what are, from the indigenous-rights perspective, key weaknesses of copyright: its time-lim-

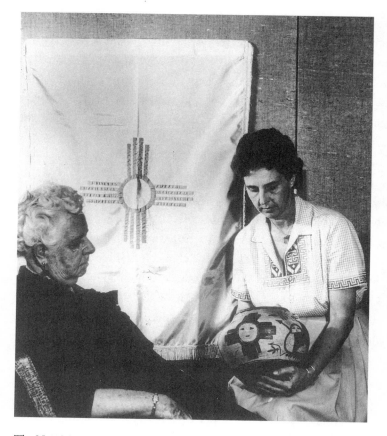

The New Mexico state flag and the Zia pot that inspired it. *Left:* Reba Mera, widow of the flag's designer, Dr. Harry P. Mera. *Right:* Betty Toulouse, curator, School of American Research, Santa Fe. Photograph probably taken in 1968.

ited quality and its inability to effect absolute control over the use of protected work. Protection and fair use are two sides of the contractual nature of copyright. Native activists stand firmly in support of protection; many oppose fair use, which they say is incompatible with their own cultural rules. That is why they have focused attention on two aspects of intellectual property law that offer enduring, comprehensive control over the use of works: trademark law and the moral-rights element of copyright, sometimes referred to as "author's rights."

At first glance, native concerns seem tailor made for a moral-rights strategy. Moral rights, unlike the economic rights associated with copyright, are perpetual. They are also designed to defend the creator against defamatory uses of a copyrighted work. This potentially cordons off material from fair use, including the selective quotation of material by someone whose views the original author finds offensive. In principle, this could provide a powerful screen of protection for indigenous cultural productions. In practice, there are obstacles. Copyright law protects discrete products defined as "works." Is a group's folklore a work or is it something else? Even if all known myths and folktales of a particular society have been transcribed and published, would the moral-rights doctrine give the group control over novel tellings of the same tales? Would such rights have limits? That is, if groups control all uses of works defined as theirs, would this effectively prevent others from quoting or borrowing from those materials in perpetuity?

An Australian study, *Our Culture: Our Future,* published in 1998, considers the implications of moral rights and other expressions of intellectual property law for native peoples. In reviewing proposed Australian legislation intended to protect indigenous peoples from "derogatory treatment" (defined as "doing anything that results in material distortion, mutilation of or material alteration to the work that is prejudicial to the author's honour or reputation"), the report allows that it will be hard to distinguish between simple portrayals of Aboriginal life and investigative reporting that documents troubling aspects of it. Critics of the proposed legislation obviously fear that it will inhibit the ability of the news media to talk about native peoples in public forums. In contrast, native-rights activists argue that the legislation is not restrictive enough, leaving too many loopholes and unanswered questions about precisely who will be able to exercise moral rights after an author's death.[4]

Despite initial hopes that principles of moral rights would provide powerful leverage for indigenous societies, little has happened on this front. As noted earlier, the moral-rights dimension of copyright is underdeveloped in the United States, a situation that seems unlikely to change. Even in places where moral rights have legal standing, the gap between Western notions of individual creativity and the concerns of native communities may be too great to be bridged. Interest has shifted instead to another key element of intellectual property law, trademarks.

A trademark is a sign or, as USPTO attorneys put it, an "indication" clearly identifying something as the product of a particular manufacturer. The use of marks has been traced as far back as First Dynasty Egypt (ca. 3200 B.C.), when pottery was inscribed with distinctive symbols that identified the maker. One of the earliest legal contests dealing with trademark infringement took place in 1618, when an English textile manufacturer sued a competitor who used the plaintiff's mark on inferior cloth with the intention to deceive.[5]

Textbooks on intellectual property law explain that a distinctive mark serves two main purposes. First, it identifies a product to buyers and assures them that they know who made it. Second, it protects the maker from other companies that might be tempted to confuse buyers by using the same mark. Anyone who travels in countries where illiteracy is common receives a rapid education in the power of manufacturers' marks. Among Indians in the Peruvian Amazon, even members of the community who cannot read are comfortable talking about *tátasham máchit* ("woodpecker machetes"), tools of Spanish manufacture whose blades are stamped with the woodpecker trademark. Ironically, trademarks have become even more important in the developed world because their stark simplicity keeps them visible amid the media-generated tidal wave of imagery. The legal scholar Rosemary Coombe suggests that trademarks are now such important signifiers of difference that they provide a parallel language that we use to communicate with others via the goods arrayed in our homes and on our bodies.[6]

Trademark thinking has become sufficiently pervasive that college and university presidents talk publicly, and with no trace of embarrassment, about the value of their "brand." Ordinary words and phrases—"Big Kids Meals," "Increase," "It's a good thing"—are trademarked, and businesses are now reaching for letters of the alphabet: in 2002, attorneys for Oprah Winfrey and her publishers went to court to defend her in a lawsuit claiming that Winfrey's publication *O, The Oprah Magazine* infringed the registered trademark of another magazine, also called *O*, that features erotic images of women in fetish clothing. (The judge ruled for Winfrey on the grounds that the plaintiff had waited too long to file suit and that the two magazines are so different that consumers are unlikely to confuse them.) As we run out of available space in the lexical domain, companies are actively exploring other sensory arenas. Jingles provide a familiar example of auditory trademarks, but perhaps not all readers know that the ticking-watch sound of the CBS news program *Sixty Minutes* is also protected, as is the roar of the MGM lion. The Harley-Davidson company attracted public attention in 1994 when it attempted to register the distinctive sound of its V-Twin motorcycle engine. (The company abandoned the campaign six years later, citing the cost of responding to litigation launched by competing manufacturers.) Trademark has begun to homestead the olfactory world as well. The European Union recently granted a trademark for the smell of freshly cut grass. This mark will identify a line of tennis balls sold under the name "Scenter Court."[7]

Unlike copyrights and patents, trademarks do not require originality, only distinctiveness. They last as long as the trademark holder uses and defends them. They may be lost if allowed to slide into common usage, which explains why companies oppose even innocuous references to trademarked material in books and magazines. The need to defend a trademark may produce litigation that fosters head-shaking cynicism about the law. In 1999 the pop musician Prince filed suit against a fan magazine devoted to his music on the grounds that it had used his identity-symbol without authorization. In response to a long-running feud with his record company, Prince dropped his name in 1993 and replaced it with a trademarked symbol. (Hence press references to him as "the Artist Formerly Known as Prince," subsequently shortened to "the Artist." He resumed use of his name in 2000.) The suit, however bizarre and ill-considered, offers an object lesson in how the expansion of trademarking threatens the fundamental ability of people to communicate.[8]

Against this backdrop, Zia Pueblo's complaints about outsiders' use of the sun symbol become more convincing. And the people of Zia may not be the most aggrieved among American Indians. Registered trademarks drawn from just three tribal names, "Navajo," "Cherokee," and "Sioux," number more than a hundred. Other tribal names and symbols are in similar if less common use in the marketplace, largely by non-native businesses.

In recent years the USPTO has begun to take this problem seriously. Existing laws allow the agency to deny registration to any mark that "consists of or comprises matter which, with regard to persons, institutions, beliefs, or national symbols, does any of the following: (1) disparages them; (2) falsely suggests a connection with them; (3) brings them into contempt; or (4) brings them into disrepute." Using these criteria, the USPTO has refused registration of the name Zia and the Zia sun symbol to a software company and a maker of cocktail mixes, citing a false association with Zia Pueblo and, in the second case, "possible disparagement of the tribe." The most prominent case in which the agency has invoked these regulations involves the name and logo of the Washington Redskins football team, whose registration the Trademark Trial and Appeals Board of the USPTO revoked after concluding that the term "redskins" was disparaging to Native Americans both today and when the mark was registered decades ago. The case was still under appeal in Federal District Court in 2002, but the tide appears to have turned against the trademark holders. Revocation of registered-trademark standing will not prevent the owners from continuing to use the name and logo. It will simply end the trademark's protected status, opening the door to unlicensed use. Given the financial stakes, loss of trademark registration is likely to put the owners under great pressure to rename the team.[9]

Crazy Horse Malt Liquor, a beverage produced by Hornell Brewing Company and Ferolito, Vultaggio & Sons, has long been the target of a national campaign to end its demeaning use of a revered American Indian leader's name. The USPTO refused to register the trademark, and the manufacturer has been publicly denounced by the U.S. Surgeon General, members of Congress representing both parties, the governor of South Dakota, and countless church groups and student organizations. In 1992 Congress passed a law that specifically banned the association of Crazy Horse's name or image with any alcoholic beverage, although the statute was subsequently overturned on free-speech grounds. The manufacturer's stubborn refusal to abandon the name eventually prompted the descendants of Crazy Horse to bring suit against the company in Rosebud Sioux Tribal Court, alleging, among other things, defamation, emotional harm, and violation of the "right of publicity"—that is, the right of a person or his estate to control the commercial use of a name and image. Subsequent litigation in federal court has focused on whether tribal courts have jurisdiction over parties operating off-reservation. In 1998 the Eighth Circuit Court of Appeals ruled that "the tribal court lacks adjudicatory authority over disputes arising from [the Breweries'] conduct." Since then, efforts of the descendants of Crazy Horse have shifted to federal court, where they filed suit in 2000. A secondary defendant in the suit, SBC Holdings, owner of a brewing company that at one time produced Crazy Horse Malt Liquor for Hornell, reached a settlement in April 2001. John Stroh III, chairman of SBC, went to Mission, South Dakota, to present "32 blankets, 32 braids of sweet grass, 32 twists of tobacco, seven thoroughbred racehorses and an apology" to the administrator of the Crazy Horse estate, Seth Big Crow, thus ending the company's role as a defendant in the lawsuit.[10]

Social critics cite the continued sale of Crazy Horse Malt Liquor as evidence of Indian powerlessness, but the relentless pressure on the product's manufacturer can also be read as a demonstration of the moral authority and political muscle that American Indians—among whom are more than a thousand lawyers—can bring to bear when confronted by egregious cultural insensitivity. In present circumstances, any corporation that emulates Hornell by using Native American names or symbols in defamatory ways must be seen as showing poor judgment, even by the standards of market capitalism.[11]

These distinct currents—commercial, political, and religious—collided in the USPTO-sponsored hearings about the trademark status of tribal insignia, which were held in mid-1999. Written submissions from the public range from the telegraphic ("NO ONE should be able to use insignia in ads, names of products, etc. that belong to Native Americans," from a Nevada resident) to sophisticated special pleading by attorneys representing DaimlerChrysler, the flatware manufacturer Oneida Ltd., and the Mohawk Carpet Corporation. Opinions offered by lawyers focused on three key issues. The first was how the law should define "tribal insignia." Attorneys representing Native Americans proposed definitions of great breadth. The Native Affairs and Development Group, for example, argued that insignias should embrace "any word, name, symbol, or device or any combination thereof used by Native Americans and/or adopted by tribal governments . . . and which is not used in commerce." A second concern was whether new protections for tribal names or insignia would be retroactive, thereby voiding long-standing trademarks of great commercial value. DaimlerChrysler, obviously concerned about the future of its Jeep Cherokee mark, argued against defining tribal names alone as insignia, citing the financial harm that current trademark holders would suffer if their marks lost protection.

The third issue concerned links between American trademark policy and global business practices. The United States is a signatory to the Paris Convention, which obliges the USPTO to honor registered foreign trademarks that are consistent with American norms. "If a foreign-owned company cannot continue to protect its established trademark rights in the United States because its mark is also the name of a Native American tribe, or a component of the tribe's insignia," wrote attorneys for DaimlerChrysler, "this could well result in foreign countries refusing to protect the established trademark rights of United States companies because of native European, Asian, African or South American tribal names and symbols." In fact, changes in the trademark status of indigenous words and symbols are already poised for adoption in Australia and New Zealand. The extent to which this would affect American trademark holders with businesses in those countries is unclear.[12]

The transcripts of the three regional public hearings held by the USPTO in mid-1999 offer a better sense of the emotions behind resistance to the use of traditional symbols for commercial purposes, or for that matter, any purpose not defined by native peoples themselves. Oral testimony also reveals the difficulty of translating these sometimes diffuse sentiments into the narrow goals of a bureaucratic entity such as the USPTO. USPTO officials heard complaints about everything from the use of the word "squaw" in local place names to the sale of Native American tarot cards in New Age bookstores. At the San Francisco hearing, a Dakota woman named Fern Mathias, who identified herself as director of the American Indian Movement in Southern California, urged officials to regulate the use of all Indian symbols, especially religious ones. "Just because the Indians didn't have copyright laws doesn't mean others can take and use their symbols," she said. She continued: "We, as Indian people, never had to regulate fairness, dignity and respect. It came naturally. But we live in America, in the modern age, and we have to protect ourselves. We need to make a list of Indian symbols, especially the religious ones, that should be excluded from commercial use. We need to create an awareness of these symbols and explain why it is offensive to use them. Every company and official organization needs to be furnished with such a list so there will not be the excuse of pleading ignorance."

Mathias urged the USPTO to protect American Indian religious symbols, tribal insignia, tribal names, and "Indian words of significant social, religious or tribal meaning." When asked how the government could best determine which symbols merit protection, she suggested that officials go to traditional religious elders rather than to tribal councils, which she dismissed as an invention of the U.S. government. In view of the government-to-government nature of relations between Indian nations and Washington—a relationship that Indian officials took pains to emphasize in the same hearings—it is difficult to see how the USPTO could bypass the formal governance structure of tribes and communicate directly with "traditional people," whose identity, Mathias herself noted, is often a well-kept secret.[13]

In the day-long hearing held at the Indian Pueblo Cultural Center in Albuquerque, the Zia sun-symbol case took center stage. After brief remarks by USPTO Commissioner Q. Todd Dickinson, Senator Jeff Bingaman, and Representative Tom Udall, the floor was turned over to Amadeo Shije, governor of Zia Pueblo. Governor Shije briefly discussed the history of Zia and its survival against formidable odds. He then turned to the subject of the hearing:

> I know there are other symbols that are important to other tribes. These tribes will speak for themselves about this . . . But I will say that the injury that my people have suffered from the disrespectful use of the Zia sun symbol has been very, very deep. The history of the European in this continent has been a long history of unauthorized taking. We are in the beginning of, I hope, a different frame of mind. I do not see how the Trademark Office in good conscience can give a person, foreign to our nation, the right to use our symbol on a chemical fertilizer or a porta-pottie or whatever business or service he is peddling. Under the existing law, other governments in this country are protected from such an affront. I understand that there are separate statutes protecting the Boy Scouts' insignia and the Red Cross. Even using western logic alone, without using any kind of compassionate understanding of our culture and our way

of life, the official insignia or symbols of the sovereign tribes should be protected as much as the symbol or insignia of municipalities, states, foreign states and so forth.

Governor Shije was followed by other speakers who emphasized the same themes: the religious importance of the sun symbol and the sadness or anger that Indian people feel when they see such images being used for commercial purposes; the possible confusion generated by labeling a product with a tribal name when it is not a product of the tribe; and the difficulty that tribes have in licensing their names and symbols when these are already in use by outsiders. Occasionally percolating to the surface in the generally cordial and measured exchanges were sentiments that if enacted into law would take trademark protection to new places. William Weahkee, executive director of the Five Sandoval Indian Pueblos, spoke of his experiences as the only Indian member of a national committee concerned with petroglyphs—rock images found widely in North America, especially in the West. Commenting on the thoughtlessness with which non-Indian people use these images for their own purposes, Weahkee said: "These things are tied in with song. They're tied in with the ritual. They're tied in with things that we cannot divulge, because what happens when we divulge something like that [is that] it's always exploited at our expense. Nothing comes back to the tribes." In response to a question from a USPTO attorney, Weahkee suggested that the more than 17,000 images and designs already documented should be shielded from exploitation that allows non-Indians "to make profit all the time and not give anything back to the Indian people at all."[14]

The USPTO's final report on the tribal-insignia issue, released in November 1999, shows the difficulty of reconciling anxiety about the proliferation of culturally significant symbols with the tightly focused and largely commercial mission of the USPTO. The agency stood by a definition of insignia encompassing only symbols used for official purposes. This kept at arm's length alternative formulations that would embrace everything from native-language words to iconography used in religious rituals and works of art. The agency argued that its current rules and procedures can meet the needs of Indians by preventing the registration of a mark that falsely implies a connection with a particular tribe. It promised more vigorous efforts to document the official seals and symbols of recognized Indian tribes, few of which had responded to the USPTO's 1994 invitation to enter their insignia in a national database.[15]

The agency's task is made difficult by the tribes' differing ideas about the proper balance between commercial and religious uses of traditional symbols. If the USPTO were to declare tribal insignia equivalent to other government symbols, as some Indian activists demand, then tribes would be unable to license them for commercial use, thereby losing a potential source of income. A recent case illustrates the volatility of claims about the appropriate use of religious symbols. In 2000 the Tigua Tribe of Ysleta del Sur Pueblo, Texas, sent the Texas Parks and Wildlife Department a letter directing them to cease publishing images of a well-known pictograph from Hueco Tanks State Historical Park, located near El Paso. The letter states that the design, referred to as the Tigua Sun Symbol, has "deep religious and cultural significance for the Tribe, symbolizing the key to the return to the mother pueblo by the last tribal member alive." Yet the tribe had already registered the pictograph design as a servicemark, precursor to a trademark, and featured it prominently in the tribally owned Speaking Rock Casino.[16]

The USPTO's counterpart agency in Canada has shown greater willingness to assist native communities seeking to control circulation of culturally sensitive images. A small Coastal Salish tribe called the Snuneymuxw (usually pronounced "Snuh-nái-mo") First Nation, most of whose lands are located in and around the town of Nanaimo on Vancouver Island, British Columbia, announced in 2000 that it had secured protection for ten petroglyph images on the nearby island of Gabriola. The images are protected under a provision of Canadian trademark law that applies to "any badge, crest, emblem or mark adopted and used by any public authority." Having registered the petroglyphs as official marks, the Snuneymuxw have the right to take legal action against anyone who uses the images without permission. The Snuneymuxw have already asked local shops to cease selling tee-shirts and other items that reproduce the registered designs. The museum on Gabriola Island declared that it would remove images of the petroglyphs from its site on the World Wide Web and no longer offer visitors material for making rubbings of the museum's petroglyph reproductions.[17]

In a telephone interview, Kathleen Johnnie, Lands and Resources Coordinator for the Snuneymuxw First Nation Treaty Negotiation Office, emphasized that the main interest of the Snuneymuxw in the petroglyphs is religious rather than commercial. Community elders want to limit frivolous uses of these potent symbols. They hope that the legal protection now afforded the images will create a framework within which they can educate the public about Snuneymuxw spiritual values and their link to ancestral designs. "In Canada," she said, "we're expected to respect other cultures, their religions and ways of doing things. That's all we're asking, for people to respect our culture. We're not using the images for commercial purposes, and we're asking people to respect that. We use them for religious purposes. They are very sacred to us."[18]

In seeking protection for the designs, the Snuneymuxw wrestled with difficult questions. The community reportedly discussed whether protection should be sought for all petroglyphs in which they have a cultural interest. After considering the pros and cons, they opted for a more limited strategy focusing on the most widely reproduced images, although they did not rule out the possibility of seeking protection for other petroglyphs. "We first created the official mark status so that people would understand that there's an intellectual property right in the images," Kathleen Johnnie said. "If they didn't want to understand that, then we provided cultural education and background on the issue. We hadn't been doing that on a regular basis before, but now we're trying to educate them as much as possible about the sensitivity of the issue and the importance of it in our culture." A paradox to which the Snuneymuxw had to reconcile themselves is that the official-mark registration process that would remove the petroglyph designs from the public domain required that facsimiles of the images be available for public inspection in the trademark database of the Canadian Intellectual Property Office.[19]

The actions taken by the Snuneymuxw can be seen either as a canny use of law for new purposes or a troubling distortion of the trademark system's intent. As Rosemary Coombe observes in her analysis of contemporary trademark practices, the legal protection of certain public symbols has several rationales. Use of the logo and name of a local police or fire department, for instance, is regulated in the interests of public safety. In a broader sense, Coombe argues, the protection afforded official symbols exists to "singularly determine the 'official' meaning of the sign and to prosecute those who give the signifier unsanctioned connotations." In securing official-mark status for petroglyph images, the Snuneymuxw people assert control over meaning, but they do so by severely limiting access to reproductions of the images. The rock art thereby becomes an anti-icon, an absence where there once was a presence. From the Snuneymuxw perspective, the analogy to public-safety emblems is accurate. They insist that any use of the images uninformed by religious understanding exposes the user to spiritual harm.[20]

The Snuneymuxw First Nation claims the petroglyphs as its own by right of oral tradition and common-law title, and some commentators celebrated the "repatriation" of the petroglyphs when they were certified as official marks of the band. By their nature, however, petroglyphs are difficult to date or to identify with specific creators, at least by the standards of Western law and science. The Snuneymuxw assertion of rights in the rock images of their traditional territory is strong because their presence in the region appears to be of considerable antiquity. In many other parts of North America, in contrast, dramatic population movements since the sixteenth century make it impossible to link rock art to existing native communities. In what sense, then, can the images be considered the intellectual property of a people? Might not the creators of the rock art have been the ancestors of other native groups of the region or of peoples who left no descendants, perhaps because they were only passing through? The Snuneymuxw's newly granted monopoly over religiously significant images is likely to become the gold standard for similar claims elsewhere, some of which will be far more difficult to substantiate. At bottom, the Snuneymuxw case, like the Zia Pueblo one, is less about intellectual property than about resistance to the uncontrolled proliferation of signs—more precisely, copies of signs—that a community considers theirs. The language of commercial gain in which trademark disputes are typically cast accommodates these religious concerns only awkwardly.[21]

Kathleen Johnnie acknowledged as much. "If the federal government or the global community would provide a different kind of protection for Aboriginal cultures, then we'd use that. We did what we had to do given the resources that were available. If the global community would come together as effectively to protect our intellectual property rights as they've come together to protect Coca-Cola or Microsoft, we wouldn't use the trademark. We'd use something else. People justify their use of the petroglyphs by saying that they've been in public view for however long. My community is ten thousand years old, so seventy-five years is just a drop in the bucket. Our arguments and our rights go back much further than that."

It is fair to say that the *Trademark Reporter* is not everyday reading for cultural anthropologists. But in 1994 it published an article by Candace Greene, an anthropologist on the staff of the Smithsonian Institution, and Thomas Drescher, an attorney, that assesses the similarities and differences between American trademark practices and graphic traditions among the Kiowa Indians. The essay tracks the history of a tipi given in 1845 to the Kiowa chief Little Bluff by a Cheyenne leader named Sleeping Bear. The gift celebrated a peace treaty concluded by the two groups several years earlier. The tipi given to Little Bluff was decorated on one side with sixteen yellow stripes, which commemorated Cheyenne war expeditions, and on the other with depictions of actual battles. To these motifs Little Bluff eventually added his own designs. Painted tipis were rare among the Kiowa, and this tipi's unusual history made it exceptionally valuable from their perspective.

As Greene and Drescher explain, tipis made of buffalo hides lasted only a season or two before they needed to be replaced. As long as he was alive, Little Bluff periodically called together a large group of men to help him renew the tipi by painting the designs on fresh hides. Over time, the designs changed to reflect new military victories, but the tipi itself was considered to be the same. The rights to reproduce the images on the tipi were regarded as belonging to Little Bluff alone. These were transferable rights, and a few years before his death he passed them to his nephew, whose name also became Little Bluff. The nephew renewed the tipi as long as he could, but confinement to a small reservation and the disappearance of the buffalo eventually made this difficult. Poverty also interrupted the cycle of tipi renewal. When the second Little Bluff sought to transfer his tipi design rights to younger relatives, few had access to the reciprocal gifts that the transfer required. Eventually, however, rights to the *Tipi with Battle Pictures* were passed to one of his sons, White Buffalo. The last recorded renewal of the tipi took place around 1916, when it was painted by White Buffalo's brother, a noted artist named Charley Buffalo. Kiowa people still remember this tipi even though it has been superseded by designs that celebrate more recent military exploits, including Kiowa participation in World War II and the conflicts in Korea, Vietnam, and the Persian Gulf.

The Kiowa zealously protect their personal rights to intangible property, in this case the right to use individual designs and to depict particular events. In fact, in times past they may have been more concerned with intangible property—what we would call intellectual property—than with material goods. This Kiowa version of intellectual property differs from Western norms in several key respects. The distinction between an idea and its expression so crucial to copyright is unknown to them: Kiowa individuals own ideas and personal life experiences. For others to depict these things, even in their own words or artistic idioms, is a violation of cultural rules. Such rights are transferable and perpetual. Their permanence and their close identification with individuals, Greene and Drescher argue, bring them closer to trademark practices than to copyright: "Whether the symbol possesses a religious 'medicine,' or a commercial 'persona,' the phenomenon is the same—the inherent capacity of symbols to be imbued with power."[22]

Critics of contemporary intellectual property laws and their effects on native peoples often insist that copyright and patents are unknown in non-Western societies, which treat information as communal property. The Kiowa case demonstrates that this claim is misleading. There exists a rich ethnographic literature detailing the complex rules about knowledge and its uses observed in countless indigenous societies. It was not unusual for Indians of Plains tribes to buy and sell personal songs, blessings, visions, and other expressions of spiritual knowledge. Among the Oto people of Oklahoma, for example, payment in goods for spiritual knowledge was a requirement, since it was believed to effect the transfer of power from seller to buyer. The problem is not that copyright or its equivalent cannot be found among native peoples. It is that the rules controlling the flow of ideas and information are often hard to reconcile with Western practices and, perhaps more significantly, with the replicative technologies spawned by the Industrial Revolution.[23]

Confronting the challenge that Western law and technology pose to indigenous cultures, some critics demand that copyright law be changed so that it protects indigenous art *styles,* not just their manifestation in concrete works or performances. Colin Golvan, the barrister who argued *Bulun Bulun* in Darwin, raises the issue in an essay exploring the possibilities and limits of copyright law for the protection of Aboriginal art. After Australian tee-shirt companies were sued for infringing the copyright of Aboriginal artists, they began to print shirts with fake designs. "Most tourist shops today are replete with examples of T-shirt designs which may appear to be works of Aboriginal art but are in fact caricatures of Aboriginal art," Golvan writes. "One issue which justifiably arises for attention is whether there ought to be protection to prohibit this bastardization of Aboriginal art, and if so, how this protection would work."[24]

Golvan's proposal that fake designs be treated as if they were authentic moves into territory that his colleagues are energetically litigating in courts throughout the industrial world: ownership of the "look and feel" of products and forms of artistic expression. In *Onassis v. Dior,* a landmark case dating to 1984, the New York State

Supreme Court ruled that the fashion designer Dior had violated the rights of Jacqueline Kennedy Onassis when it published an ad that showed an Onassis look-alike named Barbara Reynolds standing with various other celebrities who played themselves. The court in effect determined that Barbara Reynolds no longer retained exclusive ownership of her own image because it resembled that of someone far more famous. Similar disputes have arisen over the use of vocal material that can easily be mistaken for the work of popular singers. Courts have concluded that this violates the identity of the imitated vocalist. Real and counterfeit are no longer legally separable where familiar images or sounds are concerned. Shouldn't the same logic apply to native cultures, whose authentic identity is also at stake?[25]

Many writers, artists, and legal scholars worry about the trend toward aggressive protection of personal identities and arbitrary legislative extensions of copyright terms. Expressions like "strangling culture" and "stifling creativity" mark these discussions. Such fears have done little to deter the conviction of advocates for cultural protection that settler nations must somehow "repatriate" words, symbols, and culturally inflected styles back to indigenous communities. Nicholas Thomas, a respected commentator on the indigenous art of Australia and New Zealand, insists that abuses heaped on the Maori during New Zealand's colonial history "can only suggest resonances between invasions of land and of culture." "These identifications," he continues, "in turn suggest that quotations of indigenous art on the part of non-indigenous artists (irrespective of their ambivalence or complexity) are to be censured."[26]

However much one sympathizes with the idea of discouraging tasteless or hurtful quotations of native iconography or design styles, Thomas's blanket condemnation of *all* references to indigenous cultures by non-indigenous artists or writers drifts perilously close to a semiotic version of ethnic cleansing. This would be alarming if it were not so impractical. In settler democracies, native design styles have become part of the warp and weft of mass culture and visual expressions of national identity. Purging them would require draconian social engineering. Place names drawn from indigenous languages are ubiquitous in the United States and Canada, as they are in other settler nations. About half of the names of states and provinces originate in native languages, as do those of innumerable counties, cities and towns (for example, Chicago, Minneapolis, Miami), and geographical features, some of which incorporate the names of tribes (Sioux Falls) or native individuals (Seattle). Nor do native peoples always oppose the use of tribal names by outsiders. Apache religious leaders, for instance, turned out to bless the latest model of the AH-64D Apache Longbow helicopter prior to its deployment, and Apache military veterans continue to express pride in their association with such a formidable weapon.[27]

In 2000 Zia Pueblo negotiated an agreement with Southwest Airlines for use of the sun symbol on a specially painted aircraft christened "New Mexico One." According to Peter Pino, the Zia tribal administrator, the airline considered approaching the pueblo for several years but feared a hostile response. Eventually it contacted Zia's tribal government, and negotiations went smoothly. "I think that they were pleasantly surprised that we were civilized people," Pino said. At the dedication ceremony for the new aircraft, Zia officials were among the honored guests, and children from the pueblo performed a Crow Dance. The airline issued a press release that declared the company "proud to carry New Mexico's message to the 56 cities across the country served by Southwest Airlines."

As part of the agreement with Zia, the airline gave an undisclosed sum to the tribe's scholarship fund. Pino pointedly stressed that this should be described as a donation rather than as compensation. The distinction between the two underscores the pueblo's difficult balancing act. Is its interest in the sun symbol religious or commercial? When asked about this, Pino said that in the best of worlds the symbol would never have come into public circulation, since it was traditionally used only by permission of specific religious societies within the pueblo. But because the sun symbol is now ubiquitous, the community wishes to share in whatever wealth the familiar image can produce.

Zia Pueblo's quest to resolve its differences with the state of New Mexico has been less successful than its negotiations with businesses. In the autumn of 2001, New Mexico House Bill 423, which would have appropriated $50,000 to set up a special state commission to undertake negotiations with the pueblo, died in committee. Representative James Roger Madalena, the bill's sponsor, believes the measure fell victim to two forces. The first was fiscal: this was not considered a high-priority issue in a state with many claims on its modest resources. The second, which he heard mentioned by other members of the appropriations committee, was more philosophical. "How can you place a dollar value on such an important cultural and religious symbol?" they wanted to know.[28]

Behind these controversies can be detected the destabilizing influence of the copy. New technologies of duplication often threaten existing lines of social control. The advent of the printing press, which gave literate lay persons access to inexpensive Bibles, challenged the power of church authorities and helped to bring about the Reformation. The rise of motion pictures spelled the end of vaudeville. Industrialized mass production destroyed craft guilds. Computer software that encourages the free replication of copyrighted music is shaking the recording industry and may eventually transform it. The book that you hold in your hand may be destined for obsolescence now that university presses are offering electronic copies to research libraries in lieu of physical ones. Not that it matters much, since the book's royalties are already compromised by photocopy machines and Internet-based marketing systems that put used copies into the hands of customers with startling efficiency. The history of attempts to control the products of replicative technologies gives one little reason to hope that indigenous heritage will prove any more protectable than other cultural resources. Isolation affords modest shelter, but this is fast disappearing. The languages in which native songs and stories are embedded offer another barrier. Here, too, optimism finds little support: experts believe that half the world's languages will be extinct by century's end.[29]

The most pressing challenge for native societies is not the greed of businesses that traffic in indigenous symbols, although this is worthy of pointed criticism. Many firms have proved responsive to boycotts, campaigns of negative publicity, and the intervention of national and global agencies that regulate trademarks. The fundamental problem is technology, which provides new ways of reproducing information and images whose circulation was once more easily monitored. This threatens traditional authority and the authority of tradition itself. The consequences for indigenous artists may be grave. In a ruling on another Aboriginal copyright case, Justice John von Doussa, who presided over the *Bulun Bulun* trial in Darwin, notes that Aboriginal artists whose work is misused by outsiders may be barred from participation in ceremonies, denied permission to paint traditional clan images, or forced to pay damages to local authorities. More rarely, they are the victims of physical assault. Similarly, indigenous writers and intellectuals may find themselves subjected to fierce criticism within their own communities when they publish culture-specific information that has been available for decades in libraries.[30]

The increasing porosity of all societies and the strain of maintaining a firm grip on one's identity in a media-rich world generate spirited resistance. For indigenous peoples this takes the form of hypersensitivity to perceived misuse of traditional symbols. It also gives rise to dreams of separateness, of control over the stories, art, music, and religious practices of one's community. For pluralist states, a key challenge of the coming decades will be the implementation of public policies that honor indigenous sensibilities without violating basic freedoms. No sloganeering about cultural sovereignty will solve a problem rooted in the rise of revolutionary communication technologies; no appeals to free speech will settle the moral debate occasioned by thoughtless and disrespectful use of a people's iconography.

Some skirmishes in the ongoing war of signs are more theatrical than substantive. When the publicity value of one issue is played out, activists move on to others. But Pueblo Indians usually take the long view, and Zia Pueblo is determined to press on with its sun-symbol campaign regardless of the disappointments it encounters along the way. Peter Pino notes that much of the general public believes the pueblo has sued the state over the flag issue, which is untrue. Pino expresses hope that the matter can be settled without an expensive lawsuit. "We'd like to think that we're still civil enough to resolve this issue across a conference table," he said. "The sun symbol is something that we feel rightfully belongs to the Pueblo of Zia. This issue is important to us. It was a directive given by some of the elders who are no longer with us in this world. So we have a charge, and we're going to continue to work on this."

4. Ethnobotany Blues

Since the late nineteenth century, the interdisciplinary field of ethnobotany has brought together elements of anthropology, agronomy, botany, and ecology to document the practical and symbolic significance of plants in societies around the world. One branch of ethnobotany studies the progressive domestication of the crops that made settled life possible. Practitioners typically divide their time between archaeological sites, where they harvest fragments of preserved plant parts from excavated soil, and laboratories, where they painstakingly study the gleanings to understand interactions between plants and people at a given moment in prehistory. Another branch of ethnobotany investigates how native peoples classify their botanical universe. The results of this research have proved useful to cognitive scientists searching for the underlying principles by which humans organize information.

The most flamboyant ethnobotanists may be those who scour the planet in search of medicinal and mind-altering plants. For much of the twentieth century, few people other than professional naturalists took notice of their work. That changed in the 1960s. The writings of Timothy Leary and Carlos Castaneda, as well as rediscovered literary curiosities from the past—Aldous Huxley's *The Doors of Perception* (1956), Antonin Artaud's description of a Tarahumara Indian peyote ritual (1943), and Thomas De Quincey's *Confessions of an English Opium-Eater* (1821)—fueled interest in the role of psychotropic plants in religion and art. Thus began a small but persistent two-way traffic linking religious seekers in the developed world to ritual practitioners in Asia, Africa, and the Americas. One does not have to probe the alternative-spirituality scene too long before hearing stories of itinerant shamans from Mexico or Peru, sometimes bearing psychotropic concoctions, who dispense religious experiences to fee-paying customers in New York, Santa Fe, or the Bay Area. As the baby boom generation has aged and American society become less tolerant of intoxicants, interest has shifted to indigenous plant medicines thought to promote health and longevity.

The towering figure in the drug-hunting branch of ethnobotany is Richard Evans Schultes of Harvard University, who died in 2001 at the age of 86. Schultes was a paradoxical figure. In dress and manner he was the consummate Harvard professor: dignified, conservative, sometimes remote. He chose to live in a steadfastly Republican suburb of Boston and is said to have entered a write-in vote for Queen Elizabeth II in a presidential election. Yet he spent a decade and a half of his twenties and thirties engaged in difficult journeys of botanical exploration, first in Mexico and then in the forests and savannas of the South American tropics. By all accounts, he revered the native healers with whom he worked and expressed admiration for their botanical acumen. He may have been the only Republican in America who freely admitted to having sampled just about every mind-altering plant yet discovered in the New World. Schultes trained or strongly influenced several generations of ethnobotanists who went on to notable careers—among them Michael Balick, Robert Bye,

Paul Cox, Wade Davis, Mark Plotkin, Timothy Plowman, and Siri von Reis. The truest indicator of a naturalist's influence is the frequency with which his or her name has been applied to newly discovered organisms. According to Wade Davis, "Schultes" appears in dozens of species epithets and in at least three genera, including *Schultesianthus,* a member of the nightshade family, and *Schultesia,* a genus of cockroach.[1]

The work of Schultes and his students assumed broader significance in the 1970s and 1980s when environmentalists noted the accelerating rate at which the world's tropical forests were being destroyed by logging, mining, and the expansion of agriculture. As the forests disappeared, so would the great wealth of species for which they provided a home. The Amazon basin alone was thought to contain up to 15 percent of the world's known plant species plus countless others still awaiting discovery. Most faced extinction if rain forests vanished. Nevertheless, it was difficult to convince developing countries that protection of biodiversity was a good idea. For them it seemed to make little economic sense. Why should Peru or Colombia or Malaysia care about the fate of obscure plants and animals when these nations needed to feed their citizens, promote exports, and service mounting foreign debt? The insistence of well-fed scientists and environmentalists from the developed world that little-known species of ants or beetles were valuable in themselves tended to fall on deaf ears.

I witnessed this debate firsthand while working in northeastern Peru in the late 1970s. My field site in the Department of San Martín was near a new highway that for the first time linked the region to the population centers of the Pacific coast. Despite the poor quality of the road, sections of which regularly left vehicles churning in meter-deep mud during the rainy season, the surrounding forests were opened to thousands of poor farmers seeking their fortunes in lands

R. E. Schultes shares tobacco snuff with an unidentified Indian, Colombian Amazon, 1952.

that appeared fertile and, more to the point, unoccupied. Amid the turmoil of the region's moving frontier lived about 1,200 Aguaruna Indians. They held generous land grants as the result of a progressive reform of the nation's land-titling laws during the late 1960s. Holding title to land was one thing; protecting it from invasion was another. Government officials repeatedly told the Aguaruna that unless they "used" the land they had been given, it might be transferred to non-Indians who would make something of it. No matter that Indians depended almost entirely on their community lands and adjacent forest reserves for crops, wild plant foods, fish, and game. Their sophisticated knowledge of these resources gave them a diet better than that of other Peruvians, half of whom experienced malnutrition as children. This self-sufficiency, however, was held to be profligate because it produced few marketable commodities. At that moment in Peru's economic history, land use was defined largely in extractive terms: removing desirable trees for the lumber market and replacing the forest with fields of rice for urban consumers. Arguments that the Aguaruna should be seen as successful stewards of the long-term potential of the region's rain forests evoked only skepticism from local officials.

A decade later the situation had changed. Rain forests were a global mass-culture concern. Pop stars competed to be photographed painting their faces with Amazonian tribesmen. Publicists for McDonald's put in overtime hours to convince consumers that the corporation's insatiable hunger for beef was not promoting tropical deforestation. The rapid decline of the rain forests was widely lamented in the media even if the complex forces behind it were often reduced to simplistic slogans—for instance, that the policies of the World Bank were mostly to blame. Few wanted to understand the problem's systemic causes, which include high rates of population growth, the internal migration of peasants whose farmlands had been swallowed up by large-scale agribusiness, and strong U.S. and European demand for cocaine, which has tempted enterprising farmers to try their hand at coca farming in the upland rain forests of Peru, Ecuador, Bolivia, and Colombia.[2]

The global shift in awareness about tropical deforestation provided an opening for ethnobotanists to insist that everyone had an interest in preserving rain forests because their biodiversity might shelter compounds that could cure cancer, HIV-AIDS, and other diseases. No one knows more about the healing resources of tropical forests than the indigenous peoples who depended on them for centuries. The ethnobotanist Mark Plotkin makes this point emphatically in his book *Tales of a Shaman's Apprentice*. "The tribal healers," Plotkin writes, "hold the key to unlocking one of the great mysteries of our day and age—how to demonstrate the value of the rain forest in concrete economic terms and, in so doing, provide the rationale for protecting Mother Nature's ultimate creation."[3]

By the time Plotkin's book appeared in bookstores, the argument that "bioprospecting" could help to solve the problem of tropical deforestation had persuaded a few governments to forge alliances with transnational drug companies. In 1991 Costa Rica's National Biodiversity Institute (INBio) signed a contract with the pharmaceutical giant Merck that allowed the latter to search for medically useful compounds in exchange for immediate compensation, transfer of sophisticated equipment, training of Costa Rican scientists, and participation in any future royalties. Yet even as the INBio arrangement raised the hopes of environmentalists, the cry of "Biopiracy!" arose from indigenous-rights activists and critics of globalization. Public discussions of bioprospecting quickly became so toxic that by the end of the 1990s Plotkin and several other prominent ethnobotanists expressed regret that they had ever promoted commercialization of the forest's biochemical assets. A 1999 profile in the *New York Times* declared that Plotkin had renounced bioprospecting and did "not want people to search his writings or botanical collections for clues to Indian medicines."[4]

In little more than a decade, ethnobotany, which Richard Evans Schultes had helped to define as a heroic field dedicated to salvaging useful native knowledge, had become for its critics a simple instrument of theft. This was a bitter pill for ethnobotanists, most of whom had entered the profession because of their interest in, and personal commitment to, indigenous people. To understand how such a rapid transformation could take place in the image of an unusual vocation, we must make a brief detour into the converging worlds of intellectual property, molecular biology, agriculture, and pharmaceuticals, with particular attention to how technological changes in the developed world have given rise to fears that capitalism is, or soon will be, reaping immense profits by exploiting the traditional knowledge of native peoples, who themselves receive no discernible benefits.

Experts on intellectual property usually identify a 1980 decision of the United States Supreme Court, *Diamond v. Chakrabarty*, as a major turning point in the economic trajectory of biological research. The court ruled that a genetically modified strain of bacteria created in a laboratory by the microbiologist Ananda Chakrabarty, then working for General Electric, qualified for patent protection. GE and Chakrabarty had developed the organism in the hope that it would prove useful in cleaning up oil spills at sea. In granting a utility patent to Chakrabarty, the Supreme Court reversed decades of prior rulings, which held that life-forms and other "products of nature" were not patentable, although novel ways of processing and using them were. The decision opened the door to ever-broader biological patents, ranging from the controversial OncoMouse, a breed of laboratory mouse developed at Harvard specifically for cancer research, to a still-contested ruling that the firm Agracetus—whose rights were later acquired by Monsanto—holds a patent on all forms of cotton that have been, or can be, modified through the introduction of foreign genes ("transgenic cotton").[5]

This breakdown in the once-clear distinction between products of nature and products of human ingenuity was linked to advances in molecular technology and digital information processing. The completion in 2000 of the Human Genome Project, which mapped human chromosomes, turned genetic raw material into a powerful text that can be read and interpreted. Soon science will have the capacity to edit the text. So should the text be patentable? In more legalistic language, should the inherited sequence of nucleic acids that makes us who we are in physical terms be assigned to corporations as a monopoly for a limited period of time?

The question, like so many at the point of technology's wedge into the future, prompts a bipolar response. Those who see life as inherently sacred argue that reducing life's code to an item of commerce is inherently wrong. An expert on Jewish medical ethics told the *Jerusalem Post* that Judaism opposes any form of ownership of the human body. "That belongs to God," he said. These sentiments have been echoed in other quarters. Public anxiety about corporate control of the genome was sardonically expressed by a British woman, Donna Rawlinson MacLean, who filed application number GB0000180.0 for a patent on her own body. She told the *Guardian* that she sought to protect herself from "unauthorized exploitation, genetic or otherwise."[6]

Against these misgivings stands the utilitarian logic behind all intellectual property regimes. Genetic research, the argument goes, is expensive and time-consuming. It carries significant financial risks. If successfully undertaken, it leads to therapies that alleviate human suffering. What is wrong with offering economic incentives to those whose creativity and skill produce these innovations? To recast the question in personal terms, wouldn't you be grateful if granting twenty-year patent rights to a strip of the human genome made it possible for someone in your family to survive a genetic disease once considered fatal? Would you begrudge financial reward to whoever held that patent?

The utilitarian approach draws support from the medical advances of the past few decades. As a lawyer on the staff of the U.S. Patent and Trademark Office (USPTO) suggested during an interview, the principal reason that the United States and Europe lead the world in medical technology is their strong system of patent protections. As a counterexample he cited India, which has a wealth of talented chemists, doctors, and biologists but is hobbled by weak patent laws that discourage the invention of new drugs and medical techniques.

This view has merit, but it also skirts inconvenient facts. Patents and copyrights are intended to encourage innovation, yet the proliferation of overly broad patents and the aggressiveness with which corporate patent holders defend them have, according to some experts, begun to inhibit original research. This is particularly true of so-called upstream patents, assertions of control over discoveries that unlock fundamental biological processes. Research universities, once committed to the free exchange of scientific information, now guard their intellectual property, mindful of the income that it may eventually generate. Meanwhile, the global pharmaceutical industry reaps financial rewards on a scale that startles even hardened capitalists. Blockbuster drugs have yielded profit margins approaching 30 percent in recent years, a rate three times higher than that of the American corporate sector as a whole. Some of this windfall finds its way into the salaries of the companies' senior executives. The chief executive officer of Merck, for example, was paid almost $28 million in 2000—not counting unexercised stock options then worth nearly $165 million.[7]

Again, one might be willing to wink at such excesses if the industry were dedicated to the production of new drugs for treatment of the world's most serious afflictions. The for-profit nature of drug development, however, privileges the medical needs of the affluent over those of the poor. Hence the vastly greater research expenditures on conditions such as diabetes and high serum cholesterol than on malaria and diseases associated with poverty. As public-sector research gives way to private enterprise, it is easy to forget that many of the most effective pharmaceutical products of the modern era—among them the polio vaccine, penicillin, and streptomycin—went into production unburdened by licensing fees and in some cases unprotected by patents. A study published in 2001 by the organization Public Citizen showed that publicly funded research continues to be a major contributor to the development of new pharmaceuticals, which are then patented by industry. Consumers thus pay for drugs twice: first via research funded by tax revenues, then at the pharmacist's cash register.[8]

How much of the pharmaceutical industry's profits is based on products that originated in the botanical knowledge of indigenous peoples remains a subject of dispute. Indigenous-rights organizations routinely cite multibillion-dollar figures, but these are based on questionable assumptions. Business-oriented observers, in contrast, claim that ethnobotanical methods have contributed little to the pharmaceutical industry, once one rules out drugs such as digitalis and aspirin that date back to the birth of modern drugs. Even those committed to ethnobotanical methods of drug discovery admit that few, if any, traditional remedies have made the transformation to pharmaceutical products in the decade since the Convention on Biological Diversity became effective in 1993. This has not prevented developing countries from complaining about the exploitation of local plant resources by transnational corporations. And it is not only developing nations that complain. Norwegian researchers have criticized legal norms that allowed the firm Novartis to develop cyclosporin from soil samples collected in Norway without any requirement that some portion of the drug's profits be returned to the country of origin.[9]

Although indigenous knowledge of healing plants captures the lion's share of public attention, native varieties of important crop species have far greater economic value in today's marketplace. Since 1980, research on cultigens has moved steadily from the public sector to private corporations, which in turn have been consolidated into five dominant companies—among them Monsanto, Aventis, and Dow Chemical. Research universities still engaged in agronomic work have adopted industrial practices by patenting the results of their efforts. The tangle of patents affecting crop plants is now so complicated that introduction of improved varieties may be delayed while patent holders negotiate licensing arrangements. Such was the case with Vitamin A–rich "golden rice," whose distribution was held up for a year while all necessary permissions were secured.[10]

Ethnobotanists doing field studies in the 1970s and early 1980s typically found local people eager to share knowledge of their most important crops. Today, one encounters resistance to laissez-faire collection of local plant varieties. Why, farmers ask, should they give their agricultural resources away for free only to have them used by corporations that reap great financial rewards and dedicate themselves to putting the farmers out of business? Soybean cultivation in the United States benefited enormously from the arrival of genetic material collected in China by the plant breeder William J. Morse in the late 1920s, and similar collecting throughout the world has doubtless proved critical to the development of patented varieties of corn, potatoes, sorghum, peanuts, and other major crops.[11] Moving further back in history, other famous cases of botanical "borrowing" come to mind. Perhaps most familiar is the campaign of British botanists, led by Sir Clements Markham, to smuggle specimens of several species of *Cinchona,* the source of quinine, and the Brazilian rubber tree, *Hevea brasiliensis,* from South America to England and then to British colonies in Southeast Asia for industrial cultivation there. The Scottish botanist Robert Fortune accomplished a similar feat with tea, which he collected in China in the late 1840s and introduced into cultivation in India and Ceylon.

Useful plant and animal species have moved to new locations as long as human populations have been in contact with one another, of course. The signature dish of southern Italian cuisine would not exist if tomatoes, a New World crop, had not been introduced to Europe by travelers returning home. What would Chinese food be without chili peppers from Central and South America? The society often used to exemplify the native peoples of Amazonia, the Yanomami of the frontier region shared by Brazil and Venezuela, base their subsistence system on the plantain, a form of banana introduced from Southeast Asia. Dynamic Amerindian cultures, such as those of the American Plains, were radically transformed by the acquisition of an Old World animal species, the horse, obtained through trading and raiding. But the British campaigns to secure quinine, rubber, and tea arguably crossed the line from reciprocal exchange to industrial larceny.

The current corporate passion for patents develops this theme even further, intensifying concerns about misuse of intellectual property laws. Controversy continues over a utility patent issued to a Texas company for Basmati rice that India claims was developed from genetic materials originating in South Asia. In 1999 a Colorado seed company, POD-NERS, was issued a patent for a yellow variety of the common field bean that it calls Enola. The patent holders bred their variety using seeds purchased in Mexican markets. A number of organizations, including bean producers in northern Mexico and the International Center for Tropical Agriculture in Colombia, are challenging the patent, arguing that the consistent yellow coloration of the Enola is by no means novel. In 2000 a company called Appropriate Engineering and Manufacturing, based in Riverside, California, secured a utility patent for a variety of bean that pops when cooked, much like popcorn. In breeding the plant, the company made use of an Andean bean variety called *nuña* collected by the U.S. Department of Agriculture. Organizations representing indigenous farmers in the Andes protested that they had provided samples of this traditionally cultivated variety with the understanding that it would remain in the public domain.[12]

A case that evoked widespread outrage concerns a patent issued for a variety of the South American hallucinogen *ayahuasca (Banisteriopsis caapi)*, a plant that came to the attention of an international readership principally via the publications of Richard Evans Schultes. A collector named Loren Miller was awarded a U.S. plant patent for a variety of *ayahuasca* that he had obtained in Ecuador. When news began to circulate that a plant used for religious purposes by scores of native Amazonian peoples had been patented by an American, there was an immediate outcry. A federation of Amazonian Indians called COICA joined forces with several American organizations to bring suit against Miller. In the face of evidence that Miller's allegedly unique strain of *ayahuasca* was in fact documented elsewhere, the USPTO rescinded the patent in 1999, then reversed itself in 2001 in response to Miller's appeal.

In a report on the controversy, the Center for International Environmental Law (CIEL), a nongovernmental organization (NGO) that assisted Amazonian indigenous groups in their patent challenge, presents compelling evidence that Miller's *ayahuasca* variety was not distinctive enough to qualify for patent protection. The only audience that truly matters, the USPTO, disagreed. CIEL's assessment closes by noting that Miller's patent has almost no economic value.

The patent expires in 2003, and its scope is so narrow that he will have a difficult time realizing any financial gain from it. In that respect, the *ayahuasca* patent is no different from the approximately 95 percent of USPTO-issued patents that never generate royalties or licensing fees.[13]

The *ayahuasca* case and others like it have led to demands that the United States end its program of plant patents. Inspection of the patents issued in recent years, averaging about 460 annually, reveals that the vast majority are for uncontroversial ornamentals. Between 1996 and 2001, for instance, the USPTO issued 172 plant patents for geranium varieties (such as PP10,473, "a variety of geranium plant named 'Bubble Gum'"). Other prominent species include begonias, poinsettias, chrysanthemums, and impatiens. Another fact rarely mentioned in public discussion of controversial plant patents is that few of the aggrieved communities have demonstrated that the patents caused them financial harm. But the granting of patents for plant varieties based on material freely shared by farmers in other countries symbolically underscores the lack of reciprocity in relations between the peoples whose ancestors discovered or bred these plants and the corporations that now claim them as a monopoly. In a broader sense, it illustrates the ability of a powerful few to take material from something called the public domain and convert it to private property, at least for a limited period and in a limited geographical range.[14]

That a few ill-considered patents manage to slip through the USPTO's net is hardly surprising when one considers the steady growth in patent applications—6 to 12 percent per year—with which it has to contend. (In some categories, such as software and biotechnology, the increase has been far greater.) The discrepancy between government salaries and pay levels in private industry leads to high turnover among patent examiners. Examiners who stay with the agency are judged by the speed with which they process applications, a situation that invites error. One result is a rise in the number of patents that ultimately fail to survive scrutiny. Legal contestation of questionable patents is little more than a cost of doing business for large corporations, but for rural communities in developing countries the obstacles to challenging dubious patents are nearly insurmountable.[15]

At a 1991 conference in Bethesda, Maryland, experts on economic development, ethnobotany, biodiversity, and intellectual property shared ideas about how best to defend the rights of local communities in their botanical heritage while protecting endangered environments and encouraging forms of drug exploration that would yield badly needed income for the developing world. The result was a major U.S. initiative called the International Cooperative Biodiversity Groups Program (ICBG), administered by the Fogarty International Center for Advanced Study in the Health Sciences, part of the National Institutes of Health (NIH), with additional funding from the National Science Foundation and the U.S. Agency for International Development. After reviewing thirty-four applications, the ICBG awarded funding to five projects proposing to search for commercially valuable biochemical resources in eight countries of Africa and Latin America. Each project involved a partnership bringing together American and host-country scientists as well as major drug companies, including Monsanto, Bristol-Myers Squibb, and American Cyanamid.

What made the ICBG program different from earlier forms of bioprospecting, at least in the minds of participants, was its commitment to North-South collaboration. This included provision of technical training and equipment to host countries and explicit attention to the intellectual property interests of local communities. Among the guiding principles of the ICBG was that "intellectual property rights should be extended in some form to traditional knowledge." Scientists who dealt with native communities as part of the ICBG program were expected to "recognize their responsibility to provide reasonable compensation as an integral part of their business or research and development activities."[16]

Big pharmaceutical companies were not as eager to get involved in bioprospecting as is sometimes supposed. The industry is far more focused on "rational" research methods that design synthetic drugs to meet molecular requirements. Cori Hayden, an anthropologist who has studied bioprospecting in Mexico, notes that ethnobotanists and ecologists worked hard to make industry see the potential economic value of plants and, as a corollary, of the local ecosystems that harbor them. Bioprospecting, Hayden observes, is in part an attempt "to convince transnational companies that nature . . . should be taken seriously." The pharmaceutical firms that agreed to join the ICBG program seem to have been attracted by the relatively low cost of participation. The projects also stood to generate favorable publicity drawing on the romantic allure of drug-hunting in exotic locales.[17]

Even enthusiastic supporters of bioprospecting acknowledge that the odds against turning any single compound into a billion-dollar blockbuster drug are long. The pharmaceutical industry's conventional estimate of $300–500 million for the cost of bringing a successful drug to market is greeted skeptically by critics, but there is little doubt that drug development is expensive and risky. Because the intricacies of drug screening change over time, it is difficult to find agreed-upon figures for probabilities of success. Estimates ranging from one in a thousand to one in ten thousand or more are common. The period between plant collection and successful marketing of a drug often exceeds a decade, during which time researchers may modify certain chemicals to such an extent that the original intellectual property claims of the source community are diluted. The process may be even more complex if researchers find that a bioactive ingredient has a medical use different from that suggested by the original collectors. This is by no means unusual because traditional plant remedies may be effective within the framework of a society's own understanding and yet fail to satisfy the efficacy standards of Western medicine.[18]

The twists and turns in the long road from plant collection to pharmaceutical marketplace make it difficult to hammer out benefit-sharing agreements that all parties consider fair. Regional differences in living standards are another complicating factor. Host-nation workers and technicians typically are paid according to local wage scales. When seen against the multimillion-dollar salaries of Big Pharma's top executives or the immense profits realized by their companies, this looks exploitative. Even the highest wages paid to plant collectors are likely to represent only a fraction of a commodity's retail price at the final point of sale. So from the point of view of indigenous activists or critics of capitalism, the benefit-sharing practices of the ICBG projects—however progressive they may be when compared to the way things were done in the past—perpetuate relations of economic domination by turning local people into serfs of the developed world's biotech industry.[19]

Another riddle facing bioprospecting projects concerns the extent to which native peoples are explicitly recognized in research activities and benefit-sharing agreements. The ICBG program's protocols acknowledge the special rights and concerns of native populations within study areas. Yet determining precisely who qualifies as "indigenous" is straightforward in some places but surprisingly difficult in others, especially Africa and Southeast Asia. Even where this is not a problem, relations between indigenous communities and the nation-states in which they are embedded are often conflicted and legally ambiguous. Who are legitimate representatives of indigenous peoples in negotiations with foreign bioprospectors? Can the state speak for them, or must they be allowed to speak for themselves? But if they have no formally recognized governing bodies—or if the membership of those bodies is in constant flux—how do well-meaning outsiders work out durable arrangements with them? What if, as is frequently the case, the emerging leaders of these communities claim forms of political sovereignty impossible to reconcile with the state's own vision of its legitimate powers?

Despite these formidable complexities, the first ICBG projects went to work in 1994. Most seem to have undertaken their activities relatively unencumbered by political opposition, either locally or on the world stage. An exception was ICBG-Peru, a project bringing together ethnobotanists from Washington University in St. Louis, several Peruvian research institutions, and Searle Pharmaceuticals (now a subsidiary of Monsanto). The project chose to focus its bioprospecting in an upland rain-forest area occupied by Aguaruna Indians, the ethnic group among whom I conducted field research beginning in the 1970s. Most Aguaruna communities are members of local and regional indigenous federations that have become strategic points of contact with the Peruvian government and the larger world. The fortunes of individual federations rise and fall with the quality of their leadership and changing political circumstances. All are subject to internal conflict, which has sometimes prevented the Aguaruna from presenting a united front on important issues.

The ICBG researchers initially worked out collaborative arrangements with a large and influential federation called the Aguaruna-Huambisa Council. The project promised to employ and train Aguaruna workers, provide financial support for indigenous organizations, and share royalties should the project's activities produce marketable pharmaceuticals. As collecting activities began in late 1994, however, relations between the research team and the Aguaruna-Huambisa Council soured, largely over the question of the royalty rates.[20]

A key player in the breakdown of relations between the project and Aguaruna leaders was an organization then known as the Rural Advancement Foundation International (RAFI), based in Canada. A feisty NGO dedicated to resisting what it considered the global theft of genetic resources by capitalist industry, RAFI managed in a few short years to become a major clearinghouse for information about bioprospecting ventures. Perhaps because its resources were dwarfed by the public relations arms of the corporations that it was attacking, RAFI seemed compelled to portray biotechnology issues in Manichaean terms, as a struggle between the forces of Darkness and Light. In fact, RAFI claimed to have coined the term "biopiracy." This absolutism worked well when the organization was calling attention to clear-cut wrongs such as the *ayahuasca* patent. In more ambiguous situations, though, RAFI's polarizing rhetoric became another form of external manipulation.[21]

When RAFI intervened in negotiations, it assumed that the Aguaruna-Huambisa Council was the true representative of the Aguaruna people. One can argue, however, that the Aguaruna are not yet a polity in the sense that they have, or ever had in the past, a centralized political structure that defends their collective rights and resources. The Council and its controversial leader, Evaristo Nugkuag, enjoyed the support of some communities but were resolutely opposed by others. By casting its lot with the Council, RAFI inadvertently mimicked the actions of colonial powers who assumed that native people were, almost by definition, organized as tribes under the direction of chiefs. Such tone deafness to the nuances of native politics slowed resolution of the conflict. Eventually the ICBG project negotiated a new agreement with a multi-ethnic native federation called CONAP (Confederation of Amazonian Nationalities of Peru) that had enlisted the support of a significant number of local Aguaruna organizations. The controversy fostered by RAFI did have one positive effect: it helped CONAP to conclude an agreement with ICBG-Peru on more favorable terms, including higher royalty rates and a so-called know-how license, essentially fees paid to participating communities and organizations for access to their botanical expertise. During the project's plant-collecting phase, relations between the project and its Aguaruna clients remained reasonably cordial, although local objections periodically bubbled to the surface as some Aguarunas' high expectations of financial reward met the modest realities of a research project that may never score a major success in the world of commercial pharmaceuticals. During an interview in July 2001, César Sarasara, the president of CONAP, said that the ICBG-Peru agreement represented a key turning point for Amazonian Indians. "CONAP," he said, "is working to find new formulas for collaborating with industry so that we're not looking in from the outside. We're not waiting for NGOs or the Catholic Church to help us. We're looking for opportunities to exploit the economic value of our resources." His comments suggest impatience with paternalistic interventions that leave native peoples on the margins of decision-making and profit-taking.[22]

The global currents that slowed the progress of ICBG-Peru proved even more powerful in another project, ICBG-Maya, launched in 1998. The ICBG-Maya project was intended to meet the highest standards of ethically sound bioprospecting. Its principal investigator, O. Brent Berlin, could draw on forty years of close working relations with Tzeltal- and Tzotzil-speaking Indians living in the state of

Chiapas, Mexico. A professor of anthropology at the University of Georgia, where he set up shop after a long career at the University of California at Berkeley, Berlin is one the world's foremost ethnobiologists. In collaboration with other scientists, including his wife, Elois Ann Berlin, he has written five books on Maya medical knowledge and understandings of the natural world. In short, the principal investigator possessed the training, connections, and scientific expertise to lead his partners—the University of Georgia, a local Mexican institution called El Colegio de la Frontera Sur (ECOSUR), and Molecular Nature, Ltd., a small Welsh biotech firm—in a successful research venture. But Berlin could not foresee the extent to which the political situation in Chiapas would cast unfavorable light on his project.

The story of the Chiapas uprising has been told so often that it is fast moving into the vaporous space of legend. On 1 January 1994 an armed group calling itself the Zapatista Army of National Liberation (EZLN in Spanish) took control of municipal buildings in several Chiapas towns, including San Cristóbal de las Casas. For several days the rebellion was a shooting war, as elements of the EZLN, a force made up largely of Maya-speaking Indians, squared off against the Mexican army. Reliable casualty figures are difficult to find, but 145 or more people died during the first days of the fighting, mostly Zapatistas and innocent civilians who were caught in the army's heavy-handed assault on rebel positions. After two weeks, direct military confrontations subsided, to be replaced by a menacing strategy of containment by the Mexican army and, on the part of the EZLN, local organizing, a concerted campaign of negotiation with the government, and a global media blitz to publicize the realities faced by the peasants of Chiapas. As I write, an uneasy cease-fire prevails, although right-wing paramilitary groups continue to terrorize local communities in some parts of the state.[23]

The origins of the Chiapas rebellion lie in textbook conditions of economic and social deprivation, although with a late-twentieth-century twist. Beginning in the 1980s, Mexico experienced a profound economic crisis that led successive governments to open the nation's doors to private capital while dramatically scaling back state-sponsored social programs. These neoliberal economic policies satisfied international bankers, who helped restabilize Mexico's economy after the debt crisis of 1995. But the changes worsened the situation of the nation's poor. Mexico's per capita gross domestic product fell nearly 7.8 percent between 1981 and 1996, and income distribution became substantially more unbalanced, at both household and regional levels. Chiapas, nearly one-third of whose population consists of Maya-speaking Indians, was disproportionately affected by the economy's neoliberal makeover. In the mid-1990s the state's per capita GDP was only 40 percent of the national average; its maternal mortality rate was 117 per 100,000 live births as compared with 40 for the nation as a whole; the rate of malnutrition-related death was double the national average; and Chiapas residents were three times more likely to be illiterate than other Mexican citizens.[24]

For Indians whose lives depend on agriculture, new policies regarding land and markets were perhaps the most threatening development. The government privatized peasant coffee cooperatives. *Ejidos,* communal landholdings that have served as a cornerstone of rural life since the Mexican Revolution, were being dissolved in favor of a free-market approach to land tenure, a change that exacerbated economic divisions within Maya communities as well as between Maya and non-Maya farmers. NAFTA, the North American Free Trade Agreement, which went into effect the day the EZLN began its rebellion, placed Maya farmers in direct competition with large-scale corn producers in the United States, who can bring grain to market at a much lower price. These policies created opportunities for individuals to prosper but often at the expense of communities and other social groups. The total effect, according to the Mexican sociologist Sergio Zermeño, was to "dissolve the social" through "a deliberate effort by the state to dismantle inconvenient collective identities."[25]

The Zapatista uprising thus responded to a mix of social conditions, some old, some as current as today's headlines. Long-standing problems included the nearly complete absence of democratic representation for Maya peasants, even in their local *municipios,* and the failure of the central government to enforce agrarian reform laws that had been in effect for more than sixty years. To these concerns the Zapatistas added two new elements. First, the movement deployed the rhetoric of indigenous nationalism, which has become a potent force throughout the Western Hemisphere and in settler nations elsewhere, including Australia and New Zealand. Second, it opposed the opening of Mexico to international commerce, a process usually glossed as "globalization."

The chief irony of the EZLN's anti-globalization rhetoric is that globalization soon emerged as the movement's chief ally. More precisely, globalized media served as a counterweight to economic globalization.[26] The EZLN, represented most memorably by the masked, pipe-smoking figure of Subcomandante Marcos, quickly mastered the art of using the Internet and other media to mobilize international support. The Mexican government's early hope that it could isolate and dismember the rebel organization was shattered by the powerful media spotlight cast on Chiapas, which instantly became a potent symbol of grassroots resistance to the excesses of world capitalism. By March 2001, when supporters of the EZLN made a triumphant march to Mexico City to present their case for indigenous rights before Mexico's congress, the movement had become the apotheosis of radical chic for affluent social critics from the United

Cartoon portraying a guerrilla fighter of the Zapatista Army of National Liberation in the style of a Maya stela.

States and Europe. At times, in fact, the march threatened to become a carnival of globophobia—or as *Newsweek* sarcastically put it, "a sea of Europeans wearing dreadlocks and backpacks and playing Hacky Sack." This is no fault of the rebels themselves, who continue to face harsh economic conditions and sometimes violent right-wing opposition in the hamlets and towns of Chiapas. Instead, it illustrates the tendency for affluent activists from abroad to insert themselves into local conflicts that they may not completely understand.[27]

Brent Berlin surely recognized the risks of beginning a major research effort in this politically charged situation. By most accounts, his optimism about the project's prospects came from a lifetime spent building close working relationships with Maya communities and local political leaders. In its organization and its plan for benefit sharing, ICBG-Maya hoped to redefine relations between scientists and indigenous peoples. Berlin and his collaborators, for example, explicitly ratified the Mayas' economic and moral rights in their botanical knowledge as well as their right to deny access to investigators. The project worked hard to obtain prior informed consent in Maya villages. These efforts included translation of background material into the Tzeltal and Tzotzil languages and even the scripting of a play that explained issues of intellectual property and biodiversity in terms local farmers could understand. Twelve percent of the project budget would go to salaries for two dozen Maya field assistants, most of whom the project had already trained in "linguistic transcription of their own languages, field botanical survey techniques, computer literacy, laboratory techniques, plant propagation, marketing, and intellectual property rights issues." The project committed itself to finding practical uses for Maya knowledge that could be put to work immediately to benefit Indian participants—say, by identifying local plants that controlled pest populations or by helping communities to market medicinal herbs to the fast-growing natural-products industry. Finally, the project specified that Maya communities would receive one-quarter of any royalties that emerged from the research. This put the Maya on an even financial footing with the project's three institutional partners: the University of Georgia,

ECOSUR, and Molecular Nature. The Maya share was to be paid to a nonprofit organization called PROMAYA. Even communities that refused to collaborate with the project were to be eligible for PROMAYA funds. Berlin offered to seed PROMAYA with a $30,000 prize that he had won for his prior work on Maya ethnobiology.

By the summer of 1999 ICBG-Maya was ready to begin fieldwork. A number of communities had granted the project written permission to collect plants and interview residents (forty-six had signed consent documents by the summer of 2001). The project was still awaiting government permission to export plants for analysis abroad, but this was expected to arrive in due course. Toward the end of 1999, however, RAFI used its website to publish a withering critique of ICBG-Maya. The RAFI document recycled a denunciation of the project issued by a group called the Council of Indigenous Traditional Midwives and Healers of Chiapas (COMPITCH), which was allied with a range of local councils representing traditional healers throughout Chiapas. COMPITCH alleged that the project violated Mexican law, the U.N. Convention on Biological Diversity, and the code of ethics of the International Society of Ethnobiology, an organization that Brent Berlin had helped to found and had served as president. COMPITCH and its supporters also insisted that the project fomented conflict within Maya communities "as some individuals, pressured by the grave economic situation, collaborate with the researchers for a few pesos or tools."[28]

The standing of COMPITCH—an organization representing the interests of healers—in debates about ICBG-Maya was equivocal, as was the claim that its members were directly affected by the project. ICBG-Maya contended that its research protocol was specifically designed not to infringe the knowledge of Maya healing specialists. "The Maya ICBG's research is not directed at the specialized or sacred knowledge of persons who characterize themselves as 'special-ists,'" wrote Elois Ann and Brent Berlin in a response to the first wave of denunciations. The project thus targeted basic, everyday fa-miliarity with plant medicines.[29]

From RAFI's perspective, communities that cooperated with the project violated the rights of those who opted out, since they drew on knowledge shared by collaborators and opponents alike. For RAFI, then, the project was obliged to await a consensus among Chiapas communities before proceeding. But RAFI's logic created its own puzzles. After all, the Maya heartland is much broader than the state of Chiapas, encompassing adjoining regions, including parts of Guatemala and Belize. Even if all Maya-speaking peoples of Chiapas enthusiastically endorsed the project, wouldn't their participation violate the rights of Maya communities elsewhere? Later RAFI com-muniqués dealt with this issue: "Bioprospectors must assume in the absence of definitive evidence to the contrary that the same or simi-lar plants and preparations are used by different communities in the same country and very possibly by communities in other countries. Agreement must be reached in each community before biopros-pectors can consider that they have permission to proceed."[30]

RAFI took for granted that COMPITCH was a legitimate repre-sentative of the Maya people as a whole despite the organization's identity as a professional guild and special-interest group. For the Berlins, insisting that healers should control the region's botanical knowledge "is akin to claiming that the American Medical Associa-tion has the right to represent the health information held by the or-dinary U.S. citizen." These obvious problems of representativeness were quickly lost in press coverage of the emerging conflict. A report carried by National Public Radio on 1 September 2000, for example, discussed opposition to the ICBG project as if Mayas were a single people with a single point of view.[31]

As the conflict dragged on into 2000 and 2001, the name-calling intensified. Brent Berlin and his colleagues, at first simply labeled biopirates—painful enough for scientists committed to the protection of indigenous rights—were later elevated to the status of *pukuj,* "devils," in documents published by another Chiapas NGO, the Center for Economic and Political Studies of Communal Action (CIEPAC), a group allied with the San Francisco–based NGO Global Action. The journalist Barbara Belejack, whose article on the ICBG-Maya dispute offers a more nuanced assessment than most, describes wearying negotiations between the project and hostile NGOs that sapped the resolve of Mexican research partners at ECOSUR. Meanwhile, the administration of President Vicente Fox, desiring prompt settlement of the indigenous rebellion in Chiapas, had little stomach for inserting itself in the controversy. The government eventually denied the project permits for plant collection, a serious setback. Brent Berlin stood by his promise to negotiate with COMPITCH and other groups concerned about bioprospecting, but the position of NGOs opposed to the project only hardened. Position papers issued by RAFI and its Mexican counterparts rejected the concept of bioprospecting, regardless of the terms under which it took place. "RAFI does not believe that there exists any adequate mechanism—including the Biodiversity Convention—capable of safeguarding the rights and interests of local communities," the organization declared in 1999. "Therefore . . . RAFI regards all bioprospecting agreements to be biopiracy."[32]

Within indigenous-rights networks, most commentaries on the situation parroted the reports of RAFI and COMPITCH. A rare exception was the newsletter of the Canadian Indigenous Caucus on the Convention on Biological Diversity, which published a careful review of claims and counterclaims associated with ICBG-Maya. The article's author, Preston Hardison, concluded that prior in-

Brent Berlin *(left)* discusses medicinal plants with a Tzeltal-speaking Maya expert, Juan López López, 2001.

formed consent is a complex matter and that both sides made valid points in presenting their positions. He noted an odd contradiction in the views of RAFI and COMPITCH: sometimes they appealed to the idea of community consent, implying a high level of local autonomy; yet they also demanded that ICBG-Maya suspend activities until Mexico could implement a national policy regarding the exploitation of genetic resources. What Hardison might have added is that because COMPITCH represented an occupational group rather than an indigenous community, it was unclear why COMPITCH's opinion of ICBG-Maya should be regarded as decisive. "The sad thing here," Hardison concluded in a personal note, "is that all the parties in the dispute are consciously working to improve the position of Indigenous peoples in the world, and have deep ethical commitments to cultural survival."[33]

Brent Berlin repeatedly argued that he was a victim of his own honesty. While he and his colleagues communicated the goals and methods of their project in public forums and applied for all necessary government permits, less scrupulous researchers continued to collect plants and ship them off to distant laboratories for analysis. Another ICBG project long under way in northern Mexico generated little controversy, in part because its researchers chose to focus on plants purchased in public herb markets. Looking at Berlin's project with the benefit of distance, it seems unfair that an endeavor as promising as ICBG-Maya should be condemned as the ethical twin of, say, the nineteenth-century British campaign to spirit latex-bearing plants from the Brazilian rain forest to the greenhouses of Kew. The principles that underlie the project could hardly be more different, even if the terms of benefit sharing displeased the project's critics. ICBG-Maya had the bad luck to serve as a lightning rod for other struggles. Were the investigators guilty of hubris—or at least of naïveté—to undertake the project amid a low-intensity revolution? Probably. Most researchers in this position would have packed their gear and headed home, perhaps with the hope that conditions might eventually improve.[34]

More difficult questions are raised by the ICBG's formal alliance between ethnobotany and industry. Critics of academic ethnobotany have long insisted that published information on native medicinal plants represents a windfall for industrial bioprospectors. So even when ethnobotanists engage in what they consider to be purely scientific research, they subsidize commercial drug exploration—if not today, then years from now, when industrial pharmacologists rediscover useful works of the past. If the disinterested quality of science is a charade, as critics contend, scientists may as well find industrial partners, especially if those partners agree to meet higher ethical standards than characterized industrial practice in the past. Unfortunately, once you begin to dance with the devil, you are more likely to be seen as a sinner.

The role of COMPITCH in this controversy presents its own ethical gray areas. The international press pulled out every hoary cliché of the wise and inscrutable primitive when describing the organization's membership. Yet some of COMPITCH's most vocal representatives are sophisticated, well-traveled politicians who used the conflict to further their personal ambitions. To point this out is not to deny the right of COMPITCH or other NGOs to oppose ICBG's goals and methods. But interpretations that pit grasping multinationals against *huipíl*-wearing protectors of venerable Maya knowledge vastly oversimplify the conflict.

In November 2001 the ICBG-Maya project folded in the face of relentless criticism and the withdrawal of its Mexican partner, ECOSUR. In a statement released to the press, Brent Berlin declared, "The goals of the Maya ICBG were noble goals—the real losers are the Highland Maya themselves." He continued to insist that objections to the project were largely based on "rumors, distorted claims or partial truths, and deliberate lies." For its part, RAFI could scarcely contain its satisfaction in what it called a "victory for indigenous peoples in Chiapas." One must assume that RAFI saw the income lost to the project's Tzeltal and Tzotzil employees, to say nothing of abandoned opportunities for advanced training and development of local industries, as necessary casualties of war—in this case, RAFI's war against capitalism and the world intellectual property system.[35]

Steven King, senior vice president for ethnobotany and conservation at Shaman Pharmaceuticals, seems never to have wavered in pursuit of his vocational dream. As a precocious undergraduate interested in rain-forest ethnobotany, King wrote a term paper entitled "Preliminary Findings on the Traditional Pharmaceutical Medicine and General Health of the Angotere-Secoya," based on his field study of an Amazonian people living in a remote corner of Peru's Department of Loreto. After receiving his doctorate in biology, King worked for the National Academy of Sciences and the Nature Conservancy until Shaman offered him a job in 1990. One could hardly imagine a better match. Shaman defined one of its principal goals as "integrating the sciences of ethnobotany, medicine and plant natural product chemistry, and thereby pioneering drug discovery techniques that are proving more time- and cost-saving than the mass screening approaches typical of major pharmaceutical companies." To advance the goal of helping to preserve the environments in which plant resources were most abundant, Shaman established and funded a parallel nonprofit organization called the Healing Forest Conservancy, dedicated to protection of the world's tropical forests and their indigenous inhabitants.[36]

The logic of Shaman's business plan was novel to the pharmaceutical industry of the late 1980s and early 1990s, although it had been widely followed earlier in the industry's history. Companies looking for useful chemicals in the plant kingdom have two basic choices. They can undertake mass screening, paying particular attention to plant families already known for their bioactivity. This is simple but expensive. Alternatively, they can take advantage of centuries of human experience by narrowing the search to plants whose use by native herbalists and shamans strongly suggests the presence of biologically active compounds. The advantage of the latter, ethnobotanical approach is that it can cut the time needed to bring new products to market. An added benefit, according to Shaman's research scientists, is that ethnobotany begins and ends with humans rather than with chemistry. Lisa Conte, Shaman's president and CEO, translated this into language attractive to venture capitalists and potential share-holders: "The big investment we put into ethnobotany pays off." Conte told a reporter from *Business Week* that unlike large firms which screen thousands of compounds to achieve a tiny fraction of "hits," Shaman was batting nearly .500 while screening only 75 plants per year.[37]

In the early to mid-1990s Shaman benefited from a number of external considerations, including the emergence of venture-capital firms seeking opportunities to exploit new technologies, the pharmaceutical industry's rising profits, and what can only be described as the glamour factor. The company's exotic field research gave rise to articles in the popular press that juxtaposed wizened rain-forest herbalists and cutting-edge scientists such as Steven King. Shaman was mentioned in a 1991 *Time* cover story entitled "Lost Tribes, Lost Knowledge." Two years later the *Wall Street Journal* ran an article on Shaman that included a picture of Elias Gualinga, an Ecuadorian healer. The business press was intrigued but skeptical. A reporter for *Business Week* ended an article on Shaman with a smirk by labeling the firm's strategies "politically correct drug research." Nevertheless, Shaman raised enough money to begin ambitious programs of field study, drug screening and testing, benefit sharing with communities providing plant materials, and development of innovative software to track the data it collected on traditional remedies.[38]

Shaman's field research, largely concentrated in the world's rain forests, soon settled on two broad areas of medical interest: infection control and treatment of Type II (non–insulin dependent) diabetes. Records of the U.S. Patent and Trademark Office show that of twenty-two patents awarded to Shaman between 1991 and 1999, thirteen identify new agents that control blood sugar. Nine are for plant substances that show promise in combating viral, bacterial, or fungal infections. The plants in which these substances were discovered come from the forests of Africa, India, Southeast Asia, and Oceania, with a smattering from more arid regions.

By early 1994 the company's press releases declared that it had embarked on initial clinical trials of two related antiviral products, Provir and Virend, both based on a substance called SP-303. SP-303, according to the relevant patents, is found in plants of the genus *Croton,* a member of the spurge family. Most important of these is *Croton lechleri,* known in tropical regions of Peru, Bolivia, Ecuador, and Colombia as *sangre de grado* or *sangre de drago,* "dragon's blood," because of its red latex. Shaman hoped that the two commercial versions of SP-303 would prove effective against herpes—especially intractable herpes common among people with HIV-AIDS—and respiratory infections of viral origin. Several other encouraging leads were said to be under study, including an antifungal agent and substances that showed promise in the areas of analgesia and diabetes treatment. Some of these were being explored through partnerships with larger companies, including Eli Lilly and Merck.

Although the news from Shaman's labs was upbeat, reports from the company's accountants were increasingly worrisome. After a successful initial public offering in January 1993, during which shares of Shaman's stock rose to $17, the steady drain on the company's capital produced a slide in share price through the mid-1990s. A new stock offering was made in 1997 at $4.97 per share. By the end of 1998 Shaman filed papers with the Securities and Exchange Commission requesting a private offering of nearly 5 million shares at $1.50 each. Reportedly burning capital at the rate of $4 million per month, the company had to get a product to market soon if it was to survive.[39]

By 1998 Shaman's best hope lay with Provir, now redefined as a drug effective in the treatment of chronic diarrhea. Because of its potential for helping AIDS patients, many of whom must endure unpleasant side effects of existing anti-diarrhea medicines, the Food and Drug Administration awarded Provir fast-track status, which is intended to expedite the demanding and expensive Phase III clinical trials through which all new pharmaceuticals must pass in the United States. According to Steven King, Provir sailed through its final clinical tests, and every indication was that the company would secure the FDA approval that would at last generate a dependable revenue stream. But events intervened. A different fast-track drug already on the market, Rezulin, manufactured by Warner-Lambert/Parke-Davis, was implicated in a number of patient deaths. The FDA felt pressured to raise clinical testing standards for all drugs in the approval pipeline, Provir among them, and early in 1999 it informed Shaman that it would have to undertake a new Phase III study. The cost would be in the neighborhood of $25 million, money that Shaman did not have. The company was plunged into financial crisis. The *Economist* turned the news of Shaman's woes into an epitaph for ethnobotanical methods of drug discovery: "Shaman's failure to convert old-wives' tales into drugs . . . probably marks the end of the sort of selective 'botanising' that started the pharmaceutical industry."[40]

Shaman's president, Lisa Conte, proved more resourceful than skeptics anticipated. In September 1999 the company reorganized itself as a natural-products firm to market an extract containing SP-303 as an over-the-counter dietary supplement. Because dietary supplements are subject to less government regulation than pharmaceutical products, Shaman planned to use its SP-303-based product, sold under the trade name Normal Stool Formula, to generate enough revenue to keep the company afloat until it secured approval for the pharmaceutical-grade version of the drug. Financing remained precarious. Steven King was given the unenviable task of informing nearly two-thirds of Shaman's employees that they were being sacked. Shareholders who had seen the value of Shaman common stock plunge from $15, its price at initial offering, to less than 25 cents, were understandably upset.

When I interviewed King in the late fall of 2000, some of Shaman's labs had been rented to other companies, and most of the firm's offices were dark and silent. Although King remained as convinced as ever that SP-303 held great promise as an agent to control chronic diarrhea, the company's initial experience in the crowded marketplace of herbal remedies and supplements was discouraging. AIDS patients, it turned out, preferred to use diarrhea drugs subsidized by their insurers rather than shift to a supplement that, although superior and apparently safe, cost them more to buy. (In 2000 a month's supply of Shaman's Normal Stool Formula cost about $100.) A year later the situation looked brighter. Shaman Botanicals had ramped up its marketing efforts and licensed its product to the General Nutrition Corporation, which boasts a network of forty-five hundred stores. A clinical trial of the pharmaceutical-grade version of SP-303 was scheduled to begin in the United Kingdom, holding out the prospect that the company might still break into the far more lucrative market for prescription drugs, at least in Europe. Shaman's common stock, however, was trading at less than a penny a share, and it was unclear how long it could hold creditors at bay.

Despite the ups and downs of Shaman's finances, its benefit-sharing strategies have maintained a consistent course. In various publications, Shaman's nonprofit arm, the Healing Forest Conservancy (HFC), outlined its goals. These included conservation of cultural and biological diversity in the world's tropical forest regions, promotion of new forms of sustainable development, and a commitment to training local people to identify and produce medicinal plants suitable for world markets. For its part, Shaman pledged to provide upfront as well as long-term funds for communities with which it collaborated in drug discovery, although the scale of future benefit sharing was left vague in Shaman's publications and press releases.

In determining the targets of its benefit-sharing policy, Shaman faced challenging questions. Many species of healing plants are endemic to wide swaths of the tropical rain forest, crossing cultural as well as national boundaries. It would hardly be fair to focus benefits solely on the individuals or communities with whom the company worked, thereby excluding others who help to preserve the same traditional knowledge. But where does one draw the line? At the outer limits of a given native society? At the edge of a plant's geographical range? This can easily stretch the benefit-sharing network to thousands of square miles of territory.

According to King, the company settled on an imperfect but sensible compromise. Whenever possible, it would direct benefits to a given cultural group, even if this meant dealing with communities in adjoining countries. (Shaman's bioprospecting contracts stipulated that half of any profit resulting from its research was destined for government biodiversity-protection projects and half for the cultural groups with which the company was working.) The instrument for benefit sharing would be what the HFC called "compensation trust funds," small foundations created to distribute proceeds. A principal goal of the trust funds would be to distribute risks and benefits more widely, no small matter considering the odds against successfully bringing a new pharmaceutical to market.[41]

The most fully developed program that Shaman and the HFC have implemented to date is in Nigeria, where they disbursed funds totaling more than $200,000 for public-health training, development of a medicinal plant reserve, laboratory equipment for the study of parasitic diseases, and support for Nigerian scientists. The HFC worked closely with an existing trust fund, the Fund for Integrated Rural Development and Traditional Medicine. In reviewing these complex arrangements, one gets a sense of the considerable overhead involved—everything from communication costs to legal fees. The Nigerian program, according to the HFC's executive director, Katy Moran, was fortunate to be able to draw on strong local institutions. In other parts of the world, institutional frameworks for dealing with local communities may be poorly developed, slowing the negotiation process. Whenever possible, Shaman works with existing organizations to minimize the administrative burden.[42]

Despite its concerted efforts to turn drug prospecting into a platform for conservation and sustainable development, Shaman has been harshly criticized by many of the same groups that denounced ICBG-Maya. In 2000 the Coalition Against BioPiracy announced its "Captain Hook Awards" at a meeting in Nairobi. Although Shaman was spared an award, its patents based on *Croton*, the source of SP-303, were listed among the world's twenty worst by RAFI, a Coalition partner. "Shaman Pharmaceuticals went to the Amazon to get *sangre de drago*, an indigenous peoples' medicinal plant from which Shaman has isolated its patented pharmaceutical," declared RAFI. "The company talks about 'reciprocity' in its relations with the indigenous peoples who it taps for resources and knowledge; but so far the indigenous people who are Shaman's *sangre de drago* sources have received a few thousand dollars while Shaman has raised millions in the US capital market." RAFI neglects to mention that Shaman—or rather, Shaman's unfortunate investors—also lost those millions.[43]

Other critics contest Shaman's claims of reciprocity by asserting that the company's front-end support for local producers of *sangre de drago* has been paltry compared to what it stands to gain if SP-303 is brought to market as a pharmaceutical. At times it is hard to tell whether the critics are more offended by Shaman's profit motive or by its failure to realize a profit. Few mention that by its own reckoning Shaman has disbursed $3.5 million to the countries and communities with which it is collaborating. These expressions of benefit sharing include approximately $1 million for research and village-based programs focused on the sustainable management of *Croton* and $500,000 for training scientists and technicians from host countries. A more telling complaint is that Shaman's *Croton*-based patents fail to demonstrate novelty. The plant's powers as a digestive tonic, a healing agent for skin wounds, and a treatment for infections are so widely known in Central and South America that the company's patents represent little more than privatization of the obvious.[44]

The ability of firms like Shaman to turn folk medicines into approved pharmaceuticals is based partly on something that sociologists call "social capital"—in this case, recognized scientific credentials and links to prevailing networks of knowledge that permit individuals (or the corporations for which they work) to make credible intellectual property claims. Indigenous shamans and herbalists lack social capital, at least within the developed world's scientific networks. Their social-capital deficit is a factor in controversial patents granted for plant products that are widely known and used in indigenous communities. When patent examiners turn to conventional medical and pharmaceutical databases to review claims of novelty in patent applications, they are unlikely to find references to a plant's prominent role in folk medicine.

But it would be facile to blame everything on differences in social capital. There are more profound disjunctures between traditional and modern societies that groups such as RAFI conveniently ignore. The shamans and herbalists who have used a plant for centuries draw on local traditions and their own experience as healers. They participate in a folk medical system that articulates with a moral vision of life and death, sickness and recovery, crime and punishment. If *sangre de drago* fails to cure a patient, a healer may face suspicions that the treatment was a smokescreen for sorcery. Therapeutic failure and success are interpreted within a system of social control inextricably linked to interpersonal relations and local values. Medical practices in the developed world, however, answer to a different moral logic. Modern life is built on impersonal institutions that evaluate knowledge and set formal standards of professional competence. We trust our surgeon, our electrician, and the crew piloting the airliner in which we fly, none of whom we may know personally, because of their certified expertise. The maintenance of what the British sociologist Anthony Giddens calls "expert systems" requires an elaborate, highly rationalized bureaucracy that monitors professional practice and stipulates precisely how it is to be justified.[45]

To be used by licensed physicians, then, *sangre de drago* must be certified as a safe and effective medicine. This requires that it be subjected to the full battery of analytical techniques available to modern chemistry and that it meet the exacting standards of clinical trial. If it were to find its way into general practice without satisfying these requirements, doctors would be guilty of malpractice, especially if the drug were later shown to be harmful even to a small percentage of the people taking it. One suspects that the staff of RAFI would be first in line to file lawsuits were they to find themselves injured as the result of a failure to comply with these safeguards. Many social commentators have observed that our willingness to accept personal responsibility and risk appears to be in decline. We therefore insist that the institutions in which we place our trust study every possible scenario and anticipate every conceivable disaster.

The industrial processes by which a plant substance, whether familiar or novel, is disassembled, probed, purified, and tested are time-consuming and expensive. We accept this overhead as the cost of protecting society. It does not seem unreasonable, then, that those who bear the financial risks associated with rigorous testing should also be allowed the prospect of financial rewards conferred by the patent system. Other ways of organizing this process can be imagined—say, by having the government pay for all product testing in exchange for new limits on the profits of manufacturers—but such an alternative system is not visible on the horizon. When scientists employed by Shaman Pharmaceuticals publish a journal article with the intimidating title "SP-303, an Antiviral Oligomeric Proantho-cyanidin from the Latex of *Croton lechleri* (Sangre de Drago)," which includes assays of the effects of a molecule extracted from *Croton* la-tex on a range of viruses, they lay claim to a piece of knowledge-space defined according to their society's formal rules. It is not enough to say that *Croton's* healing powers are "obvious"—nor should it be.[46]

Shaman's two patents based on *Croton*, as well as two *Croton*-re-lated patents held by others, may well demonstrate less originality than is ideal in a patent system. Shaman acknowledges this imperfec-tion through its benefit-sharing policies, which it sees as a way to rec-ognize and reward centuries of empirical testing that lie behind the use of *sangre de drago* in folk traditions. (Whether those policies are adequate is subject to debate.) To date, Shaman's patents have had no negative impact on traditional use of the plant in local communities or on the importation and sale of *Croton* resin by natural-products companies in the United States and elsewhere. The company's ambi-tion has thus far produced greater scientific understanding of the plant, higher public visibility for a traditional remedy, and a moun-tain of corporate debt. Meanwhile, the clock is ticking on its patent protection for constituents of *Croton*. The patent term will be near its halfway point in 2003, with no immediate prospect of Shaman re-alizing substantial profits from it.[47]

Debates surrounding Shaman's commercialization of a familiar medicine from the New World tropics illustrate the difficulty of reconciling folk knowledge and the formal validation procedures of modern institutions. The gap becomes more evident in another widely cited case, that of the rosy periwinkle *(Catharanthus roseus)*. This species, usually described as native to Madagascar, is the source of two powerful cancer-fighting drugs, vincristine and vinblastine, that were isolated, tested, and then marketed by Eli Lilly beginning in the late 1950s. Vincristine eventually generated substantial profits for Lilly, none of which ever reached the nation of Madagascar.

Lilly's allegedly exploitative use of the rosy periwinkle has become the ethnobotanical equivalent of an urban legend. Countless books and articles claim that Madagascar was unfairly denied revenues from drugs whose discovery depended on its biodiversity and ethno-medical traditions. Fact-checking reveals a different story. First, botanists disagree about whether the plant is native to Madagascar or whether it was simply first described there. *Catharanthus roseus* is a resolutely cosmopolitan species now cultivated on six continents and thoroughly integrated into the folk healing traditions of countries as distant from one another as England, Pakistan, Vietnam, and Dominica. The botanist Judith Sumner notes that *Catharanthus* seeds were distributed to London's Chelsea Physic Garden by the Jardin des Plantes, Paris, in the mid-1700s. From London, they traveled the globe. Far from being an endangered species, *Catharanthus roseus* is regarded, at least in the state of Florida, as an aggressive exotic that gardeners should banish from their gardens.[48]

According to the scientists working at Eli Lilly, the literature available to them identified the rosy periwinkle as a folk treatment for diabetes, not as a cancer medicine. The first specimens used by Lilly were collected in India. Robert Noble, a Canadian scientist whose independent research on *Catharanthus* played a key role in subsequent developments, obtained his first specimens from a physician in Jamaica who believed the periwinkle would revolutionize diabetes treatment. At the time, no compounds that affected blood sugar could be isolated from the plant. (Some were identified years later.) Instead, scientists came upon alkaloids that proved effective as agents for treating cancer. This discovery, coupled with innovative extraction techniques, led to the development of vincristine and vinblastine, drugs that have helped doctors achieve remission rates of 90 percent or more in cases of childhood lymphocytic leukemia.

When Lilly released vincristine, under the trade name Oncovin, it was enormously expensive to produce. Norman R. Farnsworth, a distinguished researcher in the field of pharmacognosy (medical botany) who was part of Eli Lilly's *Catharanthus* research team, recalls that the company purchased purified vincristine from a producer in Budapest for $1.3 million per kilogram, making it one of the most expensive substances on earth at the time. Gordon Svoboda, another scientist who played a critical role in the research, has said that it was difficult to obtain sufficient quantities of *Catharanthus* leaves to refine more than small amounts of the two alkaloids. Concerns about the political situation in Madagascar and in India led Lilly to buy from newly established periwinkle plantations in Texas, where the leaves were harvested mechanically. Upon initial release of Oncovin, Lilly announced that it would be distributing the drug at cost. Later the company quietly shifted the drug into the for-profit category.[49]

Given this complex background, it is hard to insist that Madagascar must enjoy special standing in discussions of profits generated by the rosy periwinkle's biochemistry. Even if the species originated there, it was naturalized in other parts of the world before the dawn of the Industrial Revolution. The plant's use by indigenous and peasant communities strongly suggested bioactivity, but Eli Lilly's patents drew on properties that were not part of folk knowledge. In short, this is a weak case for those who argue that the pharmaceutical industry has reaped great profits by exploiting the ethnobotanical knowledge of particular nations or ethnic communities. The history of the rosy periwinkle is typical—not as an instance of clear-cut biopiracy but as an example of how difficult it can be to disentangle proprietary claims originating in folk traditions.

If ethnobotany is experiencing a crisis—and evidence suggests that it is—part of the blame must be attributed to the transformation of scientific practice in the developed countries. As recently as thirty years ago, most work in agronomy and applied botany was funded by governments. The results of research were made available to the public largely unencumbered by patent restrictions. This represented an implicit subsidy for industry, but it also served to maintain an intellectual commons favorable to innovation. Beginning in the 1980s, however, the U.S. government began to encourage its agencies, as well as research institutions receiving federal support, to seek patent protection for their discoveries. This privatization of knowledge has led to what some are calling the "tragedy of the anticommons." In an anticommons, multiple parties can deny access to outsiders, but none of the privileged owners control enough of the property to work efficiently. This patent logjam has begun to slow research in biotechnology, where important areas of the human genome and key processes used to study gene sequences are vigorously defended by patent holders. In theory, patent holders are free to license their rights to others, but the process of negotiating licenses is slow, expensive, and often thwarted by unrealistic expectations of gain. This has created a gold-rush atmosphere in which medical researchers are tempted to choose projects less on the basis of genuine social need than on the availability of arenas free of competing patent claims.[50]

Although most ethnobotanical work was not immediately affected by this sea-change in American science, ethnobotanists became easy targets for allegations of piracy, especially after conservationists embraced the notion that commercialization of genetic resources should play a constructive role in protecting biodiversity. No matter that the economic value of the developing world's genetic resources—with the exception of genetic material from a half-dozen major food crops—has been exaggerated. One can no longer imagine a scenario in which scientists from the developed world collect plant specimens, even in their own countries, with the same freedom they once enjoyed.

For even the most sensitive and politically engaged ethnobotanists, principles of informed consent and benefit sharing become vexed and equivocal in field situations. Rural areas of the developing world now encompass a broader range of social actors than in the past: entrepreneurs, ministry officials, journalists, representatives of regional NGOs, and leaders of emerging (and therefore often ambiguously positioned) organizations claiming to represent native communities and peasant farmers. The rule of law may be off in a distant capital, if it exists at all. This strange mix of conflicting interests and imperfect information is worlds apart from the clinical discussions of research ethics that take place in air-conditioned conference halls. To honor the interests of local communities, fieldworkers must sometimes settle for improvisational solutions that fall short of ethical perfection.

An emphasis on high-profile conflicts besetting the practice of ethnobotany risks misrepresenting the global picture. In some world regions, especially Africa and Southeast Asia, large-scale bioprospecting ventures are being undertaken without controversy, apparently because government ministries and local communities are content with the terms under which the research is proceeding. Even in more politicized contexts, such as among North American Indians, enterprising scientists have found ways to establish rewarding partnerships with indigenous communities. In British Columbia, for example, Kelly Bannister recently completed a study of the anti-microbial potential of balsamroot (*Balsamorhiza sagittata,* a plant in the Aster family) that was approved by the Shuswap Nation Tribal Council and conducted in collaboration with members of the Secwepemc First Nation, a tribe on whose traditional knowledge Bannister's work draws. Bannister is part of a new wave of ethnobotanists who recognize the inherently political quality of research and the need for sensitivity to community concerns as projects move forward. This perspective is voiced most forcefully by ethnobotanists from developing countries, who today are likely to see local flora and fauna as part of their national patrimony—a perspective that sometimes sets them at odds with indigenous-rights activists who insist that ethnic communities, rather than nation-states, are the rightful owners of local genetic material and ecological knowledge.[51]

In response to growing public recognition of the value of folkloric knowledge, a rebalancing of rights and responsibilities is already under way in many parts of the world. Governments and local communities now routinely set stringent conditions on bioprospecting projects. Foreign scientists must commit themselves to close collaboration with local counterparts, provide host-country institutions with equipment and training, and agree to profit-sharing arrangements. Indigenous leaders may demand that visiting scholars pay for access to local expertise and perhaps provide communities with badly needed health clinics or school buildings. Scientists increasingly reckon with local control of the information they collect, especially if it touches upon native religious practices.

Two recently announced profit-sharing agreements may be leading indicators of change in the relations between indigenous communities and the pharmaceutical industry. Late in 2001 a semi-independent research organization of the South African government, the Council for Scientific and Industrial Research, reached a compensation arrangement (the precise terms of which are undisclosed) with the San people of the country's Kalahari desert region. San knowledge contributed to discovery of an appetite-suppressant in a species of *Hoodia,* a cactus-like succulent long used to control hunger and thirst while hunting. A fortnight later the *Financial Times* reported that a U.S.-based group, the AIDS ReSearch Alliance of America, had agreed to share 20 percent of the profits from sale of a promising anti-AIDS drug called prostratin. Prostratin, derived from the bark of a Samoan tree, *Homalanthus nutans,* was identified by American scientists who had been sent samples by the ethnobotanist Paul Cox. Cox had learned of the plant from Samoan healers. The terms of the agreement with Samoa reportedly include making prostratin available to poor countries at low cost and providing compensation for the village where Cox collected the plant and for the families of the healers who taught him about it. According to the U.S. patent for prostratin issued in 1997, the drug is "extremely suitable for use as an antiviral agent and more desirable than other agents with anti-HIV activity." What medical researchers find particularly exciting about prostratin is its ability to purge the virus from its hiding places in the body. Used in conjunction with other drugs, it may improve prospects for a complete cure.[52]

These positive developments do little to placate hard-line opponents of bioprospecting and agribusiness. They insist that the world reinvent the intellectual property system so that the technical achievements of the last ten thousand years of human history qualify for economic compensation. It may be only a matter of time before we witness demands that the developed world make reparations to the world's centers of domestication for the "expropriation" of their crop plants. The list of potential claims is endless.[53]

Meanwhile, new technologies may be leaving the debates behind. Rational drug design, loosely defined as the process of identifying the structure of a target molecule and then finding a chemical that interacts with it in a desired way, has been made dramatically faster and more cost-effective by digital technology. In theory there is no reason why ethnobotanical techniques and rational drug design cannot complement each other. Ethnobotanists make a compelling case that their modest track record for drug discovery is explained by the simplistic way that pharmaceutical firms approach biological activity. The purification of active compounds often results in a loss of efficacy because plant-based ingredients interact synergistically with one another. Nor do pharmaceutical researchers show much interest in the precise methods by which traditional medicines are prepared for use, something that can greatly affect the remedies' power. Most ethnobotanists continue to believe that if we carefully attend to what traditional healers are saying we will eventually uncover a wealth of powerful healing agents.

Laboratory-based approaches have one big advantage over ethnobotanical fieldwork: they are largely immune to the kinds of political squabbles and bureaucratic log-rolling that played havoc with the ICBG-Maya project. Decades of systematic collecting have allowed universities and commercial firms to amass enough tissue samples to keep legions of pharmacologists and chemists busy for years. Facing the delays and frustrations of field-based bioprospecting, corporations are happy to fall back on these alternative resources and strategies. Many would be willing to pay significant bioprospecting fees and perhaps enter into profit-sharing agreements with developing countries, which would simply become part of the cost of doing business. To make this happen, however, the process of negotiating such arrangements must become faster and more transparent than it is at present.[54]

By 2002 the political climate in the United States had shifted for the pharmaceutical industry. During the scare following the anthrax bioterrorism attacks in 2001, there was widespread talk of forcing the industry to waive patent rights on Cipro and other antibiotics when demand far exceeded supply. The crisis drew public attention to the risks of drug development based on market forces rather than on national priorities. A wave of financial scandals implicating major American corporations highlighted the startlingly generous compensation packages of pharmaceutical company CEOs. Escalating health care costs and fiscal crises at the state level have focused greater attention on the high price of popular prescription drugs. Still, it would be naive to underestimate the power of the industry's massive lobbying arm to defend pharmaceutical companies against calls for increased regulation of their research and business practices.[55]

It is too soon to know whether we are seeing a permanent shift toward industrial practices that acknowledge the rights of indigenous communities in their traditional crop varieties and knowledge of local flora and fauna. What we do know is that the world's tropical forest regions continue to shrink with each passing month, and with them the planet's biodiversity. The argument that rain forests should be saved for the sake of their biochemical riches has resulted in a few encouraging developments and a great deal of polarizing conflict. The era of Richard Evans Schultes, who spent years contentedly gathering medicinal plants and interviewing shamans with few political constraints, is now definitively over.[56]

5. Negotiating Mutual Respect

Seventy miles from Sheridan, Wyoming, at an altitude of 9,600 feet, lies the Bighorn Medicine Wheel, a spoked circle of gray stones. The eighty-foot circle is sliced by twenty-eight lines that radiate from a central cairn. The wheel overlooks the Bighorn Basin, whose distant alkali flats shimmer like bleached bones in the hard sunlight of a clear day. Nine months of the year, cold winds and snow rule this part of the high country, sweeping the site clear of anything but the hardiest vegetation. When S. C. Simms, an early anthropologist, described his visit to the Medicine Wheel in 1902, he noted that his party had to negotiate snow drifts during a midsummer ascent. Arriving at the top of "Medicine Mountain," he found a "peculiar structure [that] consists of a large number of limestone slabs and bowlders of various sizes . . . Upon the projecting slabs of the eastern side of the central structure rested a perfectly bleached buffalo skull which had been so placed that it had the appearance of looking toward the rising sun. Resting on the rocks near the skull were several other bones of the buffalo." Simms had to content himself with verifying the existence of the Medicine

Wheel, because the Indians with whom he spoke declined to say much about it.[1]

The Bighorn Medicine Wheel is one of many circular stone features scattered throughout western North America. Most mark places where Plains Indians anchored their tipis. A few score of these, however, are too large and complex to be residential sites. They have a central stone cairn, sometimes echoed by satellite cairns. Circles may have concentric bands or lines radiating outward from the rim. The large cairn in the center of the Majorville Medicine Wheel, excavated in Canada's province of Alberta, contained three thousand artifacts that have been dated to as early as 3200 B.C. These included stone projectile points, tools for cutting and scraping, ground stone containers, amulets, hole-punchers made of animal bone, beads of shell and glass, ceramic pipes, and natural ammonite fossils used in medicine bundles, apparently because they bear a resemblance to bison. The layering of materials in the Majorville cairn suggests periodic use into the era of European contact.[2]

The Bighorn site has been harder to date because of a scarcity of wood or stone implements. So far the evidence points to construction sometime between A.D. 1200 and 1700. Archaeologists studying the site in the 1950s found nine glass trade beads dating from the early nineteenth century and a projectile point made four millennia earlier. Artifact scatters in the immediate vicinity of the wheel show that the area has been used by Native Americans for a variety of purposes—hunting, collecting, and religious activities—for perhaps seven thousand years. Evidence points most strongly to the presence of Crow and Shoshone peoples, but other tribes of the region, including the Arapaho, Blackfeet, Cheyenne, and Sioux, today regard the Bighorn Medicine Wheel as a powerful place.[3] When I visited in 1998, their veneration of the site could be seen in scores of religious offerings woven into the chain-link fence that protected the wheel from casual foot traffic. (The fence was replaced by a more discreet post-and-rope barrier in 2001.) There were dream-catchers, chamois bundles, tobacco pouches, mirrored pendants, and smudge sticks of sage gathered together with thread. Standing near the fence on a quiet morning before too many tourists arrived, one could hear the snap of brightly hued ribbons and the faint chink of beadwork stirred by the wind.[4]

What Native Americans do at the Medicine Wheel is not well documented. Given their recent turn to secrecy in matters of religion, detailed information is unlikely to emerge anytime soon. Some experts argue that one of the stone features on the site fits a pattern of vision-quest enclosures. A man seeking spiritual guidance removes himself to a remote place, where he fasts and prays. As privation leads him into an altered state, he lies in a hole or a ring of stones limiting vision to a circle of sky. Often, his prayers are rewarded by a powerful dream. Whether the site continues to be used for this purpose is not widely known. In the early 1990s William Tall Bull, a Cheyenne elder, told a group in Canada that the wheel "is an altar that is designed for ceremonies and also vision questing. The thing that I do when I go to the Medicine Wheel is to make atonement for all those who come and who will have no understanding of what is there, of what it's all about." Despite limited public knowledge of what takes place at the Medicine Wheel, few responsible observers doubt that it is a holy place for the region's Indians. "The Medicine Wheel and the land around it," Indian leaders say, "is our church, our Sistine Chapel."[5]

The fate of this remote place of prayer has been in doubt for decades. As early as 1915 the site was nominated for designation as a national monument. According to Fred Chapman, a state archaeologist who has long been involved in efforts to protect the Bighorn Medicine Wheel, rumors began to circulate in the 1950s that the federal

Cut Ear, a Crow Indian, praying at the eastern end of Bighorn Medicine Wheel, ca. 1916.

government wanted to move the stones to a more accessible place. Intervention by the state governor laid this plan to rest. In 1970 it became a National Historic Landmark.[6]

Americans love their favorite places to death. As highways improved and vacationers took to the road, the Bighorn Medicine Wheel saw a steady increase in visitors. About two thousand people went there in 1967. By the early 1990s there were 70,000. Fred Chapman reports that in addition to the damage inflicted on footpaths and vegetation by pedestrian traffic, tourists began to add offerings of their own to those left by Indians. These included "cigarette lighters, fish hooks, belt buckles, condoms, tampons, and other inappropriate items." To make matters worse, in 1988 the U.S. Forest Service, the federal agency responsible for the site, proposed changes that would make the wheel more accessible to the public: a paved access road and parking area, a visitor center, and an observation tower.

The proposal mobilized Indians in Wyoming and neighboring states. An advocacy group called the Medicine Wheel Coalition, which included representatives from fourteen tribes, mounted a vigorous challenge to the Forest Service's plans. Indian activism evoked a counter-response from the surrounding community of ranchers, loggers, and mining executives, a major power bloc in Wyoming politics. Discussions entered a bureaucratic labyrinth involving multiple government agencies (among them the Forest Service, the Advisory Council on Historic Preservation, the State Historic Preservation Office, and county officials) as well as two Indian organizations that sometimes disagreed about goals and strategies. Things became ugly: one Forest Service ranger was the target of anonymous death threats, and his children were taunted by schoolmates. To comprehend why an isolated religious site on public land would evoke such strong sentiments, we must first come to grips with the politics of Wyoming and of the New West that it represents.

Wyoming is a paradoxical place. The nation's tenth-largest state in size, it has the smallest population. It encompasses two of the country's most revered national parks, Grand Teton and Yellowstone, as well as vast tracts ravaged by surface mining. Once a state with a strongly libertarian live-and-let-live tradition, Wyoming has become a stronghold of the Republican party's activist wing, boasting a congressional delegation that earns near-perfect legislative scores from such organizations as the Christian Coalition, the Gun Owners of America, and the American Conservative Union. An ethic of self-reliance contrasts with the reality of ranching and mining enterprises heavily subsidized by the federal government—hence the criticism that Wyoming, like other western states, practices a form of socialism for the rich that benefits a few corporations and cattlemen ("welfare cowboys"). Known as the Equality State because it was the first to grant voting rights to women, Wyoming gives a statue of the suffragette Esther Hobart Morris pride of place in front of the handsome state capitol in Cheyenne. Visitors to Wyoming often comment on the decency and cordiality of its people, an impression borne out by my own experience. It is the kind of old-fashioned place where a Cheyenne newspaper can, without a hint of irony, carry a story about a man arrested for "violent and tumultuous behavior." Yet beneath this happy surface simmers intense hostility toward the federal government.

Washington directly controls about 50 percent of Wyoming's land area. Federal holdings include national parks and monuments, national forest lands, military bases, and areas administered by the Bureau of Land Management. Another 3 percent belongs to federally recognized Indian nations, the Shoshone and Arapaho tribes. One-fourth of the state's workers are federal employees. Although there are western states with a larger federal presence—Nevada, for instance, where more than 80 percent of the land is federally managed—Wyoming is arguably among the two or three states that most viscerally resent Washington's influence even though federal land-management practices have been extraordinarily beneficial to the state's extractive industries and ranchers.

Beginning in the late 1970s, frustration with federal land-use policies in the western states touched off what came to be known as the Sagebrush Rebellion. States demanded that federal lands be privatized or transferred to state control. Companies involved in resource extraction resisted federal attempts to classify forest lands as protected wilderness areas. Led by neoconservative ideologues such as James Watt, who was eventually named Secretary of the Interior by Ronald Reagan, and like-minded western legislators, the Sagebrush Rebellion took aim at environmental-protection policies developed in the 1960s and 1970s. Much controversy hinged on the specific meaning of "multiple use," the principle that had long guided management of federal lands. To what extent should the federal government protect fragile lands from use by loggers, stockmen, miners, energy companies, and enthusiasts of off-road vehicles while still allowing or even promoting economic development?

The Sagebrush Rebellion was more complex than a battle between resource-hungry corporations and passionate defenders of the environment. It was also a conflict between distant and local management, between long-time residents of western states and the mobile career bureaucrats who cycle through federal parks and administrative offices. Class elements figure in the equation, too: on average, federal jobs in Wyoming pay nearly 70 percent more than the state's per capita income. Even westerners with little sympathy for the neoconservative right acknowledge that federal control vastly complicates any activity that involves the land. Aside from the usual local, county, and state bureaucracies, one confronts a maze of federal agencies, each with its own rules, procedures, and tradition of foot-dragging.[7]

Opinions vary about whether the Sagebrush Rebellion ended with the departure of Ronald Reagan from the White House. The wholesale dismantling of federal control of western lands sought by the rebels never came to pass. Still, the vehemence of public debate made federal agencies more attentive to local concerns and, some environmentalists argue, more inclined to look the other way when faced with destructive land-use practices. In the 1990s the Freemen and militant Christian Identity groups found the West a congenial place to cultivate their ideology of racial nationalism. Although they represent a minority view, and a tiny minority at that, their anti-government rhetoric continues to feed public mistrust of federal agencies, as does the more conventional conservatism of regional talk radio. At the other end of the political spectrum, radical environmentalist groups like Earth First! hurl themselves into conflict with logging and mining interests through acts of civil disobedience known as "monkeywrenching." The result is a palpable edginess that surprises visitors from other parts of the country.

These currents shape another conflict over a sacred site—this one at Devils Tower, a national monument located in Wyoming's northeast corner, not far from the town of Hulett. Devils Tower rises up from gently rolling hills, a squat monolith of dark-colored porphyry that marks the core of an eroded volcano. Given its English name by Colonel Richard Dodge in 1875, the tower is known among the region's Indians as Na Kovea (Cheyenne), Mato Tipila (Lakota), T'sou'a'e (Kiowa), and other names, many of which translate roughly as "Lodge of the Bear."

At 1,350 acres, Devils Tower National Monument is a postage-stamp-sized park, especially when compared with Yellowstone National Park's 3,470 square miles, yet it welcomes nearly half a million visitors annually. About six thousand of these are rock climbers drawn to the tower's challenging vertical pitch and spectacular views. During the short climbing season, an average of fifty people a day make the ascent, some assisted by outfitters who guide climbers for a fee. From the base, visitors can see the climbers, many dressed in brightly hued clothes, working their way up the tower's columns.

In the late 1980s American Indian tribes in the region began to complain that constantly increasing use of Devils Tower by avocational climbers violated Native American religious principles. Shoshone religious leaders, for example, suggested that climbers who ascended Devils Tower showed a lack of respect for spiritual forces resident there. From Lakotas came more specific complaints that the climbers interfered with the Sun Dance that has been held annually within park boundaries since the 1980s. The shouts of the climbers and the sounds of their hammers and drills were distracting to Indians engaged in acts of worship. The presence of outsiders on such a commanding vantage point made it impossible to assure a modest degree of privacy during rituals such as the Sun Dance.[8]

The growing number of ascents also caused park rangers to worry about the environmental impact of this new human traffic. Elsewhere in the West, the introduction of hundreds of steel bolts into rock faces has damaged popular climbing sites. Climbers interfere with the nesting activities of raptors and endanger fragile high-altitude vegetation. These factors had led other parks to restrict the form, location, and frequency of climbing activities. The Devils Tower situation differed only in its religious dimension. Beginning in the early 1990s, the monument's superintendent, Deborah Liggett, opened discussions leading to the preparation of a management plan that would try to strike a balance between the needs of Native Americans and non-Indian visitors, including rock climbers and the outfitters who provided services for them. At about the same time, the National Park Service (NPS) commissioned an anthropological study of the cultural significance of Devils Tower to the region's Indians.

The consultants' report revealed that the Cheyenne, Arapaho, Crow, Kiowa, and Lakota recognize Devils Tower as a sacred site, grant it a prominent place in their mythology and oral histories, and in the past probably used it for individual religious observances. It proved more difficult to substantiate the tower's historical significance to the Eastern Shoshone, although contemporary Shoshone insist that it is and always has been a place sacred to them. The consultants delicately gloss over a sensitive issue. The Lakota declare that Devils Tower is conceptually linked to the Black Hills lying just to the east, where, they say, their tribe emerged from the underworld thousands of years ago. Anthropologists and historians see things differently. The Lakota, like the Cheyenne and several other Plains peoples, can be shown to have originated east of the Missouri River. The arrival of Europeans in eastern and southern North America unleashed social forces that rolled across the continent long before many native peoples laid eyes on a white person. Horses moved north from Mexico into the continent's heartland, while firearms were traded south from French Canada. The impact on formerly settled peoples such as the Lakota was dramatic. Horses and guns made bison hunting more productive than agriculture and nomadism more appealing than life in permanent villages. The Lakota and the other closely related groups known collectively as the Sioux pushed steadily west, using their superb equestrian ability and organizational skills to displace other native populations. Convincing evidence of sustained Lakota presence in the Black Hills cannot be found before the mid-eighteenth century or even later. This puts Lakotas within reach of Devils Tower only about a century before it was "discovered" by the cavalry officer Richard Dodge. For the purposes of determining the contemporary significance of the tower, however, the discrepancy between native and non-native views matters little. Even if, as seems to be the case, the annual performance of the Sun Dance at the base of Devils Tower owes more to the forces of contemporary cultural revitalization than to tradition, Native Americans can point to an impressive body of evidence to support their insistence that the tower is an important focus of religious sentiment.[9]

In 1994 the National Park Service invited public comment on its draft climbing-management plan for Devils Tower. The plan proposed to limit the use of climbing hardware (bolts or fixed pitons), impose seasonal closures to protect places where raptors nested, and, most controversially, request a voluntary moratorium on climbing in

June, a month when nearly thirteen hundred climbers made the ascent in 1994. The moratorium was intended to allow climbers to "show respect for American Indian concerns through their willingness to avoid climbing the tower in June." "Overall," the draft report declared, "the FCMP [Final Climbing Management Plan] will help preserve our cultural heritage and help promote amicable relations between Indian societies and the prevalent western society in the United States." The earliest draft of the plan also suspended for the month of June the issuing of ascent licenses to the several commercial outfitters who guide climbers up Devils Tower. The document warned that if the voluntary climbing moratorium failed, the NPS might impose a mandatory closure each June.[10]

In making the climbing ban voluntary, the Park Service walked a constitutional tightrope. The so-called Establishment Clause of the First Amendment to the U.S. Constitution prevents the government from enforcing any law or policy favoring a specific religion or even promoting religion in general. At the same time, several Supreme Court decisions have determined that the government and its many agencies are obliged to accommodate the free exercise of religion when possible. The distinction between promoting religion and allowing its free exercise by citizens is obviously a fine one that invites constant skirmishing in American courts.

The complex legal status of religion is further complicated by policies meant to acknowledge the special status of American Indians. The American Indian Religious Freedom Act (AIRFA) of 1978, for instance, declares that the United States will "protect and preserve for American Indians their inherent rights to believe, express and exercise [their] traditional religions . . . including but not limited to access to sites, use and possession of sacred objects, and the freedom to worship through ceremonials and traditional rites." To strengthen the sacred-site provisions of AIRFA, President Bill Clinton issued

Executive Order 13007, which requires federal agencies to "(1) accommodate access to and ceremonial use of Indian sacred sites by Indian religious practitioners and (2) avoid adversely affecting the physical integrity of such sacred sites." Another relevant legal resource is the National Historic Preservation Act (1966), which allows areas to be identified as "traditional cultural properties," a designation that affords modest protection.[11]

Laws made in Washington often look different in the places where they are applied. Park Service plans for Devils Tower quickly sparked local opposition. Immediately affected by the climbing policy were climbing outfitters, who stood to lose business during one of the season's busiest months. Some American Indians were unenthusiastic about a policy that offered only partial protection to a sacred site. "Why must the mountain be defined by your rules?" Park Service representatives were asked by an Indian attending a public forum held in Rapid City, South Dakota.[12]

Especially contentious was a related Park Service proposal that the site's name should be changed from Devils Tower, which is offensive to the region's Indians, to Bears Lodge, a name that better reflects the site's religious significance. This was precisely the sort of symbolic act that galvanizes veterans of the Sagebrush Rebellion, many of whom reflexively oppose any federal policy that expands Indian rights or acknowledges the validity of traditions other than the mythical grit and self-reliance of white settlers. In response to news stories about the possible name change, a white resident of Moorcroft, Wyoming, sent a letter of opposition to the State Office of Historic Preservation. To change the name now, she argued, would be to "forget all of the history that the Euro-Americans gave to the following generations." "Seems to me," she concluded, "that America is no longer a country where majority rules, now everything is for the minorities." Another long-time resident, the daughter of nineteenth-century homesteaders, wrote movingly of the tower's importance to her family. It had been a place for family reunions and community picnics until such activities came under the full control of the National Park Service. "The big point of my story is that in all these years and the many many trips to Devils Tower I don't remember ever seeing an Indian. I don't use the term 'Native American' because I feel that includes me, my Father and many others who are Native Americans of Crook County, Wyoming." She concluded her letter with the observation that the money required to change the name of the national monument "could better be used for the betterment of both cultures [Indian and white]." Wyoming's sole member of the House of Representatives, Barbara Cubin, pledged to block legislation that would change the name of the national monument, largely on the grounds that it threatened the local tourist industry. In a conciliatory move, the Park Service suggested that it might be possible to retain the park's current name but rename the geographical feature on official maps.[13]

It would be wrong to dismiss local opposition to Park Service policies as nothing more than racism. Not that racism is in short supply in Moorcroft or Hulett, the towns nearest to Devils Tower, hardscrabble places worlds away from the glitter of Jackson Hole, with its log "McMansions" and its seasonal air force of private jets. But local residents feel that they, too, possess a heritage worthy of protection and respect. When conspicuous symbols of that heritage are threatened by outsiders—including Indians, few of whom currently reside in this part of Wyoming—opposition is a predictable response.

The effects of this enmity were evident to Chas Cartwright, who succeeded Deb Liggett as superintendent of Devils Tower National Monument in 1998. A trim man with a lined, mobile face and graying hair, Cartwright is a seasoned NPS professional with experience at far larger parks. He expressed shock at the hostility that greeted him at his new post. At his first public meeting in Hulett, citizens opposed to NPS policies screamed obscenities and generally made him and his family unwelcome. In 1998 he received a visit by the entire Wyoming congressional delegation—two senators and one congresswoman—who came to protest a controlled forest burn that the NPS conducted at Devils Tower. The burn had been a complete success, and four months later the land was lush with grass and other vegetation. But angry locals insisted that their beloved tower had been defaced. They were even more upset when Superintendent Cartwright ruled against salvage logging of the burn site—that is, commercial removal of dead trees.[14]

Spearheading local opposition to the Park Service is an organization called the Bear Lodge Multiple Use Association (BLMUA). Multiple use—sometimes also called "wise use"—is based on the principle that public lands should not be set aside exclusively for any single purpose. Instead, they should be made available "wisely" to the full spectrum of interest groups, from environmentalist to industrial. In many areas of the West multiple use has become code language for the activities of loggers, miners, ranchers, and enthusiasts of off-road vehicles.[15]

In March 1996 the BLMUA filed suit in U.S. District Court, Wyoming, against Secretary of the Interior Bruce Babbitt, arguing that the new climbing policy at Devils Tower was unconstitutional. The BLMUA served as a proxy for the Denver-based Mountain States Legal Foundation, a right-wing multiple-use organization once headed by James Watt. The BLMUA succeeded in obtaining a court order overturning the mandatory ban on commercial climbing at Devils Tower, and several months later the NPS had made the climbing ban voluntary for all parties. But this failed to satisfy those opposed to government attempts to influence the use of public lands that Indians consider sacred.

The suit's arguments offer a fascinating tour of the philosophy of the multiple-use movement. The BLMUA organized its claim around two key assertions: that the climbing policy put the Park Service in the position of advocating Native American religious values in violation of the Establishment Clause; and that the NPS violated its own policies by restricting the activities of climbing outfitters. The latter point lost some of its punch when, prior to the filing of the suit, the NPS replaced the mandatory ban on outfitters' climbing licenses with a voluntary one. This left religious questions at center stage. The BLMUA insisted, among other things, that the Park Service's on-site interpretive program, which briefly describes American Indian beliefs about Devils Tower, "promotes or endorses the religious beliefs of some Native Americans to the general public." The plaintiffs claimed that the tour offered by interpretive rangers had caused emotional harm to students visiting from a school in nearby Hulett, presumably because it challenged their Christian values.[16]

Documents submitted by plaintiffs, defendants, and various friends of the court, as well as more inflammatory manifestos published on the Web and elsewhere, reveal deep local divisions on these issues. An affidavit filed by Romanus Bear Stops, a religious leader from the Cheyenne River Indian Reservation, states: "When I go with my relatives to Mato Tipila [Devils Tower] to participate in and perform ceremonies in which we pray for healing, rejuvenation, strength, and good life, I am worried that climbers will interfere with our prayers. The noise they make when they hammer things into the butte, clamber up its face or holler at each other as they climb the butte disturbs us. So too, does the fact that we see them on the butte." He concludes: "The climbing prevents me from practicing my religion. The climbing is a desecration of a very sacred place. The climbers don't know how to act when we are performing our ceremonies at Mato Tipila. Someone should have taught them that they should have respect for our people and not go near us when we pray . . . This is all I have to say for now. I will pray about this so that I may have more to say later." I suspect that few readers will quibble with this plea for basic respect. At the same time, one can reasonably infer that for Romanus Bear Stops and others who share his beliefs, all climbing on Devils Tower is offensive regardless of when it takes place.

At the other end of the spectrum of opinion is an anonymous group called Friends of Devils Tower, presumably associated with the plaintiffs in the lawsuit. On a Web page entitled "Tolerance not Segregation," the Friends of Devils Tower declare: "Regardless of what the Whimpy Cowardice Brown Nosing PC Access Fund, Bullish NPS, or Whining Indians may try to make you believe about their psychosomatic self induced practice of Indian religion at Devils tower . . . There is NO closure what so ever at Devils Tower." Less defamatory passages state that "Land Based Religious Practitioners"—a coded reference to American Indians—"don't want climbing or any other human activity, but theirs, at Devils Tower at any time. They are not happy with the token one month temporary closure to HUMANS, and they have made it clear that their ultimate goal is the complete prohibition of all Human Activity, but theirs, at Devils Tower and on many other PUBLIC LANDS." The document singles out Francis Brown, leader of the Medicine Wheel Coalition, as someone who favors complete closure of sacred sites to everyone but Native Americans.[17]

Francis Brown, whom I interviewed outside Wyoming Indian High School in Ethete, Wyoming, is a big man, with dark glasses and a generously proportioned salt-and-pepper mustache. He didn't hesitate to speak his mind about the Devils Tower dispute. "The

Entrance to Devils Tower National Monument, Wyoming, August 1998. The motorcyclists are participating in the annual Harley-Davidson rally held in Sturgis, South Dakota, not far from Devils Tower.

climbers say that the Constitution guarantees them the right to climb. Well I've read the Constitution, and it doesn't say anything about rock climbing. The issue boils down to religion and beliefs. My people love God better than Christians do. Christians were paid to destroy the life of my people. I don't have much use for Christianity. Those missionaries shouldn't get a tax deduction for what they do and all the lands they own." During our conversation Brown revealed considerable expertise in navigating the complex process by which sacred places can be protected by environmental easements and designation as traditional cultural properties. Federal acronyms rolled off his tongue: MOA (memorandum of agreement), HPP (historic preservation plan), and AIRFA (American Indian Religious Freedom Act), among others. A man deeply committed to traditional religious practices but also wise in the ways of government, Brown struck me as someone who would be a formidable adversary in any negotiating process. His harsh words about Christianity were consistent with assertions that his long-term goal is to close Native American sacred places to non-Indians.[18]

Chas Cartwright, the harried superintendent of Devils Tower, was mindful of his obligation to remain impartial about religious activities at the monument. He noted that Christian services have long been held at Devils Tower on Sundays, and the entry fee is waived for churchgoers. The NPS has also issued annual permits for the Sun Dance, which is held in the northwest corner of the park, at some distance from the visitor center and other heavily used areas. The Sun Dance is perhaps the most dramatic religious rite still performed by Plains Indian tribes. It requires the construction of a special lodge and altar. Those who commit themselves to the ritual as dancers must undergo days of privation—in some cases, self-torture—that may culminate in sacred visions. Standing on the Sun Dance grounds, with their unimpeded view of the tower, one quickly appreciates how distracting it must be to worship in the presence of Spandex-clad climbers whose voices carry for hundreds of yards in the still air.

The Sun Dance brings its own problems to the park, although no more than other visitor activities. Sometimes trash has been left at the site, and the organizers now must provide their own portable sanitary facilities because the park's primitive campground has proved unsuitable for events involving large groups. Sun Dance participants have been seen collecting sage, a plant in scarce supply at the park. Nevertheless, Cartwright expressed confidence that these problems would be solved through negotiation.

More difficult to accommodate are practitioners of New Age religion. In 1996 a New Age group sought permission to hold a large gathering to celebrate World Peace and Prayer Day at Devils Tower. The scale of the event was inappropriate for the park, and after protracted negotiations the group decided to camp on adjacent private land. Elsewhere in the West, parks and national forests face a phenomenon known as "New Age vandalism." Typically this consists of damage to the landscape or to fragile archaeological sites caused by ritual activities such as "smudging" (burning bundles of sage or other aromatic substances), recharging crystals by burying them in the ground, or allowing candle wax to accumulate in caves during impromptu meditation sessions. On Forest Service land just outside Sedona, Arizona, a stone medicine wheel has been rebuilt repeatedly by New Age devotees despite the efforts of rangers to remove it. In 1993 an official at the Sedona ranger station told a journalist that his staff had dismantled hundreds of newly built medicine wheels throughout the district. The situation became so serious that the Forest Service approved a flier encouraging pilgrims to make "mental" medicine wheels in lieu of real ones. When officials from Devils Tower National Monument met with Native Americans to discuss the proposed changes in climbing policy, one member of the audience voiced concern that the park would accommodate New Age religious practices as well as Native American ones. "Why does the NPS have to allow New Age activities?" park officials were asked. "There are thousands of years of oral traditions, including many ancient Kiowa stories about the tower. New Age activities have no connection with history or oral traditions at the tower." Nevertheless, park officials are obliged to honor all forms of religious expression that do not become a public nuisance or violate the integrity of protected environments and historic landmarks. Perhaps for this reason, climbers opposed to the June climbing moratorium have begun to argue that climbing is their religion and that the new policy prevents its free expression.[19]

The NPS has used the controversies surrounding Devils Tower to educate visitors about the site's significance to the region's Indians. Signs posted around the tower ask hikers to stay on marked trails because the site is sacred to Native Americans. (At other parks, it bears noting, such instructions are usually justified in terms of protecting fragile environments.) So-called interpretive guides provide background information on the tower's place in Indian mythology. Few park visitors object to such modest deference to an alien faith, especially when they are only yards away from one of that faith's places of worship. Undoubtedly some of them visit places like Devils Tower precisely because they want to know more about the West's Indians and their beliefs. National parks elsewhere in the United States show similar respect for religious sensibilities. At Arlington National Cemetery, for instance, the NPS informs visitors that the cemetery is a shrine and therefore an inappropriate spot for "recreation, picnics, or child's play." Where parks and national historic sites include Christian churches, the NPS urges visitors to be respectful during church services. Examples include the four Roman Catholic churches within the San Antonio Missions National Historic Park in Texas and the Ebenezer Baptist Church within the Martin Luther King, Jr., National Historic Site in Georgia.[20]

To the Mountain States Legal Foundation, however, Park Service policies that honor Native American sensitivities at Devils Tower are deeply threatening. "Imagine," reads one of the foundation's press releases, "if out of 'respect' for Moslems, all women had to be covered to enter federal buildings. Imagine, if out of 'respect' for Jewish dietary laws, park concessionaires were prohibited from serving certain foods. Imagine, if out of 'respect' for the religion of Native Americans, Colorado's Aspen Mountain were closed to skiing during December." The press release makes clear that the MSLF fears Devils Tower could be the next step toward conversion of public lands into zones exclusively reserved for Native American religious activities. "What is at stake . . . [is] the ability of the Clinton Administration to deny public access to federal land because it is 'sacred.' If successful in this gambit—after all, who cares about rock climbers—then the Clinton Administration can say 'no' to every use of federal land, including hiking, camping, fishing, grazing, timber harvesting, oil and gas or mineral exploration and development, or even skiing."[21]

Some of the issues to which the MSLF refers were settled in a Supreme Court ruling on the case called *Lyng v. Northwest Indian Cemetery Protective Association,* handed down in 1988. *Lyng* pitted the U.S. Forest Service (represented by Richard E. Lyng, then secretary of agriculture) against representatives of three California Indian tribes and a number of other parties, including the State of California. The Forest Service wished to construct a road and to issue logging permits in an area of national forest land called Chimney Rock, which contains archaeological sites and places that serve as "an integral and indispensable part of Indian religious conceptualization and practice," according to a study commissioned by the federal government. Although the Forest Service offered to locate the road and the logging area as far away from places of spiritual importance as the terrain would allow, Indians insisted that their religious observances required solitude and natural quiet. Wherever located, in other words, the road and the logging would make ritual activities nearly impossible. A lower court issued an injunction that prevented road-building and logging at Chimney Rock on the grounds that the project would violate the First Amendment's Free Exercise Clause as well as various environmental protection laws and AIRFA, the American Indian Religious Freedom Act.[22]

Indians in California and across the country were dismayed when the Supreme Court, voting 5–3, ruled for the Forest Service. The majority opinion, written by Justice Sandra Day O'Connor, was especially shocking because it accepted that "the threat to the efficacy of at least some religious practices is extremely grave." Justice O'Connor offered an exceedingly narrow free-exercise standard, insisting that the Constitution merely blocks the government from coercing people into acts contrary to their religious principles or punishing them when they act according to those same principles. So even if the road would "virtually destroy" the religion of the affected groups, she argued, the government had a right to build it.

Advocates for the rights of Native Americans and for religious freedom in general have penned scathing critiques of *Lyng*, denouncing it as a repudiation of the freedoms guaranteed by the Supreme Court's 1972 *Yoder* decision, which granted Amish communities in Wisconsin exemption from laws requiring public-school education for children through age sixteen. The Amish had argued that compulsory attendance of public schools by their children would undermine the fundamental values of their religion, thereby forcing the community to assimilate. Legal scholars see *Yoder* as an important model for weighing the legitimate needs of government—in *Yoder,* the government's "compelling interest" in education—against the protected practices of religious minorities. To some extent, however, subsequent decisions of the Supreme Court have backed away from *Yoder,* especially in cases involving American Indians. Experts in Indian law argue that the *Lyng* decision revealed the toothlessness of AIRFA, a measure that has proved largely unsuccessful in protecting Native American religions.[23]

The majority opinion in *Lyng* has an especially mean-spirited quality when one considers that the government's "compelling interest" involved road-building and the right to license private logging companies to harvest trees. In the grand scheme of things, the economic stakes were paltry in comparison with the potential impact on Indian communities who worship near Chimney Rock. No evidence was presented, for instance, that equivalent resources could not readily be obtained elsewhere. As one legal scholar has noted, the court might have delivered a narrow opinion in favor of the Indians by stating that it "intended only to limit the Forest Service's discretion in the land's use" without assigning the land to Indian control. Instead, Justice O'Connor focused on two issues that relate to sacred-site conflicts elsewhere. Above all, she saw the case as a direct challenge to federal sovereignty and the government's ability to use public lands. "No disrespect for these practices is implied when one notes that such beliefs could easily require de facto beneficial ownership of some rather spacious tracts of public property . . . Whatever rights the Indians may have to the use of the area, however, those rights do not divest the Government of its right to use what is, after all, its land."[24]

O'Connor's ruling also emphasized the difficulty of assessing the "centrality" of specific religious beliefs. It would be extremely undesirable, she argued, for the Court to judge the authenticity of beliefs or rank their relative importance to believers. This would, in her words, "cast the Judiciary in a role that we were never intended to play."

In response to Justice O'Connor's concerns about sovereignty, advocates for Native Americans insist that Indians have rarely demanded exclusive use of sacred sites on public lands. Nevertheless, if we take seriously the logic of Indian statements about places like Devils Tower, Justice O'Connor's misgivings are not unwarranted. A question commonly posed by Indian activists is, "How would your people feel if Lakotas used St. Patrick's Cathedral to perfect their climbing skills?" Taking this analogy to its logical conclusion, it is hard to see why a one-month pause will prove satisfactory. Indian ritual activities at Devils Tower peak in June, but there is no reason to think they are absent during other months of the year. As one unidentified Indian declared at a Park Service meeting in 1996, "I am opposed to any recreational activity at places where I do traditional cultural activities." Not only do Anglo-Americans prohibit climbers from using their cathedrals for recreational ascents, they also typically close them to skiers, loggers, picnickers, and teenagers riding all-terrain vehicles. Many Indians wish that their sacred places were treated with equal reverence. However misguided the *Lyng* decision may be, the ruling underscores the difficulty of reconciling native religious claims on sacred sites or entire landscapes with public ownership of those same places. This is especially true when the sites in question are located in heavily used national parks. So many people's rights are potentially in conflict that the best one can hope for is an imperfect, negotiated compromise based on common sense and some degree of mutual respect.[25]

That spirit has been much in evidence in decisions handed down by federal courts in the Devils Tower case. In April 1998 Judge William Downes of U.S. District Court, Wyoming, found against the Bear Lodge Multiple Use Association. Judge Downes reviewed the plaintiffs' claims and concluded that "the purposes underlying the ban [on climbing] are really to remove barriers to religious worship occasioned by public ownership of the Tower," which means that the Park Service's goal is to accommodate, not to promote, Native American religion. Attentive to the *Lyng* decision, Judge Downes insisted that as long as the climbing ban is voluntary it will withstand judicial scrutiny. Were the ban to be completely successful—that is, were the number of June ascents to drop to zero—he would see "powerful evidence of actual coercion." Absent that, the new climbing policy passes constitutional scrutiny. Judge Downes also rejected the claim that a party of children from a Hulett school had suffered injury by being "indoctrinated in the religious beliefs of Native Americans." The children had no standing in the case, he ruled, because they were not related to any of the plaintiffs.[26]

The Bear Lodge Multiple Use Association filed an appeal with the Tenth Circuit Court. The appeals court promptly affirmed the district court's decision, although on the narrow grounds that the BLMUA failed to show that its members had sustained any damage, financial or otherwise, as a result of the climbing ban. "The Climbers are clearly incensed by the NPS's request that they voluntarily limit their climbing," noted the appeals court ruling, "but standing is not measured by the intensity of the litigant's interest or the fervor of his advocacy."[27] In March 2000 the Supreme Court turned down the BLMUA's petition to review the case, thus ratifying the NPS management policy.

At the Bighorn Medicine Wheel, the Forest Service has posted the following sign:

To many people, particularly to Native American Indians, the Medicine Wheel has profound spiritual significance. Please follow these rules for the next ¼ mile. Please stay on marked trails. Please do not litter, move stones, pick flowers. Please leave the site as you found it.

The sign is one of the visible results of years of difficult negotiations between the Forest Service and parties with interests in the Medicine Wheel and surrounding public lands, a process that a Wyoming official has described as consisting of "endless revisions, bureaucratic skirmishes, internecine warfare between contending tribal factions, and a deliberate strategy of delay later openly acknowledged by Forest Service managers."[28] These protracted discussions paid off in 1996, when the parties announced an agreement about the future of the Medicine Wheel. Gone were the Forest Service's proposed access road, visitor center, and observation tower. In what must be a nearly unprecedented move for a nation dedicated to the proposition that no place is too sacred for automobiles, visitors to the Medicine Wheel now approach on foot via a 1½-mile-long road secured by a gate. (Only elderly and disabled visitors are permitted access in vehicles.) Local ranchers and loggers retain limited use of lands surrounding the site. Most important, American Indians who wish to use the wheel for prayer or ritual activities need only identify themselves to rangers. Visitors are asked to move about a hundred yards away from the wheel when Indians come to worship, a process that according to rangers typically closes the site for about half an hour a day in the summer months. Forest Service staff members, a few of whom are Native Americans, guide tourists through the site, giving the Medicine Wheel an important place in the Forest Service's educational programs.

In 1998 it appeared that the management plan was working. Some

Indian religious leaders grumbled that they would like to see the site protected more aggressively, but by all accounts most were reasonably satisfied with the new policies. Evidence of the regular use of the site for religious purposes can only increase its impact on non-Indian visitors, many of whom are probably unaware that Native Americans continue to worship in traditional ways. Unfortunately, this rosy picture of compromise was darkened in 1999 by the intervention of the Mountain States Legal Foundation. Undeterred by its judicial defeat at Devils Tower, the foundation sued the Forest Service on behalf of Wyoming Sawmills, a company based in Sheridan. In its suit, the MSLF sings a familiar refrain: at the Medicine Wheel the Forest Service has given the practice of American Indian religion a higher priority than other uses of public land, including logging, thus violating the Establishment Clause. Because Forest Service land is more oriented to commercial uses than are lands controlled by the National Park Service, the lawsuit moves closer to the circumstances of the *Lyng* decision than does the climbing moratorium at Devils Tower. But unlike the remote forest contested in *Lyng*, the Medicine Wheel enjoys a significant constituency of visitors who are moved by what they see. The MSLF may discover that its rhetoric of rights—in this case, the right to log high-altitude forests within sight of the Medicine Wheel—holds little appeal for Americans who find nothing wrong with the idea of protecting such a memorable place from commercial exploitation.

Bob Larson, one of the rangers at the site the day I visited, said that he has encountered little resistance from tourists asked to vacate the Medicine Wheel when Indians come to worship there, something that reportedly happens as often as 150 times a year. "It's surprising," he said, "but during the past five or six years I know of only one person who absolutely refused to honor this request." He paused for a moment to gaze at the parking area beginning to fill with cars and recreational vehicles. "She was a woman from Chicago who insisted on seeing what the Indians were doing. A ranger took her up there and explained the situation to the Indians. The woman left after a couple of minutes, obviously embarrassed. She later said that she hadn't believed that they were doing anything serious. As soon as she got there she realized that she was wrong."

At the heart of recent court decisions about Devils Tower and the Bighorn Medicine Wheel is the political significance of voluntarism. As long as the NPS rangers at Devils Tower merely ask climbers to refrain from making ascents in June out of respect for Native American wishes, the federal government stays within limits set by the Establishment Clause. To some extent, as Judge Downes acknowledged in his federal district court decision, the desired voluntarism is pushed by the formidable and potentially coercive power of the Park Service: strong messages in pamphlets, public signs, online documents, and on-site tours, as well as the explicit threat (at least in the earliest drafts of climbing-management policy documents) that the voluntary ban might give way to a compulsory moratorium. Thus far the emphasis has been on educating non-Indian visitors and soliciting their cooperation. Instead of a rights-based policy that essentially declares "We're prohibiting climbing because American Indians have the right to worship in peace during the month of June," the NPS's version of voluntary compliance says "We're encouraging you to refrain from climbing because it is the civilized thing to do." Voluntarism foregrounds "the processes of public justification, communication, and deliberation upon which the continuing vitality of a democratic regime depends," to borrow a formulation of the legal scholar Mary Ann Glendon. This approach requires a thoughtful conversation, in other words. If that conversation leads to greater mutual understanding, in the long run it will do more for Native Americans than would a rights-focused imposition of respectful behavior imposed by the state and enforced by its coercive power.[29]

The moral advantage of voluntarism surfaces conspicuously in the surprising decision of the Access Fund, the nation's largest advocacy group for recreational climbers, to support the Devils Tower climbing policy. The Access Fund fights for continued access to climbing sites throughout North America. In defending its support of the voluntary climbing moratorium, which evoked criticism from some members, the Access Fund emphasized both tactics and principles. The fund's officers argued that the organization could enhance its public image by cooperating with "influential interest groups such as Native Americans." Philosophically, the Access Fund favors "cooperative, non-regulatory solutions to competing uses of public lands." While the organization takes no official position on whether climbers should honor the June moratorium at Devils Tower, it encourages members to consider the wishes of all groups who use public lands. At the same time, the Access Fund has declared that NPS imposition of a mandatory moratorium would prompt it to sue. This group's position, in other words, turns on the power of moral choice and mutual respect.

The voluntary ban at Devils Tower has been reasonably successful. Each year from 1995 through 2001, June ascents amounted to only 13–19 percent of the approximately 1,300 ascents logged in 1994, the year before the moratorium began. Some of those who insist on climbing in June are foreign visitors unaware of the ban. Others are dissenters who resent the ban. Nevertheless, it is hard to see the success of the voluntary moratorium as anything other than a clear expression of deference to American Indian wishes.[30]

6. At the Edge of the Indigenous

Hindmarsh Island is a flat, grassy expanse just over nine miles long and three miles wide lying at the mouth of the Murray River in South Australia. To most observers, Hindmarsh is an unexceptional place. In the mid-1990s, however, it became the focus of a public struggle over the definition and protection of indigenous heritage. The conflict began as a conventional face-off between developers and environmentalists. The state government proposed to construct a bridge from the mainland to the island, site of a proposed marina that would shelter pleasure craft from the rigors of the Southern Ocean, into which the Lower Murray empties a short distance away. At first opponents emphasized the bridge's negative environmental and aesthetic impact, but these objections failed to stem the project's progress. Then concerns arose over the possibility that the bridge would destroy archaeological sites closely identified with the Ngarrindjeri, an Aboriginal people now scattered through the cities, towns, and farmsteads of southern Australia.[1]

Before the nineteenth century the Ngarrindjeri lived as patrilineal clans that exploited the aquatic bounty of the Lower Murray, the continent's largest waterway. All this changed with the coming of Europeans to Australia's southern coast in the early 1800s. Roving crews of whalers and seal hunters kidnapped Ngarrindjeri women and forced them into prostitution. By the 1830s and 1840s Aboriginal families had been thinned by European diseases such as smallpox and tuberculosis. Under pressure from European authorities, the Ngarrindjeri relocated to Christian missions. Interracial liaisons, forced or consensual, steadily turned the Ngarrindjeri into a mixed-race population. The relentless pressure of missionary work and the Australian education system sent the native language into decline. Today Ngarrindjeri people speak English, although their informal talk is peppered with Aboriginal terms for plants, animals, and traditional religious concepts. Older people retain vivid memories of living on the land. They also recall the repressive conditions of life under white rule, including the official practice of removing Aboriginal children to white foster homes. As one might expect among a people whose culture was so thoroughly unhinged by colonial history, the Ngarrindjeri have moved in multiple directions. Many continue to live in and around the towns of the Lower Murray. Some have adapted to urban life in Adelaide and other cities. Like Aboriginals elsewhere in Australia, Ngarrindjeri are more likely than non-native Australians to be unemployed, to receive public assistance, and to suffer from serious health problems. Most Ngarrindjeri are at least nominally Christian, although many continue to identify with Aboriginal religion even if they do not practice it overtly. They see Christianity as complementary to traditional beliefs, which represent Ngarrindjeri culture in a broad sense.[2]

In 1994 the government of South Australia concluded that concerns about archaeological sites on Hindmarsh Island did not justify cancellation of the bridge and marina projects. By this time the anti-bridge movement had expanded to include several Aboriginal advocacy groups, including the Aboriginal Legal Rights Movement and the Lower Murray Aboriginal Heritage Committee. Doreen Kartinyeri, a Ngarrindjeri woman employed by the South Australian Museum in Adelaide, undertook a study of the cultural significance of Hindmarsh Island. She reported the existence of previously undocumented women's ritual knowledge in which the island played a key role. Under the terms of a federal law, the Aboriginal and Torres Strait Islander Heritage Protection Act, development activities that may interfere with the exercise of traditional Aboriginal religion are subject to government review.

Here the Hindmarsh Island affair entered a labyrinth of claim and counterclaim from which it has never emerged. Doreen Kartinyeri's assertions prompted the office of the federal Minister for Aboriginal and Torres Strait Islander Affairs to hire a consulting anthropologist to investigate the matter. A second anthropologist was hired by the Aboriginal Legal Rights Movement to conduct her own study. After extremely short periods in the field, both consultants affirmed the existence of secret knowledge, known only to a few senior Ngarrindjeri women, in which the island was said to play a central role. Although no Ngarrindjeri have resided on the island since 1910, and despite the absence of evidence that Hindmarsh is currently a site of traditional Aboriginal religious activities, the consultants argued that construction of the bridge would so thoroughly violate the religious principles of Ngarrindjeri women that it endangered the foundations of their cosmology and values. The report of one of the anthropologists, Deane Fergie, included material that her interviewees described as confidential religious information ("secret-sacred" in the parlance of Australian anthropology) appropriately shared with women only. The pertinent government minister, Robert Tickner, honored this condition and asked a female staff member to review the material.

After considering the information available to him, Tickner deemed the claim of potential desecration convincing and ordered the bridge project suspended.

Then something unexpected happened. A dozen respected Ngarrindjeri female elders came forward to say that the information about "women's business" on Hindmarsh Island was a fabrication. They declared that the island's religious significance had never been mentioned to them by older relatives, that before 1995 they had not heard of important ritual activities taking place on the island, and that they therefore believed claims of the island's sacred status to be false or mistaken. Meanwhile, the ministerial ban on construction of the Hindmarsh Island Bridge came under scrutiny in the Australian court system. In February 1995 a federal court reversed the ban, arguing among other things that Minister Tickner had erred by declining to read the confidential women-only documents central to the claim of the island's cultural importance. The court concluded, not unreasonably, that an official decision made without full knowledge of the pertinent facts was a flawed decision.

By then the battle lines were drawn in public forums across Australia. On one side were supporters of the bridge and marina projects. Of these, some were broadly opposed to the expansion of native claims anywhere in Australia. Others simply felt that the specific evidence presented by the anti-bridge faction was false. On the opposing side was a loose coalition of Aboriginal activists, anthropologists, environmentalists, and ordinary citizens who saw the case as a test of Australia's commitment to Reconciliation, the national movement to improve relations between the country's Aboriginal and non-Aboriginal populations. Straddling the fence were many concerned people who although committed to Reconciliation were skeptical about the evidence presented in the Hindmarsh case. Almost everyone saw the case as an acid test of Australia's commitment to Aboriginal rights in the wake of the *Mabo* decision, which broadened the circumstances under which Aboriginal groups could press claims on lands they had traditionally used. Although the Ngarrindjeri were not asserting ownership of Hindmarsh Island, opponents of the bridge asserted that the land was a traditional cultural property over which they wished to exercise certain rights. The reluctance of government agencies to concede this was seen by Aboriginal activists as a discouraging step backward from the promise of *Mabo*.

Various observers of Australian affairs argue that the collapse of colonial policies occasioned by the *Mabo* decision prompted an upwelling of public concern—approaching obsession, in some cases—with the sacred, especially as embodied in Aboriginal peoples and their links to the land. This fixation is especially resonant because the classic formulation of the sacred in modern Western literature, Emile Durkheim's *The Elementary Forms of the Religious Life* (1912), used Aboriginal religion as its raw material. In today's Australia, Aboriginal assertions that a landscape or place is sacred evoke two basic responses. One is awed support, as if by honoring Aboriginal claims of sacredness non-Aboriginals can somehow reinvigorate their own lives and the life of the nation. The other is resentment, apparently driven by the belief that Aboriginal religion receives too much attention and too much protection. Those threatened by claims of sacredness—developers, mining firms, and the like—either insist that the claims are false or reject them on the grounds that they represent an expression of mysticism that should not be allowed to slow the rational exploitation of Australia's natural resources.[3]

Another factor driving the polarization of the Hindmarsh debate was the allegedly sacred "women's business" that held center stage for anti-bridge activists. Although the women-only affidavits submitted to government officials were confidential, their general outline emerged in public documents and the work of concerned anthropologists. The most detailed account is offered by the anthropologist Diane Bell in a sprawling, passionately written book with the tongue-twisting title *Ngarrindjeri Wurruwarrin,* published in 1998. In Bell's opinion, oral testimony certifies that Hindmarsh Island was the site of women's activities directed to the regulation of Ngarrindjeri fertility. These included puberty rites, menstrual seclusion, childbirth, and abortion—the last most often directed to fetuses fathered by white men. Women's generative knowledge and the practices once associated with it maintained crucial links between land and people, both living and dead. The island was, as one local woman told Bell, "the hub of the Ngarrindjeri nation" and a place whose symbolic power came from its location at the union of salt and fresh waters, creating a rich environment once central to Ngarrindjeri subsistence. By joining the island to the mainland, the bridge would destroy this generative symbolism and threaten the future of the Ngarrindjeri people.[4]

The theme of women's mystical ways of knowing exerts a powerful fascination for middle-class women in Australia, Europe, and the United States, as can be seen from the proliferation of books and personal-growth workshops devoted to it. Although Diane Bell takes pains to distance herself from the New Age movement, the Hindmarsh case became a cause célèbre partly because it resonated with popular interest in women's spirituality. To question the claims made by Ngarrindjeri women was to silence an expression of women's notions of the sacred that supposedly had survived centuries of oppression.

Critics of Bell's book insist that it must be seen through the prism of her own history and loyalties. She has been a vigorous proponent of the view that prior to the 1970s anthropology was negligent in its portrayal of women's understandings, a position with which few male anthropologists would disagree today. Her previous fieldwork produced a well-regarded study of the ritual life of Aboriginal women from Australia's central desert region. A key question in the Hindmarsh case was whether institutions found among Australia's desert peoples could be substantiated for the culturally distinct Ngarrindjeri of South Australia. In recent years Ngarrindjeri self-definition seems to have shifted subtly toward the emulation of central desert groups. These peoples have emerged as exemplars of Aboriginal authenticity, much as the Lakota or the Hopi are for Indian groups undergoing cultural revitalization in the United States.

Unfortunately for the anti-bridge movement, few cultural records gathered prior to the controversy supported the claim that Hindmarsh was a sacred site or that important women's rituals took place there. When experts consulted a major ethnographic study published by two of the country's leading anthropologists, Catherine and Ronald Berndt, who studied the Ngarrindjeri in the late 1930s and early 1940s, they found that the preponderance of evidence contradicted bridge-related claims. In fact, the Berndts declared the Ngarrindjeri unusual in the degree to which women's understandings and interests were integrated into everyday public life, not separated into a distinct sphere. This was especially telling because in principle Catherine Berndt would have had access to the opinions of Ngarrindjeri women. And as an anthropologist familiar with Australia's desert peoples, she would have been sensitive to the nuances of secret women's knowledge, had it existed. Other written sources are more equivocal. Authorities on both sides of the issue concede that the relevant cultural records are marked by silences and empty spaces. These gaps are easily explained away as the inevitable result of European sexism and the understandable desire of the Ngarrindjeri to protect religious secrets from hostile eyes. Harder to account for was the resolute insistence of some Ngarrindjeri women—elders whose cultural credentials seemed as convincing as those of the anti-bridge faction—that claims about the existence of a secret women's ritual sphere were patently false.

Skepticism about reports filed by the anthropologists assigned to the Hindmarsh case led the Australian government to convene a Royal Commission to investigate. The commission met for six months in 1995. One can hardly imagine a less effective way to explore the complexities of tradition. Even Chris Kenny, a journalist openly hostile to the opponents of the Hindmarsh Island Bridge, found the spectacle disturbing. "There was something at once impressive and farcical in the array of legal talent assembled at the opening session," he wrote. "Almost twenty lawyers were present, including some of the most prominent in the country." Aboriginal advocacy groups issued angry manifestos. Noisy rallies denounced the event as a witch-hunt and a violation of religious freedom. Objections were lodged at the United Nations. A story circulated that the Ngarrindjeri opposed to the bridge had brought along a Pitjantjatjara woman who would lay curses on anyone who questioned their views. It was days before the commission heard actual testimony. Testimony, in turn, was slowed by the adversarial format of the proceedings, which were conducted like a court hearing or a trial. Doreen Kartinyeri and most of the other "proponent women"— those arguing that Hindmarsh Island had sacred significance—refused to be questioned. Transcripts of the hearings ran to thousands of pages.[5]

In the end, the Royal Commission ruled that claims of sacred knowledge and women-only rituals on Hindmarsh Island were false, useful fictions deployed to halt construction of the bridge. But the commission's report did little to quell the determination of the anti-bridge faction. The developers of the marina project went into bankruptcy and then launched defamation suits against groups and individuals who had spoken out against the bridge, including the

Demonstrators marching in protest against the Hindmarsh Island Bridge Royal Commission, Adelaide, October 13, 1995.

consulting anthropologists. Fear of legal retribution prevented some people with knowledge of the case from speaking publicly.

The threat of civil action does not completely explain the vehemence of the Hindmarsh struggle, which was startling to observers from abroad. To some extent it reflects the size of the Australian social world. Despite the country's immensity, it has only 19 million citizens (slightly less than 7 percent of the population of the United States), most of whom live in and around the cities of the nation's eastern and southern rim. People sharing a profession often grew up in the same neighborhood and studied at the same university. Public debates quickly turn personal, giving them a jagged intensity disproportionate to the issues being contested.

Australians have also struggled more openly with issues of native rights than have Americans. Aboriginal land claims and sacred-sites conflicts make the newspapers almost daily, perhaps because Aboriginal people are more visibly a part of everyday Australian life than are their counterparts in North America's major population centers. Australia's attempt to come to grips with its history was brought to center stage at the 2000 Olympics in Sydney, when the national flag and the Aboriginal flag were flown side by side. It is difficult to imagine something similar happening in the United States.

A criticism leveled against white Australia's Reconciliation campaign is that it implicitly lends new legitimacy to the nation by identifying it with the Aboriginal history and culture that it once attempted to destroy. One wonders whether the emotional resonance of the Hindmarsh case stems in part from the resolute unwillingness of some Aboriginals to share religious information with outsiders. The concern with ritual secrecy among many Aboriginal groups evokes mixed feelings in non-natives. Some are drawn to the sense of mystery that secrecy produces. Others perceive it as a form of negation, a sharp rebuke to those who wish to enter more fully into Aboriginal understandings as part of a process of national soul-searching.[6]

The Hindmarsh controversy split academic departments, ended friendships, sundered families. It also raised disturbing questions about the credibility of anthropology. In July 1999 the *Sydney Morning Herald* published an article entitled "Trouble in the Myth Business," which examined the role of anthropologists in identifying sacred sites and other elements of heritage that merit protection under Australian law. The article contends that consulting anthropologists, for both political and economic reasons, are under pressure to produce the conclusions that their Aboriginal clients desire—namely, that a given place is sacred and therefore protected by law. This finding offers clients leverage in negotiations with the state and other key players, especially mining companies.[7]

The role of consulting anthropologists in heritage-protection cases raises genuine ethical concerns, but the problems highlighted by the newspaper account emerge at levels deeper than financial self-interest. By definition, heritage looks backward. It is something received from one's forebears. The creation of heritage-protection laws by settler nations such as Australia, New Zealand, and the United States acknowledges that colonized native peoples were deprived of access to their cultural birthright and the conditions that allowed it to be sustained. Because cultures must change to survive, the question of what constitutes a group's heritage quickly becomes knotty. Heritage thus suffers from some of the same problems as tradition and the broader concept of culture. The core difficulty lies in the tension between the retrospective dimension of heritage and the need to redefine tradition in response to new conditions. In practice, judges, lawmakers, indigenous activists, and other political actors move uneasily among these contradictory features of heritage, a situation that promotes inconsistent policies and contradictory rulings.

Another challenging dimension of the Hindmarsh Island controversy concerns authoritative knowledge. Whose opinion counts most when attempting to determine whether a concept or social practice is part of a community's heritage? "In an oral culture," asserts Diane Bell in relation to the Hindmarsh case, "knowledge is restricted to certain persons; for the system to work, those who are not privy to the 'inside knowledge' must accept the authority of those persons who are privy, and the wisdom of the restrictions. They must be willing to believe without 'knowing,' but be prepared to participate in the system nonetheless." As a generalization about oral cultures, Bell's declaration is debatable, yet it does capture an important feature of many Aboriginal societies, in which knowledge may be compartmentalized along lines of age and gender or unevenly shared between ritual experts and lay persons.[8]

Diane Bell and other supporters of the anti-bridge faction of the Ngarrindjeri are understandably reluctant to grapple with a more difficult question: How *few* people can hold a belief or engage in a practice before we must regard it as idiosyncratic and therefore unrepresentative of a group's heritage? Is one person enough? Two? A dozen? In the Hindmarsh case, perhaps half a dozen individuals, out of a population of more than three thousand, were said to be privy to the secret knowledge; hence the unease felt about the case by otherwise sympathetic observers. The compartmentalization of knowledge provides a perfect rationale for discounting contrary opinions, even those of other respected members of the community. Sure, the argument goes, a dozen elders say the claims about the ritual significance of Hindmarsh Island are rubbish. But they can't prove that secret knowledge about the island doesn't exist. Their statements reveal only that they themselves were never in on the secret. Ironically, some women's groups have been as quick to discount the skeptics among the Ngarrindjeri as developers were to discredit the anti-bridge faction. A women's newsletter portrayed the elders who denied the island's ritual importance as dupes and victims of colonial policies that suppressed traditional women's knowledge. The lucky few who retained these sacred understandings, according to the newsletter, are "viewed through the lens of patriarchal Eurocentric values, with women's business holding little value except as a curiosity or as amusing drama."[9]

There were occasional voices of calm amid the shouting. Robert Tonkinson, an anthropologist with considerable research experience among Aboriginal peoples, concluded that although it was possible that the Ngarrindjeri's secret women's knowledge did exist, "serious questions arise as to how such a hugely consequential body of knowledge could have remained so restricted, and how its status as a secret-sacred *category* could have failed to leave a visible social imprint of any kind." But common sense does little to counter the rage felt by those committed to what academics call "radical alterity," forms of otherness that resist the logic of Western institutions and thought processes.[10]

Echoes of the Hindmarsh affair can be heard at Point Conception, California, a scenic stretch of Pacific coast that lies between Vandenberg Air Force Base and the fast-growing city of Santa Barbara. In a region beleaguered by suburban sprawl, this undeveloped spot is a visible reminder of California's original beauty. Photos of its picturesque lighthouse regularly turn up on calendars. Environmentalists treasure its rich marine resources, including migrating whales and a small population of the endangered Guadalupe fur seal.

In the late 1970s Point Conception was the focus of a major conflict over the proposed construction of a liquefied natural gas terminal at nearby Little Cojo Bay. A coalition of Native American groups, supported by environmentalists and local ranchers, staged an occupation near Point Conception to protest the plan. The longest occupation, which sporadically involved as many as a hundred Indians and supporters, lasted from mid-1978 until March 1979. Delays created by this opposition, as well as the deregulation of the natural gas industry, raised questions about the project's economic rationale, and it was eventually killed by the governor. More recently, off-shore oil drilling and a proposal to expand Vandenberg Air Force Base have prompted new efforts to protect this pristine coastal area.

Central actors in the campaign to save Point Conception from development are California Indians now known as "Chumash peoples." Chumash claim descent from Indians who lived in the Santa Barbara area prior to European contact. With few exceptions, their ancestors were relocated to Spanish missions administered by the

Franciscan order. The California missions, in common with others throughout the New World, were designed to separate Indians from settings in which their former beliefs and practices could survive. They were also sites of ethnic mixing, first across the permeable ethnic lines that separated Indian groups and later between Indians and Spanish and Mexican settlers, a process that hastened the decline and eventual extinction of the region's native languages. In this respect California history resembles that of South Australia, although California's greater ethnic diversity made it possible for some people of native descent to take on social identities—identified by terms such as Californios, Mexican Americans, and later chicanos—which although politically inferior to that of whites were considered preferable to identification as an Indian. Others maintained distinct Indian communities from the mission period to the present. The name Chumash, an anglicized version of a Barbareño Indian name for residents of Santa Cruz Island, emerged in the early twentieth century as a term applied to a network of ethnically mixed but still identifiably Indian people who had survived the mission experience.[11]

The mission system and subsequent treaty violations by the United States separated the Indians of the Santa Barbara area from most of the land they had formerly occupied, including the Channel Islands lying off the coast. Today only one small Chumash community, Santa Ynez, is a federally recognized Indian reservation. Its sovereignty allowed it to launch a gaming venture that has brought full employment to reservation residents. Other groups asserting Chumash ancestry have initiated land claims and petitions for federal recognition, although at present their prospects for success do not appear bright.

Beyond this basic sketch, it is difficult to say anything about the Chumash that isn't contested by anthropologists, journalists, and the Chumash themselves. For example, the *Encyclopedia Britannica* declares that "fewer than 100 Chumash descendants remained in the late twentieth century." In contrast, an article in a respected anthropology journal proposes a figure of approximately three thousand, based on census data and interviewee self-identification. Yet even the larger figure is rejected by some as too low. At the heart of the discrepancy are genealogies developed from mission records. Many experts on California mission history believe these records are reliable and comprehensive. People unable to identify ancestors in the records, however, dismiss them as flawed, some even going so far as to assert that it is ethnocentric and racist to frame identity issues in terms of European notions of descent.[12]

These ambiguities led to controversy in 1997, when two anthropologists, Brian Haley and Larry Wilcoxon, published an article that names a prominent group of Chumash "Traditionalists" as people who assumed an Indian identity in the 1960s. For this group, Haley and Wilcoxon argue, knowledge of Chumash heritage comes from "creative assumptions, borrowings from non-Chumash spiritualists, popular stereotypes, and anthropological publications." They further allege that Traditionalists receive greater public attention and resources than do those Chumash who, despite stronger social and genealogical links to Indian peoples, are less picturesquely "native" in the way they present their heritage. Predictably, these assertions outraged some members of the Indian community and the anthropologists who work closely with them. Those unfamiliar with California historiography will find it difficult to sort out the twisted branches of multi-ethnic family trees reaching back more than 150 years—a process that, by all accounts, is a fractious one for Chumash families as well. Haley and Wilcoxon's analysis of the intensification of Chumash interest in Point Conception is easier to grasp.[13]

Ethnographic accounts from early in the twentieth century—fragmented and contradictory, much like those about the Ngarrindjeri of South Australia—emphasize that some local Indians considered Point Conception a special place. A handful of oral testimonies identify it as the site where the souls of the dead leave the world of the living and enter the afterworld. These sources differ in emphasis and credibility, and some experts trace them to the recollections of a single woman, María Solares, who was interviewed by the anthropologist John P. Harrington during research that he conducted sporadically between 1912 and 1928. Harrington's notes leave unresolved a number of important questions, including whether this belief was widely held.

By the 1970s, when local ranchers, environmentalists, and Indian activists geared up their campaign to block the proposed natural gas plant near Point Conception, the site's ambiguities vanished quickly. The place had become the "Western Gate," and its traditional protectors, the Chumash, were "Keepers of the Western Gate." The writer Peter Matthiessen, who in the mid-1980s published an account of the Point Conception struggle sympathetic to Indian demands, quoted the statement of one activist that Point Conception "is the most sacred site in all of California." A Luiseño Indian from the San Diego area told Matthiessen, "Indians as far away as Utah and Arizona knew about 'That Place.'" Matthiessen's description of the Point Conception occupations drew heavily on the views of Archie Fire Lame Deer, a Lakota medicine man whom Matthiessen describes as a key spiritual advisor to the Chumash. Lame Deer told him, "Indians come from South Dakota, Montana, Oregon, and throughout the nation to be present in support of our Chumash brothers and sisters, and in support of our Mother Earth." Pan-Indian interest in Point Conception suggests the increasingly cosmopolitan influences that have shaped Chumash thinking. A Chumash interviewed by Haley and Wilcoxon said: "I learned about the Western Gate from Indians and non-Indians. If you read the culture, you know what is there. There are lots of non-Indians who believe in the

Western Gate. Many people snub it, but people who are into psychic things, crystals . . . know all about the Western Gate." The Chumash Traditionalists' religious mentor, Archie Fire Lame Deer, eventually went on to market "Lakota Sweat Lodge Cards" that are sold in New Age bookstores.[14]

This unstable mixture of oral history, ethnography, pan-Indian thought, and New Age improvisation shapes contemporary belief in Point Conception's special religious significance. Haley and Wilcoxon discovered that after the popularization of the Western Gate theme in the late 1970s some Indians began to identify a site in Long Island as the Eastern Gate, where souls reenter the world. A Northern Gate may be in the process of emerging among the Inuit of Greenland. A Southern Gate does not yet seem to exist, but it cannot be long in coming. In arguing for the recency of a fully developed notion of the Western Gate, Haley and Wilcoxon take pains to emphasize that the expressed sacredness of Point Conception is not a hoax, a term used by critics of the Hindmarsh Island claims in Australia. Those who insist on the sacredness of the Western Gate, both Indian and non-Indian, seem genuinely to believe in its power. But these ideas are impossible to separate from the emergence of a vocal group of self-identified Chumash whose claims to native descent are controversial—according to some, completely spurious.[15]

Like the Hindmarsh Island case, the Point Conception controversy is clouded by conspiracy theories and skeins of self-interest. Some consulting anthropologists depend on the support of Indians for their livelihood; hence the temptation to tell clients what they want to hear. The same is alleged about consultants hired by developers, energy companies, and government agencies. Native claims may set the stage for cash settlements, lucrative environmental monitoring contracts, and even federal recognition, a critical step toward the establishment of reservations that can launch gaming enterprises.

Yet the Point Conception conflict cannot be reduced to economic or political agendas without doing violence to the subtle processes by which collective self-definition is forged in crisis. The transformation of a group into Keepers of the Western Gate may be—most likely is—perfectly sincere at the level of belief. But should this expression of cultural creativity merit legal protections different from those offered to other congregations or communities that do not claim to be indigenous? Current thinking in international circles generally supports the view that the Chumash case and others like it demand special legal remedies. A key U.N. policy document, for example, states that governments "should take immediate steps, in cooperation with the indigenous peoples concerned, to identify sacred and ceremonial sites, including burials, healing places, and traditional places of teaching, and to protect them from unauthorized entry or use." But what standards are we to use to ascertain whether the people in question are "indigenous"? With what members of such groups must we consult or negotiate? And how do governments verify that a place is indeed sacred?[16]

Merely asking these questions invites accusations of insensitivity. As in Australian debates over Hindmarsh, there are people who insist that Chumash spirituality is inherently incomprehensible to outsiders—radical alterity again—and that, even if the Chumash could cross this great conceptual divide, they have no reason to share their understandings with the oppressor. One commentator on the Point Conception controversy declares simply, "Humility dictates that neither I nor any other non-Chumash person will ever be able to know." The possibility of anything approximating intercultural understanding is thereby foreclosed.[17]

In the Hindmarsh Island case, the legal status of belief emerged as a central issue. Government agencies and courts were charged with determining what Ngarrindjeri people believed and whether their assertions of belief were real or invented. But belief resists documentation. Observers cannot know what a person thinks or feels. They can know what she says she believes, what others say she believes, and how she and the people around her act on those presumed beliefs. Given the elusive nature of belief, actual practice—demonstrable social behavior—must be taken more seriously than expressed opinion. We lend credence to declarations of faith by a Mother Teresa because of her lifetime of good works. Similar claims of Christian devotion are less persuasive when they come from an industrialist whose factories produce munitions. We can go further to say that in the face of actual behavior, statements of belief or motive may be unnecessary. Even if few of the participants fully understand the purpose of an event, the willingness to participate expresses commitment to its underlying power.[18]

Questions of practice, as opposed to those of belief, gave rise to the strongest doubts about the Hindmarsh Island claims. Even if we accept that the island and the water that surrounds it defined the traditional Ngarrindjeri cosmos in a way that a bridge would desecrate, there was little evidence that people acted on this belief in observable ways, now or in the recent past. Ngarrindjeri opponents of the bridge did not claim, for example, that Hindmarsh Island had been a site of ritual activity during the last half-century. They offered only fragmentary and contested evidence of Ngarrindjeri opposition to earlier modifications of the island's ecosystem, including construction of a pontoon bridge from Hindmarsh to the mainland in the 1930s. In short, the plaintiffs made a weak case that construction of the bridge and marina would prevent the continuation of Ngarrindjeri customs as they currently exist.

Similar difficulties arise in the Point Conception case. Compelling evidence of cultural activity at Point Conception between the mid-nineteenth century and the 1970s has not been presented in any public forum. Assertions about the site's sacredness foreground belief rather than practice. Peter Matthiessen describes ritual activities conducted on the site soon after the court-ordered eviction of Indian occupiers in 1979. But those rituals were undertaken by his Lakota friend, Archie Fire Lame Deer, rather than by someone native to California.

Examination of legal struggles over cultural *practice* reveals the relative weakness of claims based solely on declared *belief.* In 1985 the Zuni Tribe of New Mexico was drawn into unwelcome conflict with a landowner over the tribe's right to conduct ritual pilgrimages through a trail on his ranch. The destination of the pilgrimage was a site called Kolhu/wala:wa, usually translated as "Zuni Heaven," located in Arizona, to the west of the Zuni reservation. The Zunis consider Zuni Heaven sacred because it contains caves in which religious leaders can communicate directly with spiritual beings. A party of Zunis makes the 110-mile horseback trip to Zuni Heaven at least once every four years around the time of the summer solstice. In violation of government promises, the pilgrimage site was not included in the Zuni reservation when formal boundaries were defined by the United States government. Through the early part of the twentieth century Zunis petitioned for title to the site and surrounding lands. Like other Pueblo tribes, they were reluctant to provide information about their religious practices, but this reticence did not prevent them from maintaining pressure on the government to respond to their land claims. Their persistence bore fruit in 1984, when after protracted negotiations involving the tribe, the state of Arizona, and federal agencies, they were granted title to eleven thousand acres containing the site and its immediate environs.

The following year, however, a private landowner vowed to prevent Zuni pilgrims from using a section of the trail that crossed his lands. His motives, to the extent that he was willing to articulate them, seemed largely to involve asserting the right of private property, which in his case encompassed one of the largest holdings in the state. The tribe had no choice but to seek legal help from the federal government, which secured a temporary restraining order to prevent the landowner from blocking the pilgrimage. Continuing legal maneuvers culminated in a 1990 trial to determine whether the tribe should have a prescriptive easement—in essence, the right to use someone else's land without permission—that would permit unhindered travel to Zuni Heaven.

A fascinating element of the trial is that the pueblo's attorneys presented their case not as a religious-freedom issue but as an easement petition. Witnesses for the tribe, including several anthropologists, had relatively little to say about Zuni motives in undertaking the pilgrimage or the religious meanings of the event. Instead, they sought to establish that Zunis had traveled the same trail for centuries and that their use of it—although not its specific religious purpose—was widely known in the region. The judge promptly ruled for the tribe on the grounds that it had substantiated the easement claim to his satisfaction.

Legal observers note that the Zunis were wise to emphasize land use rather than religion in their case against the landowner. Constitutional protections against the establishment of religion prevent courts from valuing one group's right to practice its religion more highly than other rights, including property rights. The case might have gone against the tribe had it been framed in terms of religious rights. Hank Meshorer, the federal attorney who represented the tribe in the easement trial, notes several other factors that contributed to their success. Zunis were resolute in their determination to continue the pilgrimage. No internal divisions distracted the tribe from pursuit of this goal. Meshorer also believes that the expert consultants brought their extensive knowledge to bear in ways that compensated for what he calls the "secretive nature of the pilgrimage" and the "natural reticence of the Zunis."[19]

Admittedly, there are differences between the Zuni Heaven case and the disputes over Hindmarsh Island and Point Conception. The Zuni Tribe operates from a base of sovereignty possessed neither by the Ngarrindjeri nor by most self-identified Chumash people. It bears noting, however, that Zunis prevailed because of their unity and because they offered compelling evidence of sustained, verifiable cultural practice in the form of a quadrennial pilgrimage. Religious secrets or group sentiments were not a prominent part of the picture. Evidence of the pilgrimage's antiquity, regularity, and familiarity to local residents was sufficient to convince a judge that the Zunis' right to travel trumped the property rights of a stubborn landowner. Had similar conditions been met in the Hindmarsh and Point Conception cases, the outlook for defining both sites as irreplaceable cultural resources would almost certainly be different.

A focus on belief leads inexorably to concern with feelings. Diane Bell's account of the Ngarrindjeri routinely circles back to her informants' feelings about Hindmarsh Island, which Bell sees as inseparable from their knowledge of it. Bell claims an initial uneasiness with talk about the island's emotional power, which "sounded too much like getting in touch with my inner child and the intuitive self that New Age workshops promise to deliver." But she eventually came to share the sense that Hindmarsh contains sacred places that evoke particular feeling states. These place-related feelings, which Bell sees as central to Ngarrindjeri heritage, in her view merit protection by the state.[20]

Sensitivity to the feelings of fellow citizens has increased steadily in liberal democracies since the beginning of the twentieth century. Samuel D. Warren and Louis D. Brandeis comment on this in their landmark essay on privacy. Civilization, they observe, has progressed from a concern with life and property to a "recognition of man's spiritual nature, of his feelings and his intellect . . . [and] recognition of the legal value of sensations." Since the 1960s this trend has become a major social project. James L. Nolan Jr., a sociologist who has examined the ascent of therapeutic perspectives in American life, sees the emergence of an "emotivist" ethic as a reaction to the rationalizing and utilitarian power of capitalism. Today's therapeutic social policies, he argues, attempt to reunite public and private in a new synthesis. This leads the state to become more involved in the legitimation of personal feelings and the protection of citizens' emotional well-being through programs that promote self-esteem.[21]

The rhetoric surrounding Hindmarsh Island and Point Conception follows this therapeutic script. Supporters of the anti-bridge faction of the Ngarrindjeri objected to the work of the Royal Commission on the grounds that such rationalistic fact-finding was incompatible with Aboriginal religion and its unique ways of knowing. At times, Diane Bell's rendering of Ngarrindjeri philosophy is hard to distinguish from the New Age emotivism that she deplores. "Feelings and sentiment are acted upon," she writes. "They carry important messages, are reported, analyzed, nurtured, and remembered . . . The notion that one could know by feeling goes against the rationalist grain. If it can't be proved or disproved, can it be considered knowledge? As heirs of the scientific method, westerners tend to be afraid of feelings and sentiment. It is disconcerting to be told that only by letting go will one know truth; or find a particular place." Here Bell uses a bit of strategic Occidentalism to characterize Westerners as fearful of feelings, when in fact our public discourse is awash in sentiment. If anything, we fear that we are not sentimental *enough,* and this is why her accusation of insensitivity hits home.[22]

Like others involved in controversies over sacred sites, Bell says that the law must protect feelings but cannot submit them to scrutiny. Hence the conflict between attempts to create legal mechanisms to protect native heritage and the frequent rejection of those mechanisms when heritage claims are tested in court. In connection with another sacred-site case in California, for example, the state's Native American Heritage Commission declared: "Archaeology cannot determine religious and cultural significance. Only the Indian people can determine those values." Much the same has been said in the heat of the Hindmarsh Island case in Australia. The state must protect heritage, but it cannot inquire about what that heritage is, where it came from, and where it might be headed. These things can be known only to the bearers of the heritage, who have feelings to guide them. This argument carries considerable weight in the context of today's therapeutic values. It is made even more convincing by romantic views of indigenous peoples as possessing a spiritual and emotional authenticity missing in the larger society.

Feelings matter. No just society rides roughshod over the feelings of citizens, whatever their ethnic origin. But when heritage-protection laws move in an emotivist direction by aiming to protect the feelings of native populations from every possible indignity, they travel down a dangerous road—one that, among other things, invites similar demands from groups whose goals and values may be distasteful or destructive. Insistence that questionable, poorly documented assertions based largely on expressed feelings should trump all other considerations reveals cynicism and, perhaps worse, willful blindness to the negative impact these claims may have on the broader native-rights situation.

In a mordant assessment of contemporary heritage struggles, the geographer David Lowenthal offers a critical distinction between history and heritage. History, he argues, strives for value-free truth. It never achieves this goal, of course, but at least it remains open to test and refutation. In contrast, heritage "is not testable or even a reasonably plausible account of some past, but a *declaration of faith* in that past." Heritage makes use of history, "but these tales and traces are stitched into fables that are open neither to critical analysis nor to comparative scrutiny." Heritage is not about what people do, Lowenthal says; it is about who they are. Those who attempt to prove heritage through empirical research engage in a pointless activity.[23]

Lowenthal may overstate the difference between history and heritage, but his assessment brings into focus the difficulty of squaring the emotivism of heritage claims with the factual demands of law. The most aggressive proponents of sacred-sites protection insist that the central issue is sovereignty—in this case, the epistemological sovereignty of allegedly different cultures. They ask, Who are you to tell us what we believe? Within the relative sovereignty of reserves and tribal lands, native peoples hold an undisputed right to define their own values. In liberal democracies such as Canada and the United States, even landless native peoples are free to believe what they like and to reinvent their cultures as they see fit. But when groups make claims on public space as part of their process of cultural revitalization, basic fairness dictates that they bolster their assertions with evidence. Declarations of belief must be affirmed by proof of past and present practice, especially when invoking laws that give native rights special standing. Admittedly, this puts reemerging or newly constituted native groups at a disadvantage relative to communities that have already achieved a degree of nationhood. Advocates for native rights see this disparity as unfair. Why, they ask, should Chumash people be penalized for having suffered greater cultural dislocation

than the Inuit or the Navajo? And what justification is there for seeing those who claim Chumash identity as less legitimate, less deserving of cultural and political recognition, than other individuals or
communities already recognized as indigenous?

These questions cannot be addressed without consideration of
broader patterns of ethnic self-ascription in settler nations. In the
United States, for example, the number of people self-identified as
American Indians increased almost five times faster than the population as a whole in the 1980s. Most of this increase, the sociologist
Angela Gonzales points out, represents "ethnic switching," elective
changes in personal identity. Demographic trends, including high
rates of marriage between Indians and non-Indians, suggest that by
the year 2080 the U.S. Indian population will surpass 15 million,
nearly 90 percent of whom will have less than 50 percent Indian ancestry, as measured by blood quantum. The same trend is evident in
Australia, where as much as half of the reported increase in Aboriginal population in recent years has been caused by changes in the way
people identify themselves to census-takers. In both nations, this
should be taken as a hopeful sign. An improved political climate
leads people to conclude that it is now safe to reveal their indigenous
origins.[24]

But this shift in self-ascription creates problems of its own. An
Australian demographer notes that because of marriage between
Aboriginals and members of other ethnic groups, "indigenous births
to non-indigenous parents are experiencing logistic lift-off, and will
increasingly boost natural growth of the indigenous population way
beyond the growth trend of the rest of the Australian population."
This expert's assumption, which seems warranted by the evidence, is
that all who *can* claim a native identity will now do so. Many of these
"recovered" indigenous individuals have few ties to functioning na-

tive communities, raising questions about whether they should have the same legal status as members of recognized native nations.[25]

It is easy to overstate the importance of descent as a factor in determining who should be considered indigenous, even if it remains a standard by which most U.S. tribes define membership rights. Native peoples have long welcomed outsiders into their midst through intermarriage or adoption, and in the United States several key court decisions—notably *Morton v. Mancari* (1974)—have weakened the legal link between descent and native identity. But substituting culture for race does little to clarify the status of individuals or groups seeking to be recognized as indigenous. Native-rights activists often reject notions of culture rooted primarily in language, religion, co-residence, or shared leadership. What remains are such things as collective sentiments and oral traditions shared by networks of friends and kin—a diffuse basis for asserting a distinct social identity that collectively merits recognition as a "nation."[26]

In a much-cited essay, the anthropologist James Clifford reflects on the unsuccessful attempt of the Wampanoag Indians of Mashpee, Massachusetts, to secure restitution of lands alienated from them by non-Indian residents, developers, and local governments over the course of two centuries. The case turned on the question of whether the Mashpee Wampanoags constitute a tribe as defined by federal law. Clifford's text moves deftly between the author's musings on the complexity of Indian identity in the late twentieth century and his descriptions of the forty-one-day trial that resulted from a lawsuit known as *Mashpee Tribe v. New Seabury Corp.*, in which the Mashpee Tribal Council asked a federal court to right what the Wampanoags represented as a series of historical wrongs.

Clifford presents *Mashpee* as a borderline situation. Depending on how one looks at the evidence, itself a hotly contested category, the town's Wampanoags are either assimilated Americans or people who have "managed to keep alive a core of Indian identity over three centuries against enormous odds." His sympathies lie with the tenacious Wampanoags and, more pointedly, against an adversarial system that reduces courtroom exchange to trivial questions about whether a red bandanna worn as a headband qualifies as "Indian regalia." One cannot read the trial transcripts without concluding, along with Clifford, that an injustice was done to the Indians. Like most academic observers, however, Clifford dismisses the fear of white landowners, some of modest means, that the granting of tribal status to the Wampanoags could imperil their homes and life savings. Yet when long-time members of a community suddenly assert that they are really something separate and distinct, something that qualifies as a "tribe" or a "nation" and can lay claim to much of the land in the area because of a long-forgotten legal irregularity, their neighbors are bound to be upset. Such a sweeping and subversive assertion raises questions that courts can deal with only awkwardly.[27]

Although the issues contested in Mashpee, Massachusetts, are complex, they seem straightforward when compared with the situation of groups emerging under the rubric of the Mexica Movement in the region around the U.S.-Mexican border. People who call themselves Mexica (pronounced "Me-sheé-ka") explicitly reject identities as chicanos, Latinos, or Hispanics in favor of a reconnection with what they see as their indigenous roots. A militant wing of the movement, represented by the Chicano Mexicano Mexica Empowerment Committee, declares that it is working to use the resources of Mexica history and culture to "rebuild our indigenous identity" and to create "a great and independent non-Eurocentric future for all of our people." Leaders of the more spiritually oriented offshoots of the movement take on Aztec names and issue statements of solidarity with the religious vision of Native North Americans. The House of the Sun, they say, "is the legitimate heir and bearer of the philosophical principles of Mexicayotl, the Red Road, and of the religious tradition of our pre-American ancestors." In some cities, such as El Paso, Texas, the Mexica movement is engaged in outreach activities that focus on instilling cultural pride in young people and providing them resources for job training and artistic expression.[28]

One could easily dismiss this small movement as a minor side show in the tumultuous arena of American identity politics, but it has already affected policy discussions regarding vulnerable sacred sites. At Hueco Tanks State Historical Park, located a half-hour drive from El Paso, two local Mexica groups, the Kalpulli Tonal Teocalli and the Kalpulli Tlalteca, have been granted temporary religious permits allowing them special access to the park's fragile pictographs. With these permits they joined recognized American Indian tribes, including the Tigua, the Kiowa, the Mescalero Apache, the Comanche, and the Pueblo of Isleta, that are officially recognized as having "special ceremonial ties" to the park's spectacular images. The status of the Mexica groups' religious-use permit was still under review in 2002. It may eventually be revoked if park administrators conclude that the Mexica fail to meet the standard set by the National Register of Historic Places, which requires a pattern of "use or continued value" for at least fifty years for a site to be ruled a "traditional cultural property." Although the Mexica groups claim to have venerated the pictograph images for a thousand years, their current practices are less than twenty years old, well below the statutory minimum.[29]

A more bewildering case of indigenous reemergence is provided by the Washitaw, a separatist group based in Louisiana and largely consisting of African Americans. The Washitaw Nation, ruled by a woman who calls herself the Empress Verdiacee "Tiari" Washitaw-Turner Goston El-Bey, claims sovereign control of millions of acres of the American South. Her claim is based on the group's insistence that its members descend from Africans who peopled the lower Mississippi thousands of years ago and who built the mound complexes—now identified as sacred sites by the group—conventionally thought to have been constructed by Native American peoples.

The Washitaw Nation caught the eye of law-enforcement officials when it began to issue birth certificates, driver's licenses, and vehicle registrations. Its leaders also claimed that by virtue of its political sovereignty, citizens of the Washitaw Nation were exempt from state and federal taxes. Despite the African identity of most of the group's two hundred members, the Washitaw forged an alliance with a white separatist organization called the Republic of Texas, with which it shares an ideology of local sovereignty and common-law control. This link to extremists known for overt racism has not prevented the outlandish claims of the group's Empress from receiving sympathetic attention from certain black nationalist organizations.[30]

With little fanfare, Native American intellectuals and political leaders in the United States and Canada are turning their attention to the growing problem of ethnic fraud: claims of Indian descent motivated by a desire for personal gain or spiritual fulfillment. With public and private resources for Indians already scarce, the prospect of dramatic increases in the number of claimants has caused tribes to tighten membership requirements and universities to demand more background information from students seeking fellowships targeted to Native Americans. Perhaps more than their non-native counterparts, these leaders recognize that an erosion of standards for defining native cultures and native identities risks precipitating a crisis of legitimacy for *all* native rights.[31]

Nevertheless, universally accepted standards for indigenousness are likely to remain elusive. Equally challenging are efforts to develop acceptable legal definitions of sacredness and protocols for dealing with the diverse and often contradictory opinions arising within indigenous groups themselves. These issues complicate the work of judges and policymakers seeking to accommodate the religious activities of indigenous people (whether legally recognized or newly emergent) on public lands.

The Hindmarsh Island Bridge was inaugurated in March 2001, but reverberations of the controversy surrounding it still rattle Australia. Six months after the bridge opened to traffic, a federal court ruled against the marina developers who insisted that they had been bankrupted by the government-mandated delay in construction. After 146 days of legal wrangling, including testimony from 70 witnesses, Justice John von Doussa—the same federal judge who presided over the *Bulun Bulun* trial in Darwin—found that the plaintiffs' company had already been in financial trouble before the government suspended the bridge construction. The bridge dispute, he concluded, was not a significant factor in the developers' misfortune. More controversial was his rejection of the plaintiffs' claims of gross negligence, directed at the consulting anthropologists whose testimony supported the anti-bridge faction of the Ngarrindjeri. His reason: "Upon the evidence before this Court I am not satisfied that the restricted women's knowledge was fabricated or that it was not part of genuine Aboriginal tradition." Behind the double negatives, Justice von Doussa was saying that he believed the claim of secret women's knowledge was true, not the fabrication that the Royal Commission had found in 1995. He sidestepped direct refutation of the Royal Commission's findings by noting that the civil trial had considered testimony unavailable to the commission. The press was quick to jump on the implications of von Doussa's ruling, stirring passions anew. Among the Ngarrindjeri there seemed to be universal agreement about only one thing: that the dispute had caused deep and lasting divisions within their community. Meanwhile, the aggrieved developers vowed to appeal.[32]

Among the avalanche of words set off by the Hindmarsh Island case, the ones that retain a prophetic ring, because they suggest new ways of thinking about similar disputes elsewhere, are those of the Australian writers Ken Gelder and Jane Jacobs. Emotional public debate about an allegedly sacred site, Gelder and Jacobs argue, "transforms that place into nothing less than a 'site of significance,' with such immense reach and such powers of affect that even the skeptics succumb to it." Which is a roundabout way of saying that intense public conflict may imbue places with a sacredness that they never before possessed.[33]

7. Native Heritage in the Iron Cage

The common eider *(Somateria mollissima)* is a large, thick-bodied duck native to the polar regions of North America and northwestern Europe. The species is distinctive for the male's dramatic black and white markings, which contrast with the dowdier grays and browns of the females. Among northern peoples, eiders are considered good eating, but they are even more prized for their down, one of the world's best insulating materials. Eider populations, like those of other migratory game birds, dropped precipitously until Canada and the United States began to regulate hunting in the first decades of the twentieth century. Their numbers have recovered since then, although the status of some nonmigratory subspecies is still in question.

Among these is the Hudson Bay eider, which overwinters in areas of open water not far from the edge of the ice pack. Scientists' efforts to study the Hudson Bay eider are hampered by the region's harsh winters. But the area's permanent residents are uniquely positioned to observe every nuance of eider behavior and population dynamics. These residents are the Inuit, whose travels and hunting activities take them to places where ducks feed, breed, and find shelter. When Inuits were asked in the late 1980s to determine the size of eider populations by surveying nesting colonies, they established that the Hudson Bay eider population was much larger than scientists' sketchier information had indicated. Inuit observers also reported that eiders gathered in specific places according to environmental factors previously unreported by scientists and that their populations were subject to massive die-offs caused by local ice conditions. This information has implications for efforts to protect eider populations throughout the Arctic.[1]

Inuit understanding of the behavior and life cycle of the Hudson Bay eider exemplifies what has come to be known as traditional ecological knowledge (TEK), local lore drawing on centuries of observation and engagement with particular environments. For the past twenty years, many policymakers have advocated integrating TEK into land management, especially in endangered arctic and subarctic ecosystems. Although this idea seems obvious, it presents a challenge. TEK tends to be tacit rather than explicit, context-dependent rather than free-floating, and thus hard to codify and communicate. Categories basic to science, such as the distinction between the animate and the inanimate, may have no standing in indigenous knowledge systems. This makes it difficult to translate TEK into the utilitarian language of policy and management. Bureaucratic models of expertise, typically based on formal training, are hard to square with TEK's experiential roots.

Professionals in conservation ecology and rural development acknowledge these problems but take the commonsense position that traditional farmers, hunters, and herders know useful things about their environments. Local knowledge, long ignored by outsiders, ought to figure prominently in the quest for sustainable development. Although everyone agrees that some elements of TEK are incompatible with modern planning, much of it translates into policies readily understood by bureaucrats and legislators. At the very least, systematic attention to local perspectives helps to make regional planning more democratic and ultimately more successful.[2]

Nevertheless, objections to the use of TEK have arisen on both sides of the exchange. Some critics hold that the incorporation of TEK into environmental planning strips indigenous understandings of their original context and obscures their true meaning. Organizations representing indigenous peoples voice objections to the use of TEK on the grounds that it violates their intellectual property rights. Precisely what they mean by this is hard to ascertain. Sometimes the complaints refer to authorship: reports that include TEK do not often list indigenous consultants as coauthors. Sometimes critics object to the circulation of information that they define as culturally sensitive. More often, though, references to intellectual property reflect a belief that TEK has inherent economic value.[3]

Professional planners have not been universally enthusiastic either. In 1997 the Canadian press reported an unusual bureaucratic tussle involving the government of the Northwest Territories (now called Nunavut) and a senior policy adviser named Frances Widdowson. In a Canadian policy journal Widdowson and a coauthor asserted that TEK does not have the same standing as scientific knowledge because it is infused with what they labeled "spiritualism." "The integration of traditional knowledge," they wrote, "hinders rather than enhances the ability of governments to more fully understand ecological processes since there is no mechanism, or will, by which spiritually based knowledge claims can be challenged or verified." They also noted the paradoxical fact that bureaucrats are now required to consider traditional knowledge even while native leaders are refusing to divulge it on the grounds that it is proprietary. According to newspaper accounts, this public airing of doubt cost Widdowson a week's suspension without pay.[4]

These skirmishes in the policy world echo more ponderous exchanges in academic venues. Critics of Western science hold that it is inherently reductionistic or worse—a "male-oriented and patriarchal projection which necessarily entail[s] the subjugation of both nature and women," according to the feminist scholar Vandana Shiva. By contrast, TEK is held to be holistic and inherently sensitive to humankind's dependence on nature. Because the two approaches are irreconcilable, according to the critics, any attempt to bring them together will contaminate and undermine indigenous knowledge. Taiaiake Alfred, a Mohawk political scientist, accepts that Indians must be educated in the ways of the non-indigenous world if they are to defend their ways of life. But he insists that if a behavior "fails in its primary reference to inherited ways, beliefs, and values" it cannot be considered "traditional or authentically indigenous." These arguments proclaim indigenous cultures to be inalterably different from the mass cultures in which they are embedded. More important, they assert that the integrity of native heritage must be defended from the corrupting influence of alien categories. Every effort should be made to keep them from overlapping, either in public policy or in everyday life.

There is little question that communities may hold values that are both nonnegotiable and difficult to reconcile with those of other citizens. It is also true that such incommensurables are easily exaggerated. Resisting another group's conceptual framework is a proven strategy for solidifying social identity and asserting agency in situations of conflict. Conversely, a group's sense of insecurity may prompt a movement to purify categories threatened by different ways of looking at things. These complementary tendencies help to explain why many indigenous-rights advocates reject modification of existing laws to protect elements of indigenous culture on a piecemeal basis. It is argued, for instance, that indigenous art is so deeply entwined with every aspect of daily life that it is not a distinguishable activity or body of material. Since the 1992 *Mabo* decision in Australia, a line of argument has emerged which holds that land is inseparable from any aspect of Aboriginal culture. Therefore rights in land create rights in everything else, including ideas, design styles, rituals, and even biological species.[5]

Resistance to piecemeal protection of native heritage has inspired proposals that indigenous cultures be shielded in their *entirety*. If it is difficult, say, to separate religious beliefs from traditional healing practices, then patent laws designed to defend the knowledge of indigenous healers from bioprospecting will inevitably tear apart cultural elements that should remain intermingled. The proposed solution is a benign form of quarantine that safeguards all elements of cultural life. Entire cultures would thus be defined as off-limits to scrutiny and exploitation. Within this sheltering legal umbrella, communities would remain free to devise appropriate ways to defend their philosophical or scientific or artistic achievements. For lack of a widely recognized cover term for this broad-gauged approach, I will call it Total Heritage Protection.

If there is a canonical text that makes the case for Total Heritage Protection, it is a slim U.N. document entitled *Protection of the Heritage of Indigenous People* (henceforth, the Daes Report), released in 1997. The Greek jurist Erica-Irene Daes issued the report after extensive consultation with indigenous leaders and a range of experts. The document's sponsor, the United Nations, has proved an invaluable forum for voicing native grievances too often ignored at home. The organization's multinational character symbolically confers upon indigenous peoples the nationhood to which they aspire. The U.N.'s key role in the area of universal human rights gives it a moral standing useful for indigenous peoples even when their concerns are only awkwardly encompassed by a human-rights framework. But yoking the United Nations and aboriginal aspirations exacts a price. The rise of what has been called the "global cocktail circuit" promotes the emergence of a world-traveling indigenous elite and contributes to divisive internal struggles over resources and local accountability. On balance, however, the alliance has been useful to aboriginal peoples.[6]

The Daes Report declares bluntly that a society owns its heritage, defined as "everything that belongs to the distinct identity of a people and which is theirs to share, if they wish, with other peoples." "In summary, then," the document says, "each indigenous community must retain permanent control over all elements of its own heritage. It may share the right to enjoy and use certain elements of its heritage, under its own laws and procedures, but always reserves a perpetual right to determine how shared knowledge is used."[7]

To advance the cause of heritage protection, the Daes Report encourages native peoples to itemize their cultural resources, calling inventories "an essential tool in the identification and recovery of cultural property." This may not be easy to do, the report admits. "Apart from the overwhelming complexity of the task and the confidentiality of much of the information required, there is a danger that such a catalogue would encourage outsiders to think that the heritage of indigenous peoples can be sold." And who is to determine the content of what to include on each society's list of cultural elements? "What tangible and intangible items constitute the heritage of a particular indigenous people must be decided by the people themselves."[8]

Although the Daes Report offers practical suggestions about how

Indigenous representatives at United Nations Headquarters, New York, 1997.

existing laws can serve indigenous interests, its tone shifts from technocratic murmur to passionate aria when making the case for Total Heritage Protection: "Indigenous peoples regard all products of the human mind and heart as interrelated, and as flowing from the same source: the relationships between the people and their land, their kinship with other living creatures that share the land and with the spiritual world . . . All elements of heritage should be managed and protected as a single, interrelated and integrated whole." Existing laws and policies "would have the same effect on [indigenous peoples'] identities as the individualization of land ownership, in many countries, has had on their territories—that is, fragmentation into pieces, and the sale of pieces, until nothing remains."[9]

The Daes Report is more a grab-bag of laws, resolutions, and legal precedents than a closely reasoned policy statement. But one can abstract basic principles from it. It assumes that throughout the world indigenousness is readily identifiable, both in individuals and in cultures. Members of such communities own their heritage, including its "works, arts, and ideas," and they can manage it in a conscious fashion like any other resource. A people may specify precisely what their heritage consists of and what the rules for using it are to be. Other groups, including the state, must honor those definitions and rules.

Equally eloquent are the report's silences. Although it characterizes indigenous cultures as "part of the common heritage of all humankind," it says nothing about the world's cultural and intellectual commons or whether one should even exist. Put another way, the Daes Report takes for granted that indigenous people are not part of any public other than their own enclosed conceptual universe and the piece of territory to which it belongs. From the report one can reasonably infer that any social group that qualifies as "a people," indigenous or not, enjoys equally absolute rights over its cultural productions. The document remains mute about what implications this might have for the conduct of everyday life in pluralist societies. Can the cultural elements of complex societies truly be sorted and reorganized so that each is returned to its point of origin? What would be the social and political costs of such a campaign?

The most startling feature of the Daes Report and the many similar documents it has inspired is how little their authors worry about the impact that new regulatory regimes are likely to have on indigenous life. This terrain was mapped by Max Weber nearly a century ago, and his insights continue to haunt anyone who struggles to understand the modern condition. A powerful current of modernity, which Weber famously linked to Calvinist theology and the rise of capitalism, is the replacement of moral thinking by impersonal, calculating rationalism. For Weber, rationality is inherently neither good nor bad. It may encourage social progress and improve many aspects of everyday life. But those improvements have their costs—

among them a loss of spontaneity, passion, and a sense of wonder. Hence Weber's memorable reference to capitalism's "iron cage," a prison-house of soulless affluence and procedural uniformity.

Of special interest are Weber's observations on law and bureaucracy, the purest institutional expressions of human reason. Laws stand in a constant tension between their formal logic and their intended goals. In the interests of equity, we institute ever more complex legal procedures that diffuse responsibility so completely that when things go awry it is difficult to assign blame. Procedures foster the growth of bureaucracy, "with its specialization of trained, technical work, its delimitations of areas of responsibility, its regulations and its graduated hierarchy of relations of obedience." In other words, highly rationalized and formalized systems generate their own internal logic, understood only by a specialist class of mandarins. Weber considered bureaucracy inescapable and in his darkest moments saw it as the framework for humanity's progressive enslavement.[10]

At high levels of complexity, rules and procedures may have negative consequences unanticipated by the people who devise them. Zoning ordinances designed to keep communities attractive are now seen to have abetted America's epidemic of suburban sprawl. Mandatory-sentencing laws for minor drug infractions fill our prisons, diverting funds from public education and other civic needs while doing little to hinder the drug trade. Legally mandated safety devices in automobiles prove lethal to small children, requiring new laws and policies to undo the harm. One might reasonably expect that anyone concerned about the vitality of indigenous societies would hesitate before turning them into another experiment in the Law of Unintended Consequences.

A different cautionary note is sounded in the work of the French social theorist Michel Foucault. When law encompasses formerly undefined elements of social life, Foucault argues, it has a pronounced tendency to impose regulatory frameworks that shift power to regulators. This occurs even when laws are intended to protect and guarantee freedom. Law's universalizing power strips away history and contingency, replacing them with forms of policing and control that serve institutional needs. From the Foucauldian perspective, as soon as indigenous heritage is folded into comprehensive regimes of protection it becomes another regulated sphere of activity, something to be managed, optimized, and defined by formal mission statements. In the context of what some are calling a "global society of control," there is reason to be wary of legislative proposals that would interpose a novel regulatory architecture between human beings and their most powerful forms of expression. The risks of such interventions do not disappear if the regulators are themselves indigenous. Legal restrictions on the use of symbols and other cultural assets would give ruling factions considerable power over internal dissidents, no small matter in an era when native nations are becoming more internally diverse because of increased social mobility and inter-ethnic marriage.[11]

The practical effect of these abstract forces can be assessed by a look at cultural-protection laws currently in force in the United States and other countries. In the United States, the Native American Graves Protection and Repatriation Act (NAGPRA) of 1990 is arguably the most important of these. Although NAGPRA is, on balance, a reasonable law, it has sometimes fostered conflict between Indian tribes and given tribal governments new power that undermines customary rules of ownership. Because NAGPRA's reach is limited to physical objects and human remains, its impact falls far short of the complete control over cultural symbols promoted by advocates of Total Heritage Protection.

More relevant as a test case is the Indian Arts and Crafts Act of 1990, which strengthened similar legislation passed in the 1930s. The broad intent of the law is simple: to guarantee the authenticity of Native American art by prohibiting the sale of products falsely claimed to be made by American Indians or Alaska Natives. The law was designed to protect native artists who find their livelihood threatened by counterfeit goods, some produced on near-industrial scale in Mexico, Pakistan, India, Thailand, and the Philippines. One might think that certifying works as authentically Native American would be a straightforward business, but it is not. The law defines as Indians and Alaska Natives only those officially registered as members of a recognized tribe or community. One result is that people who are clearly Indians, but who lack the requisite tribal membership, are prevented from identifying their work as Native American. The law may benefit Indian arts and crafts in the aggregate, but it does so at the expense of many deserving artists who are legislatively exiled from their heritage. The Cherokee artist Kay WalkingStick has likened the law to the registration of Indians begun during the reservation period. She accepts that producers of fraudulent work should be subject to punishment. "Yet through this law," she insists, "some of our most important artists may be stopped from exhibiting their work and affirming their identity."[12]

Similar problems arise from an Alaskan certification plan called the Silver Hand program. The Silver Hand is a tag that identifies a work of art as an "Authentic Native Handicraft from Alaska." Artists are issued the tags after submitting an application that includes verification of Alaska Native identity (blood quantum of one-fourth or greater) and a pledge that products to which the tags are affixed are made entirely by the applicant, in Alaska, and using materials defined as "natural." There is no fee for the application, and the pertinent forms are simple by bureaucratic standards. Nevertheless, many artists do not use the tags. Some do not know about the program. Some are discouraged by the paperwork. Some resist the characterization of their work as "Native" because they feel the term confines their art to traditional genres. Still others are working in innovative materials that fail to qualify as natural. The Silver Hand seal is attractive to consumers, and the number of artists using it is increasing. Yet many legitimate Alaska Native artists decline to participate in the program. The absence of the Silver Hand tag on their work implicitly casts doubt on its authenticity. In a broader sense, the program— in some respects one of the most effective of its kind—generates an awkward tension between artistic freedom and the rationalizing power of bureaucratic control. If comparatively simple laws regulating the authenticity of native art already marginalize artists of mixed heritage or cosmopolitan inclinations, then more comprehensive controls risk compounding the damage by extending it into the most intimate zones of personal and collective identity.[13]

Elsewhere in the world there have been few comprehensive attempts to regulate intangible culture, aside from a recent flurry of legislation protecting local knowledge of plant and animal species. A South Korean statute called the Law for Protection of Cultural Properties has been praised for its role in preserving the nation's folk traditions. In the mid-1990s Brazilian legislators came close to passing a broad set of regulations designed to protect key cultural resources in the country's indigenous communities, but the legislation failed to emerge from a full-scale review of its constitutionality. Panama succeeded in passing such a measure in 2000. Among the articles of the Panamanian law is one that makes it illegal for dance troupes to "highlight all or part of an indigenous culture" unless the troupe has secured permission from traditional authorities or integrated representatives of the culture into the performance.[14]

The law professor Paul Kuruk, who works closely with African NGOs that defend the intellectual property rights of traditional communities, has assessed existing folklore-protection regimes in Africa. African governments have tried to accommodate common-law traditions regarding ownership of artistic and musical styles, and regulations for their public use are on the books in Ghana, Nigeria, Congo, Mali, and Senegal. Most of these countries have state-run folklore authorities or authors' guilds that review requests to use folklore for commercial purposes. Permit fees are supposed to find their way back to source communities. Kuruk endorses the African approach as useful and expresses regret that no nation has yet adopted a model law developed by UNESCO that would, among other things, criminalize "failing to acknowledge the source of folklore; misrepresenting the origin of expressions of folklore; and distorting works of folklore in any manner considered prejudicial to the honor, dignity, or cultural interests of the community from which it originates." In the United States, legislation that declared these kinds of speech a criminal offense would doubtless have a difficult time passing constitutional muster.[15]

To the extent that Total Heritage Protection has been enshrined in law, then, it gives rise to troubling contradictions. To defend indigenous peoples, it promotes official boundaries that separate one kind of native person from another, and native persons from non-native ones, thereby threatening the fluidity of ethnic and family identities typically found in aboriginal communities. In the name of defending indigenous traditions, it forces the elusive qualities of entire civilizations—everything from attitudes and bodily postures to agricultural techniques—into ready-made legal categories, among which "heritage" and "culture" are only the most far-reaching. In the interest of promoting diversity, Total Heritage Protection imposes procedural norms that have the paradoxical effect of flattening cultural difference.[16]

Contemporary willingness to redefine culture as a protectable resource reflects broader debate about culture's political status in pluralist democracies. In anthropology, which probably more than any other academic discipline gave culture high standing as an analytical category, culture's stock is at its lowest point in nearly a century. Its critics dismiss it as inherently totalizing (meaning that it implies an internal coherence that doesn't exist in reality), essentialist (implicitly reducing complex human behavior to a limited set of forces or essences), and tied to boundaries that are difficult or impossible to identify. The situation is not helped by the way people talk about culture in the mass media. One now hears frequent references to the culture of corporations or occupational groups, and some observers of contemporary social life feel comfortable declaring that gays and lesbians, the disabled, and even women have distinct cultures, an assertion whose accuracy many—although probably not all—anthropologists would reject.[17]

The inherent ambiguities of the culture concept have not prevented it from becoming a cornerstone of public debate on identity and social justice, especially for multiculturalists who demand that the state guarantee conditions under which distinct cultures can flourish. Multiculturalism is informed by a notion of culture with deep roots in German philosophy, which identifies within each society a *Volksgeist,* the spirit of a people, that sets the society apart from all others. In this view, cultures are self-contained moral universes that define values, practices, and identities. Cultures may change, and they interact with neighboring cultures in ways that may be mutually transformative, but they are nevertheless seen as all-encompassing and readily identifiable. As a corollary, individuals "belong to" or are "members of" a single culture that shapes everything about them. Proponents of multicultural politics typically hold that in the interests of fairness an individual's rights should be calibrated according to the needs of his or her cultural group. Liberal states are morally bound to construct a legal canopy of protection for minority cultures. In other words, the law should recognize that cultures, and not just individuals, have rights. Traditional liberalism is held to focus only on the rights of individuals and therefore to overlook the essential role that cultural communities play in shaping the individual. In fact, however, few liberal theorists deny that groups have important rights that merit legal protection. The struggle is not over cultural versus individual rights but over where society draws the line of demarcation between the two.[18]

The case for cultural rights is strongest when directed to education and language policies and to questions of local political control and representation. When applied to matters of heritage protection, however, cultural-rights perspectives reveal serious shortcomings. Because culture is an abstract concept, its boundaries are contested and evanescent. Exactly where does one culture end and another begin, both in space and time? On what grounds should one group's claim to an element of culture be considered more compelling than another's? Although it is relatively easy to determine whether an individual qualifies for membership in a particular group, how does one decide whether that person "belongs to" a particular culture?

As we have seen, it is often hard to determine whether specific individuals qualify as indigenous even when the general category is undisputed. In everyday political relations between native peoples and the state, this ambiguity may not be a major issue. Indigenous communities are left to sort out membership for themselves, and they do so tolerably well. But when we propose to cordon off segments of the collective idea-space along ethnic lines, the stakes are much higher. At the very least, it seems reasonable to acknowledge the inevitable fuzziness of cultural identity when pursuing solutions to problems of cultural ownership.

The absence of standards for assessing the well-being of a culture—as opposed to that of an identifiable community, which can be evaluated using a range of established metrics—creates openings for extravagant, unprovable claims of cultural damage. In an otherwise instructive essay devoted to questions of Native American intellectual property, for example, a legal scholar observes that naming Washington's football team the Redskins "is part of a pattern and practice that causes irreparable, substantial harm that has a direct effect on the survival of a culture within the United States." Even if we accept that continued use of the name "Redskins" is undesirable, how persuasive is the assertion that it causes "irreparable, substantial harm"? Native American cultures have survived five centuries of pestilence, military conflict, and dispossession. Compared to these catastrophes, in what meaningful sense does the name of a professional football team put their survival at risk? One could argue just as convincingly that petty insults actually promote cultural survival by bringing Indians together in solidarity against the dominant culture. For the article's author, the Redskins case signals the direction in which legislation must go: toward the aggressive protection of symbols "whose deprecation would have an impact on cultural survival." Here we enter a funhouse world in which any use of symbols that a society (the whole society? merely a segment of it?) finds offensive becomes a mortal threat.[19]

A curious feature of cultural-rights approaches is that their portrayal of native societies bears only a faint resemblance to the way indigenous peoples actually live. In the United States, the 1990 census revealed that 56 percent of American Indians lived in urban areas. In Canada, Australia, and New Zealand, the corresponding figures for aboriginal peoples in the 1990s were 70, 73, and 83 percent. In these four settler democracies, then, residence and everyday social relations are difficult to reconcile with the Daes Report's assumption that a people harbors a culture in a given patch of real estate. Admittedly, this massive diaspora is often a matter of necessity. In the United States, Indians have long moved to cities in search of education, jobs, and adequate medical attention. Some have been induced to relocate by assimilationist government policies, now largely abandoned. Whatever the reason for their choices, a majority of the indigenous citizens of these four countries live in multi-ethnic settings removed from the daily life of autonomous native communities. They have embraced at least some of the values of the occupational groups, schools, churches, and other institutions in which they participate. Many take marriage partners from different cultural backgrounds. Their children are likely to be bi- or even tri-cultural, regardless of whether they are officially recognized as members of a native nation.[20]

This polycultural experience has given rise to fresh and distinctive artistic forms. In the Arizona borderlands, musicians of the Tohono O'odham Nation issue CDs featuring tunes such as "Juan Rios Mazurka" and "Cheek to Cheek Polka," a startling fusion of Native, Mexican, and European music. Among the nearby Hopi, according to a journalist, young people's music of choice is reggae: "Reggae is the music that speaks for them and the preciousness of their heritage." The outspoken writer Sherman Alexie, a Coeur d'Alene Indian, plays in a blues band. When asked to justify his appropriation of an African-American musical form, he insisted that his music is "Indian blues," or "Crazy Horse with a slide guitar." Much the same has been said for variants of country-western and rock music perfected by Aboriginal artists in Australia. One could assemble countless examples of hybridity from other areas of indigenous life: graphic arts, dance, textiles, ceramics, architecture, agriculture, healing practices, religion. Hybridity moves in every possible direction. Studies of new religious movements suggest that indigenized forms of Christianity, heavily influenced by traditional religious practices from Africa and Latin America, will be among the fastest-growing faiths in twenty-first-century North America. The ubiquity of these processes of cultural recombination must not be seen as compromising the authenticity of indigenous individuals or groups, but it does underscore the folly of cordoning off heritage as a discrete domain that can be defined and defended by law.[21]

Despite the narrowing gap between native and non-native practices (or perhaps because of it), proponents of Total Heritage Protection are strongly inclined to overstate the otherness of indigenous peoples. An obsession with difference drifts inexorably toward the proposition that only indigenous people should be allowed to speak for and about their societies. In some venues, native-rights activists contend that they own their history, which has previously been taken from them by non-native scholars. We need only to review colonial history to comprehend the sentiments that drive these assertions. For centuries, the means for disseminating ideas about subject populations were controlled by the colonizers. The language of acceptable cultural description and the social credentials needed to speak this language were beyond the reach of native peoples themselves. Happily, that era is coming to an end, if it is not already concluded. Native intellectuals have found their way into the world's seminar rooms, native leaders to its cabinet rooms, native voices to its airwaves and optical fibers. Questionable statements about indigenous societies rarely go unchallenged. The sins of scholars past are regularly paraded about for public expiation, as they should be.[22]

Casper Lomayesva *(right),* a Hopi Indian reggae artist, performing at a club in Phoenix, Arizona, 1999.

In 2001 the U.S. Public Broadcasting Service aired the documentary *Who Owns the Past?* which uses a dispute about the possible repatriation of the human remains known as "Kennewick Man" as a microcosm of the larger contest over prehistoric burials in North America. In characteristic PBS style, the documentary ends with short, aphoristic statements by individuals representing both sides of the struggle. Susan Shown Harjo, a prominent Indian activist, says, "We know who we are and we know where we came from." Seconds later, Armand Minthorn, who has actively campaigned for the repatriation of the Kennewick remains to the Confederated Tribes of the Umatilla Indian Reservation, echoes Harjo's sentiments: "We already know our history. It may not be written down, but we already know our history."[23]

Would we so readily nod our heads in agreement with Harjo and

Minthorn if they were officers of the Sons of Confederate Veterans, an organization dedicated, in its own words, to "preserving the history and legacy of these heroes, so future generations can understand the motives that animated the Southern Cause"? What if they were Serbian nationalists or Shining Path cadres? As a rhetorical strategy, a group's insistence that it, and only it, knows its history may be useful; as public policy in a multicultural state, it is patently suicidal. The reality of pluralist democracy is that groups living together must be free to talk about one another's history and culture. Without these exchanges, they cannot build a durable civic life. All societies indulge in a degree of self-mythologizing. Outside perspectives offer necessary correctives. U.S. history would be wildly distorted without Native American views of it. Native American history and U.S. history are inseparable. Much the same could be said about the histories of Peru, Mexico, New Zealand, Canada, South Africa, and other settler nations.[24]

Standing in the way of this shared historical vision is the principle of sovereignty. The word has talismanic properties. Its influence explains the tendency for native peoples to describe their societies as nations and, borrowing a usage favored by the leaders of federally recognized tribes in the United States, to insist on the "government-to-government" quality of their negotiations with the state. Sovereignty is inseparable from the principle of self-determination, the idea that a people has an inherent right to live according to its own norms, values, and forms of governance. This typically includes control of territory as well as the people and resources within it, through the application of customary law. As the native-rights movement has become globalized, the North American version of native sovereignty has spread to other parts of the world, although with distinct nuances reflecting local histories and political realities.

The sovereignty principle has an appropriately weighty role in indigenous peoples' efforts to redefine their political relationship with the nation-states in which they find themselves. When applied to complex cultural flows, however, sovereignty is only a metaphor, and a deceptive one at that. Many—perhaps most—elements of culture do not answer to a logic of possession and control, to a vision of hermetically sealed social units realizing their destiny in complete autonomy. Culture is simply too performative, too elusive and at the same time easily replicated, to lend itself to systematic regulation. One must ask: Does any society, no matter how wealthy and privileged, control its culture? If so, why has the United States spent the last two decades embroiled in a "culture war" between groups who advance different visions of what American culture has been and should be in the future? The internal diversity that makes national cultures difficult to specify, and certainly difficult to manage, is no less evident in indigenous communities.[25]

The sovereignty principle has led proponents of Total Heritage Protection to focus on customary law as the solution for conflicts over intellectual property. "I would like to suggest to you that there is a very simple way of settling the legal issues surrounding indigenous people's cultural and intellectual property rights," Erica-Irene Daes, author of the U.N. study of indigenous heritage, said in 2000. "The solution is to resolve any dispute over the acquisition and use of indigenous peoples' heritage according to the customary laws of the indigenous people concerned." Daes identifies this as an instance of *lex loci*, "the law of the place," the principle that prevents one nation from imposing its laws on another.[26]

Unfortunately, many conflicts over intangible expressions of culture involve information long alienated from identifiable communities. Parties may disagree about where the elements originated or whether the usage under dispute has been modified so much that its cultural roots become irrelevant. Because these disputes typically take place outside an indigenous society's territory—assuming that it has one—*lex loci* offers little in the way of plausible solutions. To declare, in effect, "The use of what we claim to be our information must be subject to our laws" ends the discussion right where it must begin. The principle of self-determination, of course, allows indigenous peoples to decide how cultural resources are used within the boundaries of their communities. They should be encouraged to formulate clear policies about the circulation of information and to develop procedures for dealing with technologies that have no precedent in their cultural history. But the greater challenge is to find a framework for agreement between cultural groups, not within them. Therein lies a collision of fundamental values.

Indigenous leaders argue for control over cultural resources they define as uniquely theirs. Neighboring communities, sometimes including other native ones, may contest these claims or insist that honoring them would violate principles of equal sacredness: freedom of speech, freedom of religion, and freedom from unwarranted intrusion into the work of artists, musicians, and intellectuals. Arguments framed in terms of rights have limited usefulness because all parties have important rights hanging in the balance. If prevailing national and international laws affecting information, artistic expression, and access to sacred sites are hurtful to native communities—and evidence suggests that some are—then those laws and policies should be modified through political negotiation.

In their struggle for just and dignified treatment of cultural productions, native communities face formidable opposition, including corporations committed to the privatization of knowledge in its multiple forms. Total Heritage Protection is seductive because it promises a legal framework strong enough to counterbalance these forces. Yet it is a totalizing model, and such approaches have a disturbing tendency to reshape the world in unforeseen and harmful ways. In this case they are likely to foster bureaucratized and lifeless cultures that operate by a proprietary logic perilously close to that of the corporations they seek to resist.[27]

The arctic and subarctic regions have produced more than their share of vivid narratives, accounts that lodge in memory and renew one's faith in the human capacity to find beauty in unforgiving places. One of the most artfully written chronicles of the north—a book that I have profitably returned to time and again—is Hugh Brody's *Maps and Dreams,* published in 1982. In the late 1970s Brody took up residence among the Beaver Indians (or Dane-zaa, as they call themselves), an Athabascan-speaking people of northeastern British Columbia. He devoted himself to learning how the Beaver use and think about the land. His practical goal was to gauge the impact of a planned natural gas pipeline that would slice through their hunting territories. To accomplish this, he apprenticed himself to knowledgeable older men in the community. They took him into the bush to fish, hunt, and sometimes do little more than pay attention to his surroundings.

When it came time to write, Brody decided to alternate chapters that foreground scientific description—the "maps" of the book's title—with chapters based on the Beaver view of things, in which dreams play a critical role. The latter chapters tend to be experiential and poetic, reflecting the oblique and often playful way that Brody's mentors chose to educate him. The cumulative effect of the constant movement between two visions is to make the reader increasingly aware of the gap between Beaver and non-Beaver ways of knowing. For British Columbia's planners and entrepreneurs, the land is little more than a basket of resources to be analyzed, parsed, and consumed—with appropriate "remediation," of course. For the Beaver, Brody shows, the land is a livelihood, a legacy, and a moral community.

Having demonstrated how far apart the worlds of whites and Indians are in British Columbia, Brody might have concluded that traditional environmental knowledge is simply too different, too vitally linked to a community's spiritual core, to figure usefully in matters of public policy, a position that would have foreshadowed critiques of TEK that emerged two decades after his book was published. Instead, he argues the opposite. The survival of the Beaver against overwhelming odds tells us that they know things to which we should give serious consideration. They cannot, as Brody says, "withdraw into some bizarre and insular domain of their own." We must listen to them, for their sake and for our own, even if a perfect translation is impossible. There is a middle ground that, despite its inability to embrace all the subtleties of aboriginal tradition, suggests creative strategies for both using the land and protecting it for future generations. This middle ground is only one of many things that may be lost if TEK and other forms of indigenous knowledge are, in the name of heritage protection, removed to new reservations of the mind.[28]

8. Finding Justice in the Global Commons

In 2001 a university archivist faced an ethical dilemma concerning materials that had recently come under her care. The collection consisted of interview tapes and correspondence bequeathed to the archives by an anthropologist and his Native American collaborator, who had worked together on a study of an Indian tribe in the region served by her university. Now tribal officials were asking that the collection be closed to the public because it contained esoteric religious information that some members of the tribe did not wish to see circulated. The archivist consulted a range of experts interested in questions of cultural property. She offered to talk with me about the case on the condition that her institution not be identified until the issue was settled.

According to the university's legal counsel, there are no flaws in the deed of gift that transfers the collection to the archives. This means that the university owns the physical documents and holds a copyright to their contents. In accepting the gift the archives agreed to honor the wishes of the donors, now both deceased, that the material be made available to researchers. The tribe wishes to review requests for use of the documents and to decide who will be given access to them, applying whatever criteria it deems appropriate. This would potentially violate the ethical guidelines of the archivist's professional guild, which stipulates that all patrons be treated equally. It would also break an impressive list of state and federal laws prohibiting discrimination on the basis of religion, gender, or ethnicity.

On the other side of the ledger is the archives' responsibility to the public. Members of the tribe are citizens of the state where the repository is located even though their federal reservation enjoys a high degree of political sovereignty. Tribe members attend the university as students. Others serve on the university's staff. In short, they are part of the public that the archives are obliged to serve, and their wishes must be acknowledged even if they cannot be granted in their entirety.

The archivist and her staff are searching for creative ways to respond to the tribe's concerns without flouting the donors' stated desires and the ethical standards of archival practice. The university has considered establishing a joint review board to develop ground rules for use of the collection. For instance, researchers might be allowed to listen to the interview tapes but not to quote them in print. The archives might also employ informal tactics for protecting tribal interests, perhaps by delaying preparation of finding aids that make the collection easier to use. For now, the documents and tapes remain sealed as negotiations continue. The staff is training members of the tribe in records-management practices that will be put to use in tribal offices. This relationship is helping to counter misunderstandings about archives and the constraints under which they operate, but neither party to the dispute is likely to be entirely satisfied when negotiations conclude.[1]

The archives case illustrates a version of liberal pluralism that might be called "multiculturalism without illusions." This approach accepts that conflicts over values are inevitable when societies encompass groups that practice different ways of life. The optimistic view that a culturally diverse citizenry can hammer out a shared vision of the good society has become harder to sustain in the face of new forms of identity politics, rising immigration rates, and the collapse of the melting-pot model of assimilation that helped the United States absorb the last major wave of immigrants early in the twentieth century. This shift in attitudes toward cultural diversity has been effected through appeals to the idea of rights, both of individuals and of cultural communities. Such "rights talk," as it has been labeled by the legal scholar Mary Ann Glendon, has made politicians and citizens more sensitive to issues of social justice. Nevertheless, Glendon and others worry that its simplistic quality gives rise to forms of political discourse that undermine social peace. It is in the nature of rights to seek absolutes. Rights have a finality that silences debate and possibilities for negotiation. When one group's notion of a right prevails, the legitimacy of the solution remains in doubt. In complex, highly diverse societies, it is simply impossible to satisfy everyone's idea of what their rights are or should be, especially in the absence of an offsetting discourse focused on responsibilities.[2]

Complementary to Glendon's skepticism about current versions of rights talk is the pragmatic "value pluralism" advanced by the British political philosopher John Gray. Gray holds that the search for consensus values is fruitless in pluralist democracies, which can sustain themselves only through compromise and the eternal quest for a modus vivendi. That does not mean that all compromises are morally acceptable. Value pluralism allows for the protection of basic human rights and, conversely, for recognition that certain forms of behavior are genuinely wrong. With the exception of a small set of core protections, however, everything is subject to negotiated solutions that Gray insists are "usually perceived to be more legitimate than legal procedures which end in the promulgation of unconditional rights." The major advantage of political solutions is that they are never final: they can change to reflect changing sentiments and shifting local realities.[3]

In the 1990s New York City wrestled with a conflict illustrative of value pluralism. During Lunar New Year celebrations, New York's Chinese community has long punctuated its public processions with fireworks. In the traditional Chinese view of things, fireworks are an essential element of the ritual. Whether the purpose of the explosions is to rid the world of evil spirits or to awaken the dragon who brings spring rains (interpretations vary), the ritual is incomplete and flawed without pyrotechnics. But fireworks are prohibited in New York for reasons of public safety. After several years of talks, the city and the Chinese community reached a compromise. A professional pyrotechnics company, supervised by the New York Fire Department, detonated safe fireworks that simulated the sound and the flash of the illegal variety. Naysayers grumbled, but the annual festival took place with reasonably satisfying explosions. Through pragmatic compromise, the conditions of a successful ritual were met.[4]

In the continuing encounter between the archives and the Indian tribe, both parties navigate uncharted waters, without benefit of laws or formal rules that mandate censorship or repatriation of culturally sensitive information. The advent of the Native American Graves Protection and Repatriation Act (NAGPRA) has brought these questions to broader public attention. Yet NAGPRA does not deal with information as such, however much some Native American leaders would like it to do so. Instead, what has moved the archives to enter into extended negotiations with the tribe is a combination of professionalism—a commitment to serve the institution's multiple publics as faithfully as possible—and simple decency. Skeptics will dismiss the case as anomalous, a unique situation reflecting the intervention of an enlightened archivist or the good will of the parties involved. My interviews with cultural resource managers in the United States and Australia suggest that in fact this situation is more the rule than the exception today.

Negotiations provide openings for unique, culturally appropriate solutions that can subtly alter dominant cultural ideas of ownership (or, for that matter, of religion, or art, or social relationships). One sees this in action at Devils Tower National Monument. The June moratorium on ascents of the tower is precisely the kind of awkward half-measure deplored by advocates of indigenous rights. If Devils Tower is sacred to American Indians, isn't it sacred all the time? What about the two hundred or so people who climb in June in defiance of the moratorium? Yet a visit to the place left me with a feeling that something positive was happening there. The park's improvised and quintessentially political solution is not a legal end point. It is a beginning. Native American leaders have developed sound working relationships with park officials. Visitors to the monument are absorbing educational messages about its religious importance to the region's Indians. These changes were nudged forward by federal laws and presidential executive orders. Nevertheless, the outcome reflects the convergence of multiple interests advanced by groups that cover the spectrum of civil society in the American West: tribal governments, indigenous-rights organizations, climbing associations, lobbyists for expedition outfitters and the local tourism industry, right-wing legal foundations, and a range of religious denominations.

Zia Pueblo's drive to reassert control over its sun symbol is a variation on the same theme. The tribe has used an instrument of the state, trademark law, to assert control over a powerful symbol. Zia's licensing agreement with Southwest Airlines uses another tool: the desire of commercial firms to project a positive public image. Both strategies, as well as the tribe's formal petition to the state of New Mexico, serve to remind the general public that Zia religious symbols are not to be trifled with. To be sure, efforts to control use of powerful cultural symbols raise knotty questions of free speech. Yet to the extent that they inspire a public conversation about fundamental values, they serve a vital purpose. They create the possibility, as Clifford Geertz puts it, "of quite literally, and quite thoroughly, changing our minds." This outcome would be less likely if the federal government were to issue an edict declaring all Native American symbols off-limits for reproduction on the grounds that they are a form of cultural property.[5]

As these cases show, the dynamism and flexibility of civil society can play a key role in the rebalancing of relations between indigenous peoples and nation-states. This shift is evident in worldwide efforts to right historic wrongs through the restitution of lands, the payment of reparations, and the modification of legal systems to open new political spaces for formerly subordinate groups. Few believe that money or land alone can undo a history of genocide. Formal restitution has profound limitations, and sometimes it may be little more than window dressing for states in search of new legitimacy. But by acknowledging the injuries of the past, restitution helps to lay the groundwork for new and better ways of living together.[6]

If a central goal of the indigenous-rights movement is to move the global community toward cultural-protection policies that are both effective and ethically sound, it is vital to make a distinction between matters of economic justice and the broader goal of protecting "cultural integrity"—an emerging code word for respectful treatment of indigenous symbols, religious practices, and knowledge. The Total Heritage Protection approach rejects this distinction, calling it ethnocentric and a violation of the right of a people to define the world as they see fit. For better or for worse, however, intellectual property laws are organized around financial incentives. The doctrine of moral (or authors') rights represents a feeble nod in the direction of non-economic concerns, but it is limited in scope, problematic from a free-speech perspective, and almost completely absent from the legal system of the United States, the single largest actor on the world's commercial stage. Some experts worry that both intellectual property law *and* indigenous cultures might be harmed by efforts to turn copyright into an instrument for protecting cultural integrity. One has only to recall the case of H. R. Voth's photographs to see how risky it would be to redefine them legally as the intellectual property of the Hopi. The precedent would create pressures to extend the term of all copyrights even further, a prospect appealing to the world's largest media corporations. A law that automatically conferred ownership of historical photographs to their subjects, or their subjects' descendants, would inhibit the work of historians and documentary filmmakers in harmful ways. These might be acceptable hazards if they genuinely protected Hopi religion, but there is little reason to think that Voth's photographs of Hopi rituals would cease to be available to anyone seriously interested in examining them.[7]

A market-based framework provides considerable room for reforming and broadening intellectual property law to accommodate the unique features of creativity in traditional societies. The *Bulun Bulun* decision in Australia shows that the special relationship between indigenous artists and their communities, at least where religious images are concerned, merits distinctive treatment. In the United States, trademark regulations make it increasingly difficult for companies to use Native American names and symbols as identifiers for commercial products in the absence of formal licensing agreements with pertinent tribes. Patents, especially in the biotechnology arena, remain the most problematic element of the system. Opposition to overly liberal treatment of patent applications is growing even in business circles, suggesting that infringement of indigenous interests in plant products is at least partly a systemic problem that should be treated as such. In 2002 the business magazine *Forbes* published an article alleging that the U.S. Patent and Trademark Office's lax standards had turned the patent into a "blunt instrument for establishing an innovative stranglehold." When a publication that calls itself "The Capitalist Tool" begins to denounce the oppressiveness of current intellectual property practices, one may infer that the system's swing in the direction of ever greater restrictiveness may be coming to an end.[8]

Critics of the world intellectual property system are most persuasive when they question current understandings of the public domain. At present the public domain encompasses all folkloric knowledge as well as formerly proprietary knowledge whose protection has lapsed. Elements of this communal resource can be privatized, albeit temporarily, through copyrights and patents provided that an applicant meets the state's standard of originality. In the case of copyright, standards of originality are low, but so are the protections that copyright affords. Most of the economic injustice associated with the imitation of indigenous music and art arises not because the appropriator "takes something away" from someone else, for copyrights stand little chance of directly blocking the activity of a native performer or artist. The inequity lies instead with the appropriators' social capital, which leaves them better positioned than their indigenous counterparts to reap financial reward. This is manifestly unfair, but it is symptomatic of broader social realities, not of a failure of intellectual property law as such. Patents are another matter, because in principle patents confer monopolistic control. Under close scrutiny, most publicized cases of biopiracy fail to qualify as outright theft, and few have realized profits in the marketplace. Still, there are enough instances of questionable "invention" that the system cries out for reforms that would recognize the proprietary interests of local communities in public-domain information. These interests rarely qualify as absolute, but they surely merit a place at the table when profits are distributed.

Stepping outside the indigenous-rights debate, one finds progressive legal thinkers arguing passionately for more freedom to borrow, blend, and ultimately create new artistic and technological forms. These same voices lament enclosure of the intellectual commons by corporations whose predatory approach to copyright and patent law makes it increasingly difficult to innovate. Such arguments tend to assume the existence of an undifferentiated public domain. From the indigenous-rights perspective, the public domain is the problem, not the solution, because it defines traditional knowledge as a freely available resource. Harmonizing the two positions will not be easy. Advocates of the indigenous "we own our culture" perspective find themselves in the odd position of criticizing corporate capitalism while at the same time espousing capitalism's commodifying logic and even pushing it to new extremes. This position fragments what should be broad public opposition to the ways that the Microsofts and Mercks and Disneys and AOL Time Warners of the world manipulate the intellectual property system to their advantage.[9]

A possible exit from this cul-de-sac is outlined in the Bellagio Declaration, issued after an interdisciplinary conference sponsored by the Rockefeller Foundation in 1993. The Bellagio Declaration proposes reducing the scope of intellectual property rights in already established arenas (copyright, patent, trademark) while creating new protections for traditional arts and technologies. At the same time, the document affirms the signatories' commitment to continued health of a public domain "from which all people, from all nations, are free to draw." Like most statements on this subject, however, it is vague about the details of the "neighboring rights" that would protect the content of indigenous cultures. As we have seen, when actually enacted as law these new rights tend to create as many problems as they solve. This helps to explain why advocates of Total Heritage Protection routinely endorse the idea of neighboring rights but rarely commit draft legislation to paper.[10]

Since Bellagio, a number of legal thinkers have called for a radical downsizing of global intellectual property rights. Lawrence Lessig, an outspoken critic of current copyright practices, proposes reducing copyright to five-year terms renewable to a maximum of seventy-five years, considerably less than today's standard of life plus seventy years. Lessig also suggests that the U.S. Patent and Trademark Office be required to undertake empirical studies to determine whether existing patent laws encourage or stifle innovation. Others argue that if the goal of intellectual property law is to serve the public good we should adjust the terms of biotechnology patents according to the social need for the product or process. Thus drugs for the treatment of male-pattern baldness might be eligible for short patent terms, whereas a malaria vaccine would be awarded a longer term, reflecting the product's greater value to society and the difficulty of recovering development costs from the vaccine's low-income target population. The longer term, of course, would be contingent on the patent holder's willingness to make the vaccine widely available at low cost.[11]

The disposition of genetic resources may present the most difficult challenge to the world's intellectual property system, especially where food crops are concerned. Research and innovation are vitally necessary if the food supply is to grow with the planet's burgeoning population. The privatization of crop research and its control by a handful of corporations have aroused hostility in many countries, creating obstacles to continued progress. In the best of worlds, states would declare research on major food crops to be a public good free of intellectual property encumbrances, but that seems an unlikely scenario at present.

The legal scholar Carol Rose has suggested helpful new ways of thinking about genetic resources and other natural products. In an analysis of changes in legal understandings of property in the face of new technologies, Rose identifies a hybrid property form that she calls "limited common property" (LCP). LCP is neither completely public nor completely private. It typically takes the form of community resources that insiders are allowed to use but from which outsiders are excluded. Insiders enjoy a degree of latitude in their exploitation of LCP, but ties of social solidarity and economic reciprocity constrain abuses from within. The problem, according to Rose, is that LCPs are often invisible to outsiders whose notions of property assume overtly private forms of ownership.[12]

An obvious way to treat natural products and public-domain folk knowledge would be to implement a version of compulsory licensing. Compulsory licensing arose in response to technological innovations such as player pianos, jukeboxes, and commercial radio. If radio stations were required to obtain prior permission before broadcasting each song, the transaction costs would be overwhelming, and programming would grind to a halt. Compulsory licensing allows for use of copyrighted material without permission; at the same time, it requires commercial users to pay reasonable fees to copyright holders. It is a "liability rule" rather than a "property rule." The system strives to balance the rights of copyright holders against society's need for the circulation of art and information. It also accepts that a copyright system is workable only if transaction costs are low.[13]

A licensing system for natural products would acknowledge that local populations, especially indigenous ones, have legitimate proprietary interests in the flora and fauna of their region. In other words, these resources, and local knowledge about them, qualify as limited common property. At the same time, a group's interests in natural products can rarely be judged exclusive, for the simple reason that knowledge about flora and fauna is unlikely to be limited to a single community or ethnic group, except perhaps in the unusual case of island environments.

At present, misguided application of sovereignty rhetoric stands in the way of implementing licensing systems that would benefit indigenous peoples. The position of the Rural Advancement Foundation International (RAFI) in the dispute over the ICBG-Maya project illustrates the problem. In its "Ten Points on Piracy," RAFI recognizes that many neighboring indigenous societies may utilize the same plant species. RAFI concludes that "agreement must be reached with each community before bioprospectors can consider that they have permission to proceed." This requirement would do little more than spread the tragedy of the anticommons, identified in Chapter 4 as a problem of the biotechnology industry, to indigenous societies. The likelihood that anyone could negotiate a viable agreement amid so many conflicting claims is prohibitively low. In its sheer impracticality, RAFI's position fails to confront a key feature of all property regimes: their cost. As Carol Rose observes, "It costs something to define rights, to monitor trespasses, and to expel intruders." Because natural products and knowledge about them are rarely localized, it is easy for potential exploiters to seek out alternative sources that entail lower costs. This is especially true for crop plants, since the agrotechnology industry benefits from more than a century of systematic collection of specimens and their relocation to facilities in the developed north.[14]

Rather than setting impossibly high standards for prior informed consent, it would be preferable for national governments—or better still, for consortia of states sharing major biogeographic regions such as the Amazon—to impose easily explained licensing fees whose proceeds would be distributed to all recognized indigenous groups, on the assumption that over time short-term inequities would balance out. Payment of these fees, which should include a percentage of royalties on commercially successful products, would authorize companies to negotiate research agreements and know-how licenses with local groups. At the local level, the sovereignty principle would apply: communities would be free to collaborate, or decline to collaborate, with individual projects as they saw fit.

A law with this general form has been proposed in Peru, and similar legislation is under consideration elsewhere. Given the track record of many governments, one has to be skeptical about their willingness to redistribute fees to indigenous communities as promised. If administered efficiently and fairly, however, such a plan would strike a balance between the proprietary rights of local communities and the pragmatics of technological innovation by industry. Putting it into place would not imply agreement with aggressive American interpretations of patent law—such as the patenting of biological life-forms—that many countries find objectionable. It would merely set minimal conditions for undertaking commercial research within a biogeographic region.[15]

Other effective strategies might be imagined along these lines. Some would require adaptation to specific types of material. What works for crop genetic resources is probably not the best approach for protecting proprietary interests in indigenous music or ceramics. But viable solutions will be hard to implement as long as the intellectual property regime is expected to control the movement of knowledge and modes of expression identified with indigenous communities. However flawed it may be in its current form, the world's intellectual property system is designed to encourage rather than constrain the circulation of ideas.[16]

The goal of maintaining cultural integrity, inseparable from questions of collective privacy and a desire for dignity in the face of unwanted interest by outsiders, will be far more difficult to achieve through legislative means. By its nature, law strives for uniformity and precision. But in matters of getting along, as the sociologist Alan Wolfe has pointed out, precision is rarely desirable: "Just as diplomats try to find ambiguous wordings in treaties so that all sides can claim to be winners, commonsense morality suggests solutions to difficult moral dilemmas that allow as many people as possible to retain their self-respect." The ambiguity required to foster social peace, Wolfe argues, is found in civil society, not in the state or the marketplace.[17]

Pivotal elements of civil society include professional associations, which influence occupational networks through codes of ethics and best-practice standards; religious denominations and the moral guidance they offer congregants; educational institutions, which provide forums for exploring multiple perspectives on values; advocacy groups that push for one agenda or another; service organizations concerned about living conditions in underprivileged sectors of society; labor unions, charged with protecting the interests of their members; and writers and documentary filmmakers, who strive to take their audience into the social realities of different communities. Addressing questions of cultural property through the diverse institutions of civil society is a slow, demanding process that cannot solve all social problems. Yet this approach offers distinct advantages over Total Heritage Protection strategies focused narrowly on law and mechanisms of state power. It exploits existing links between indigenous people and national societies: churches (a powerful force in Latin America, where native peoples are joining evangelical congregations in growing numbers), fraternal organizations of military veterans, labor unions, nongovernmental organizations (NGOs)—the list is long. It lays the foundation for solutions that fit local conditions. It minimizes expensive litigation and takes advantage of forms of voluntarism that draw communities together. It avoids codification and the perils of formal laws about culture. It encourages culturally appropriate remedies without instituting a system of group rights that would, to quote Mary Ann Glendon, "tend to pit group against individual, one group against another, and group against state."[18]

Underestimation of the power of civil society is inevitable once sovereignty thinking is allowed to push aside other ways of crafting solutions to social conflicts. If indigenous societies are "nations," then all negotiations should take place with the state. In subtler ways, advocates of indigenous sovereignty find it threatening to acknowledge that native peoples, at least in the economically developed settler democracies, are deeply embedded in the broader civil society. Such an admission seems to undermine the separateness upon which cultural-rights claims are based. Instead, multiple social entanglements should be recognized as offering opportunities for communication and mutual comprehension. Used effectively, these vital links strengthen public understanding of indigenous self-determination and improve its prospects for realization.

Civil society also provides an opening for cultural claims based on social practice, as distinct from assertions of belief. One of the thorniest questions concerning native rights is how to accommodate emerging (or reemerging) groups that assert an indigenous identity. At present they are obliged to demonstrate clear continuity with ancestral practices, something that may be difficult or impossible to do. The modern history of pluralist democracies, however, suggests that majority populations are willing to open social and political spaces for groups whose lived practice becomes a visible part of everyday life. An example is the remarkable history of Mormonism, formally known as the Church of Jesus Christ of Latter-Day Saints. The church arose in the 1830s from an obscure corner of New York State to become, by the 1840s, the target of religious hatred as extreme as any in American history. Yet today it is one of the most prosperous religious sects in North America, as well as one of the fastest growing, and its members serve in high positions in state and federal government. Multiple factors account for this reversal of fortune, including changes internal to Mormonism. Above all, the church simply persevered. People got used to having it around, even if they did not always agree with its theology and tactics. It is easy to imagine a similar destiny for, say, the newly emerging Mexica groups of the American Southwest if they manage to endure for a generation or two.

The advantage of practice-based claims is that they do not depend on the presence or absence of "tradition." They are unlikely to prove helpful in land claims, whose justification is mostly retrospective, but they create new avenues for indigenous cultural redefinition. Sovereignty, as the Sioux writer Vine Deloria Jr. once noted, is not primarily a question of political boundaries: "It involves most of all a strong sense of community discipline and a degree of self-containment and pride that transcends all objective codes, rules, and regulations." These are matters more readily transacted in civil society than in the arena of state power.[19]

Civil society, of course, cannot be assumed to exist everywhere. Social critics question its vitality in the United States and other countries that have allowed market relations to overshadow other forms of civic engagement. In parts of the developing world, a recognizable civil society may be almost completely absent. Neither general lawlessness nor totalitarian order offers promising ground for the protection of cultural integrity, and in these situations indigenous communities focus, as they must, on collective self-defense of the most elemental kind. One happy effect of globalization is that civil society now has an international face. Today few countries are so disorderly or so hermetic that foreign NGOs are not working there. As we saw in Chapter 4, the limited accountability of NGOs may encourage mischievous and divisive tactics. In general, however, the presence of international organizations makes even the most oppressive government vulnerable to external scrutiny in ways that were unknown a few decades ago.

The matter of human rights and their precarious standing in many places raises the question of power. The forces arrayed against indigenous peoples in their struggle for control of cultural resources are undeniably strong. The market capitalization of some of the corporations pushing for more restrictive intellectual property laws exceeds the gross domestic product of entire nations. The close relation between financial power and intellectual property is evident in the periodic legislative rescues of Mickey Mouse: whenever the Walt Disney Company's copyright on the familiar rodent is about to expire, it gets renewed by the U.S. Congress. But power takes many forms. It would be a mistake to underestimate the moral weight of aboriginal claims, which have far more influence in the world than one might expect of a population that, depending on who does the counting, represents somewhere between 4 and 8 percent of humanity. The current political situation in Latin America reveals the growing importance of indigenous peoples as agents of progressive social change. Despite the region's history of military rule and indifference to human rights, indigenous groups have fundamentally reshaped national politics in Ecuador, Peru, and Bolivia. Less sweeping but still significant impacts have been felt in Mexico, Brazil, Venezuela, Colombia, Nicaragua, and Panama. In the Amazon, small but determined indigenous groups have sent international oil companies packing. Even more powerful indigenous movements have arisen in New Zealand and Australia, where Aboriginal-rights issues are now near the top of national agendas.

The symbolic power of indigenousness can be a mixed blessing. It sparks in outsiders a romantic interest that sometimes threatens the way of life they so greatly admire. But it also provides a global network of sympathizers who quickly rally to the cause in times of crisis. For corporations that worry about their public image, the power to shape opinion is never to be taken lightly. In October 2001 Maori leaders announced a settlement with the Danish toy company Lego over the firm's unauthorized use of Maori names to identify figures in a new game. Lego reportedly agreed to desist from the use of Polynesian names in other products, and it pledged to "develop a code of conduct for cultural expressions of traditional knowledge."[20]

In their struggle for dignity and self-determination, indigenous peoples fight an uphill battle, but the slope is not as steep as it might be if economic power were the only relevant factor. The reality of a power imbalance underscores the importance of forging strong and durable alliances between the native-rights movement and groups that are defending the integrity of the public domain. Both have a vested interest in protecting the world's cultural commons and in achieving a fairer balance of rights and responsibilities.

Civil-society strategies that spurn legislative solutions in favor of negotiated ones run counter to an influential strain of judicial thought that sees law as the most effective instrument for shaping attitudes and social norms. Proponents of this view hold that negotiation takes place, as the expression goes, "in the shadow of the law."

Without laws that define rights and mark limits, parties have little incentive to negotiate. Legal scholars like to point out that, in liberal democracies, laws work as much through networks of information as by overt practices of enforcement. We follow the law because we are socialized to do so. Hence the importance of law that creates social incentives for proper behavior.[21]

The case studies presented in this book strongly suggest that in the United States and Australia, and quite possibly in Canada and New Zealand as well, laws and public policies have already created a formidable legal overhang, in the shadow of which groups are successfully negotiating workable solutions to disputes about sensitive cultural information and access to sacred sites. In the United States, for instance, NAGPRA has given American Indians considerable clout with museums in matters lying beyond the law's limited scope. More than anything, NAGPRA promoted the creation of new institutional arrangements—joint-use committees, review panels, and repatriation offices—that have redefined relationships between museums and indigenous communities. Consultation has become an element of everyday practice in museums and archives whose holdings include American Indian materials. Discussions inevitably move beyond artifacts and human remains to other matters. Existing laws and policies, in other words, have changed attitudes toward the management of sensitive cultural information despite the absence of laws making such change obligatory. The considerable progress already achieved without anything approximating Total Heritage Protection calls to mind the remark of a French diplomat to Madeleine Albright, then the U.S. secretary of state, while discussing an aspect of European bureaucracy: "It will work in practice, yes. But will it work in theory?"[22]

There is doubtless a place for sharply focused legislation that confers limited rights in cultural information and community symbols, especially to groups that can show how misuse of such resources by others would cause genuine harm. The problem is that advocates of Total Heritage Protection are edging toward insistence that *all* representations of native cultures merit legal regulation. I can think of few contemporary rights claims that are at once so vast, so vague, and so frankly separatist in intent.

This raises a central question conspicuous for its absence in debate about the future of native cultural property: To what extent should Aboriginal Australians, Native Americans, Maoris, and other indigenous peoples be considered part of a global commons? There is general agreement that native communities everywhere have been victimized since the Age of Exploration. Most commentators accept that indigenous peoples should be free to maintain distinct, vibrant societies that enjoy a reasonable standard of prosperity. A key element of native self-determination is the power to decide what sort of research takes place in indigenous communities, and under what terms. Beyond these basic tenets, however, vistas remain clouded. Should the public domain be something to which native peoples contribute as full participants? Or does sovereignty imply that they are opting out of the public domain as currently understood? If they *are* opting out—to my mind, a discouraging prospect—how can they do so without severely impairing the ability of social groups to talk to and about one another, a basic requirement for peaceful relations?

The hybrid nature of indigenous cultural life today argues against rigorous separation of indigenous knowledge from the public domain of global society. Native people increasingly depend on non-native languages to communicate even in the intimacy of their homes. Language barriers, which have helped to shield indigenous traditions from outside scrutiny and influence, are eroding nearly everywhere. Meanwhile, indigenous citizens move steadily into the everyday life of nation-states. One struggles to imagine a system of laws that could reverse the cultural mixing now taking place. It is even harder to understand why native leaders would want to put national governments in charge of efforts to defend the purity of their heritage. The long history of state paternalism offers too few successes, and too many disasters, to make this an attractive prospect.

To recognize the hybrid character of indigenous cultures is not to suggest that their assimilation is inevitable, nor is it to endorse the assimilationist policies of the past. Despite five centuries of relentless pressure, many core elements of native cultures retain their vitality. Some may be undergoing a renaissance. Indigenous societies include a growing number of intellectuals and political leaders equipped to move with agility from one social world to another—from meetings of village elders to corporate boardrooms, from the sweat lodge to the conference podium. It is their right, as well as their responsibility, to defend the dignity of their communities in public forums. Settler democracies must be held accountable for failure to honor their obligations to indigenous citizens. Formal law has a useful role to play in this process of cultural reconstruction, but we must also remain mindful of law's limitations and hazards.

A vivid memory of my college years is of a public dance that I attended at Hopi—probably in the village of Songoopavi, although the details have faded with time. It was the summer of 1970, and I was visiting Hopi during a weekend off from my job as a summer school teacher on the Navajo reservation. During the event, the austere, deliberate movements of the dancers alternated with the antics of clowns usually called Mudheads because of their clay-colored masks. Mudheads, like other Pueblo clowns, play a complex role in rituals. They intensify the presence of the sacred by epitomizing, sometimes to an alarming degree, characteristics of the profane. They parody behaviors of other categories of people—Indians, Hispanics, and Anglos—to illustrate, usually with devastating humor, why Pueblo culture is superior. In the early 1970s Pueblo clowns were especially fascinated by hippies, those strangely hirsute Anglos who assumed they had a natural affinity with their native brothers and sisters.

On this day, a Mudhead working the large dance plaza moved to a spot just below where I sat watching from a rooftop. Fixing me with an unsettling stare, he shouted in English, "Hey, Jesus! Jesus Christ! Come down for the Last Supper!" Although I probably failed to qualify as a hippie, I had the requisite facial hair, and his comments sparked raucous laughter from the mix of Navajo adolescents and Hopis around me. I laughed, too, although less comfortably than my companions. A few minutes later the Mudhead returned and shouted angrily, "Jesus, come down for the Last Supper, goddamit!" It was clear that he expected me to climb down. People made way amid general laughter. His fellow clowns set up a table in the middle of the plaza. Other visitors were called out: a middle-aged Anglo man, a Navajo youth, and a Hopi elder. We were seated at the table and given food—fried trout, as I recall, and the delicious corn bread called *piki*. To my great relief, the Mudheads turned their attention elsewhere, performing little skits that mocked themselves as much as others. We ate quickly and returned to our places on the rooftops. In what I later learned was typical of Hopi rules of reciprocity, the clowns had fed us to forestall hard feelings about their jokes at our expense. A goal of the ritual is to renew life, in part by bringing people together in happiness. Provoking ill will, even from outsiders, endangers the event's sacred purpose.[23]

Pueblo public rituals include elaborate forms of cross-cultural imitation. Clowns may dress as missionaries, Girl Scouts, anthropologists, or tourists, burlesquing the behavior of these strange outsiders in elaborately staged presentations. Other Indian tribes are not spared attention. Probably the most flamboyant example is the Comanche Dance, performed in several villages in northern New Mexico, in which groups of dancers abandon the strict dress code of Pueblo ritual in favor of gaudy interpretations of Plains Indian powwow garb. Jill Sweet, an anthropologist who studied the dances of Tewa-speaking Pueblo communities, describes something called the Navajo Dance. As many as forty men and women don Navajo-style hats, jewelry, and sunglasses. Toward the end of the dance, they pass around a jug and begin to act like drunks. When Sweet observed the dance, "the Tewa audience laughed uproariously at these antics because they consider such behavior typical of Navajos but not of themselves." Sweet interprets this humorously disparaging performance (which in today's litigious climate probably qualifies as group libel) as a symbolic effort to work through Tewa ambivalence toward the Navajo, who are both trading partners (and sometimes spouses or lovers) and traditional antagonists. "By mimicking the Navajos," she says, Tewa people "ritualize and defuse years of interaction, including some dangerous confrontations."[24]

These examples of intercultural play highlight the complexity and moral ambiguity of the kinds of borrowing and imitation dourly summarized by a term like "cultural appropriation." Members of different societies need to talk about one another if they hope to get along. The fluid dance of imitation and contrast, reticence and disclosure is an essential part of social life in pluralist societies. It is suppressed only with difficulty and at some cost in creative freedom. To make this observation is not to defend commercial exploitation or gross insensitivity. Nor is it to claim that movement of cultural elements between the politically weak and the politically strong is equivalent to exchanges among equals. I wish simply to point out the risks of taking too rigid a view of cultural ownership, especially when technological and social changes are making cultural boundaries ever harder to identify.

Advocates of Total Heritage Protection fail to offer a comprehensive vision of what the world will look like after they have imposed the institutions of surveillance, border protection, and cultural purification that some call for. They talk of respect, cultural survival, and economic justice for indigenous communities. These are admirable goals. All of us should work to advance them. Nevertheless, history suggests that the legal regulation of culture is at best a fruitless enterprise and at worst an invitation to new forms of manipulation by the powerful. As a Turkish proverb says, "A weapon is an enemy even to its owner."

If I am critical of those who seem eager to defend a world of discrete, perfectly bounded cultures that never existed, it is because I am so impressed by the hope and pragmatism of indigenous elders, museum curators, archivists, and cultural-resource managers who are negotiating their way to more balanced relationships. They, far more than the activists and academic theorists who set the terms of debate about cultural ownership, understand that progress will be built on small victories, innovative local solutions, and frequent compromise. They recognize, too, that a world ruled solely by proprietary passions is not a world in which most of us want to live.

Notes

Sources on Indigenous Rights

Acknowledgments

Index

Notes

Introduction

1. "Aborigines up in Arms over Symbols," *Australian,* 29 Jan. 2002, 2, accessed via Lexis-Nexis; "Peruvian Farmers and Indigenous People Denounce Patents on Maca," *ETC Genotype,* 3 July 2002, <www.etc group.org>, accessed 2 Jan. 2003; "Pure World Botanicals Launches MacaPure, Scientifically Proven Libido and Sexual Function Enhancer," <www.pureworld.com/news/maca.html>, accessed 2 Jan. 2003; Tina Rosenberg, "Patent Your Heritage," *New York Times Magazine,* 15 Dec. 2002, 107–108; Jonathan Milne, "Toy Website Using Maori Goes Offline," *Daily News* (New Plymouth, N.Z.), 12 Nov. 2002, 2, accessed via Lexis-Nexis; "Maori Cyber-Terrorists Attack BZPower," <www.bz power.com>, accessed 2 Jan. 2003; "Rockefeller Foundation Initiative to Promote Intellectual Property (IP) Policies Fairer to Poor People," press release, 4 Nov. 2002.

2. Deborah Root, *Cannibal Culture: Art, Appropriation, and the Commodification of Difference* (Boulder, Colo.: Westview, 1995), 18.

3. Lawrence Lessig, *The Future of Ideas: The Fate of the Commons in a Connected World* (New York: Random House, 2001), 21.

4. Charles C. Mann, "The Heavenly Jukebox," *Atlantic Monthly,*

Sept. 2000, 41; quotation from the Phoenix meeting is from my notes, "Field Records at the Millennium" conference, 3 May 1999. See also Walter Benjamin, "The Work of Art in the Age of Mechanical Reproduction," in *Illuminations,* ed. Hannah Arendt (1935; New York: Schocken, 1968), 217–252.

5. Robert Conquest, *Reflections on a Ravaged Century* (New York: Norton, 2000), 18.

6. Lionel Trilling, *The Liberal Imagination* (New York: Viking, 1950), xiv–xv.

7. Sir Isaiah Berlin, *Fathers and Children* (London: Oxford University Press, 1972), 51.

1. The Missionary's Photographs

1. Fred Eggan, "H. R. Voth, Ethnologist," in *Hopi Material Culture: Artifacts Gathered by H. R. Voth in the Fred Harvey Collection,* ed. Barton Wright (Flagstaff, Ariz.: Northland Press, 1979), 2.

2. Cathy Ann Trotta, "Crossing Cultural Boundaries: Heinrich and Martha Moser Voth in the Hopi Pueblos, 1893–1906" (Ph.D. diss., Northern Arizona University, 1997), 129–130, 196–198; Eggan, "H. R. Voth," 6.

3. Don C. Talayesva, *Sun Chief: Autobiography of a Hopi Indian,* ed. Leo W. Simmons (New Haven: Yale University Press, 1942), 252; Trotta, "Crossing Cultural Boundaries," 230. Eggan reports that some Hopis accused Talayesva of having aided Voth in his research on the Soyal ceremony, accusations that led to Talayesva's exclusion from the ritual for a time. Although the chronology of events is not clear from Eggan's account, it may be that the vehemence of Talayesva's description of Voth is partly an attempt to distance himself from the controversial missionary's activities. Eggan, "H. R. Voth," 6.

4. See Albert Yava, *Big Falling Snow: A Tewa-Hopi Indian's Life and Times and the History and Traditions of His People,* ed. Harold Courlander (Albuquerque: University of New Mexico Press, 1978), 36–38.

5. Letter dated 12 Jan. 1994 in my possession. Most of it is quoted in

Jonathan Haas, "Power, Objects, and a Voice for Anthropology," *Current Anthropology* 37, supplement (1996): S4.

6. For one repatriation case, see William L. Merrill, Edmund J. Ladd, and T. J. Ferguson, "The Return of the Ahayu:Da: Lessons for Repatriation from Zuni Pueblo and the Smithsonian Institution," *Current Anthropology* 34, no. 5 (1993): 523–567.

7. See Nancy Rockafellar and Orin Starn, "Ishi's Brain," *Current Anthropology* 40 (1999): 413–415; Nancy Scheper-Hughes, "Ishi's Brain, Ishi's Ashes," *Anthropology Today* 17 (Feb. 2001): 12–18.

8. In 1996 the Hopi Tribe filed a complaint against Time-Life Books with the Indian Arts and Crafts Board, alleging that the publisher was offering Navajo-made "authentic kachina dolls" to buyers who subscribed to a series of books on American Indians. Time-Life subsequently agreed to purchase the kachinas from Hopi artists. See Faith Russell, Statement before Senate Committee on Indian Affairs, 17 May 2000, <www.doi.gov/iacb/pdf/iacbtestimony.pdf>, accessed 20 Nov. 2001.

9. Sources are the video *NAGPRA and Southwestern Tribes* (Museum of Indian Arts and Culture, 1998) and a related document, *Southwestern Tribal Peoples and NAGPRA Conference* (Museum of Indian Arts and Culture, 1997). My thanks to Sibel Melik for making these available to me. And see Christopher Smith, "Navajos and Hopis at Odds over Remains of Anasazi," *Salt Lake Tribune,* 22 Nov. 1999, <www.sltrib.com/1999/nov/11221999/utah/50693.htm>, accessed 18 Aug. 2000; Zarana Sanghani, "Descendants of the Anasazi?" *Gallup Independent,* 29 Apr. 2000, <www.cia-g.com/~gallpind/4-29-00.html>, accessed 17 Aug. 2000.

10. See Michael J. Harkin, "Privacy, Ownership, and the Repatriation of Cultural Properties: An Ethnographic Perspective from the Northwest Coast," paper presented at the conference "Categories, Culture, and Property," Chicago-Kent College of Law, 28 Sept. 2001. I am grateful to Harkin for making a copy of this paper available to me.

11. See "New Age Rites at Sacred Place Draw Indian Protests," *New York Times,* 27 June 1994, A14. Quotations are from "Mutant Mes-

sage Downed!!!" at <www.newage.com.au/panthology/mutant.htm>, accessed 4 Aug. 1997. On Morgan's book see L. R. Hiatt, "A New Age for an Old People," *Quadrant* (Fitzroy, Victoria), June 1997, 35–40. In the indigenous-rights movement, New Agers seem to be the group that everyone loves to hate. See, e.g., Paul C. Johnson, "Shamanism from Ecuador to Chicago: A Case Study in New Age Ritual Appropriation," *Religion* 25 (1995): 163–178; Alice B. Kehoe, "Prima Gaia: Primitivists and Plastic Medicine Men," in *The Invented Indian: Cultural Fictions and Government Policies,* ed. James M. Clifton (New Brunswick, N.J.: Transaction, 1990), 193–209; Wendy Rose, "The Great Pretenders: Further Reflections on Whiteshamanism," in *The State of Native America: Genocide, Colonization, and Resistance,* ed. M. Annette Jaimes (Boston: South End Press, 1992), 403–421.

12. "Hopis Trying to Halt Class on Holy Rites," *Arizona Republic,* 24 Apr. 1993, B1. And see Armin W. Geertz, *The Invention of Prophecy: Continuity and Meaning in Hopi Indian Religion* (Berkeley: University of California Press, 1994); Peter M. Whiteley, *Rethinking Hopi Ethnography,* Smithsonian Series in Ethnographic Inquiry (Washington: Smithsonian Institution Press, 1998).

13. Marilyn Masayesva, contributor, *Dialogue with the Hopi: Cultural Copyright and Research Ethics* (Hotevilla, Ariz.: Paaqavi, 1995), 8. And see James D. Nason, "Traditional Property and Modern Laws: The Need for Native American Community Intellectual Property Rights Legislation," *Stanford Law and Policy Review* 12, no. 2 (2001): 255–266.

14. "The Kachinas Sing of Doom," *NFL Superpro,* no. 6, Mar. 1992, Marvel Comics.

15. I am grateful to Marcie Rendon for permission to quote from her play and to William A. Wortman, archivist of the Native American Women Playwrights Archive, Miami University Libraries, Miami, Ohio, for assistance in obtaining a copy of it.

16. See Nancy Oestreich Lurie, "Women in Early American Anthropology," in *Pioneers of American Anthropology,* ed. June Helm (Seattle: University of Washington Press, 1966), 53. Densmore's letter quoted in the Minnesota Public Radio documentary *Song Catcher: Life Story* (Stephen Smith, producer, 1997), transcript accessed at <news.mpr.org/

features/199702/01_smiths-densmore/docs>. Also see Nina Marchetti Archabal, "Frances Densmore: Pioneer in the Study of American Indian Music," in *Women of Minnesota,* ed. Barbara Stuhler and Gretchen Kreuter (St. Paul: Minnesota Historical Society Press, 1977), 94–115; Charlotte J. Frisbie, "Frances Theresa Densmore," in *Women Anthropologists: A Biographical Dictionary,* ed. Ute Gacs et al. (New York: Greenwood, 1988), 51–58. Bullhead quoted in National Public Radio, *All Things Considered,* "Frances Densmore, Native American Music Chronicler," 26 Nov. 1994, transcript provided by NPR.

17. One approach that has not yet figured significantly in indigenous-rights discourse is group libel litigation, lawsuits seeking damages against the authors of publications that allegedly subject groups to collective vilification. See "A Communitarian Defense of Group Libel Laws," *Harvard Law Review* 101 (1988): 682–701; Rebecca Tsosie, "Reclaiming Native Stories: An Essay on Cultural Appropriation and Cultural Rights," *Arizona State Law Journal* 34 (2002): 343.

18. Thomas Axtell, "Connecting Nunavik (Arctic Canada)," <www.megantic.net/axtell/act/CN.htm>, accessed 26 Jan. 1999; Department of the Army, *Cultural Resources Management,* Pamphlet 200–4, 1997. Searches on Lexis-Nexis and several other databases failed to turn up any works that explicitly formulate the nature and scope of "cultural privacy."

19. Samuel D. Warren and Louis D. Brandeis, "The Right to Privacy," *Harvard Law Review* 4 (1890): 195, 205, 193; Ellen Alderman and Caroline Kennedy, *The Right to Privacy* (New York: Knopf, 1995), xv. See also Michael A. Weinstein, "The Uses of Privacy in the Good Life," in *Privacy,* ed. J. Roland Pennock and John W. Chapman (New York: Atherton, 1971), 88–104.

20. Edward J. Bloustein, *Individual and Group Privacy* (New Brunswick, N.J.: Transaction Books, 1978), 181. See also Ferdinand D. Schoeman, *Privacy and Social Freedom* (Cambridge: Cambridge University Press, 1992).

21. See, e.g., Christopher Anderson, ed., *Politics of the Secret* (Sydney, N.S.W.: University of Sydney, 1995); Gilbert Herdt, "Secret Societies and Secret Collectives," *Oceania* 60 (1990): 360–381; Ian Keen, *Knowl-*

edge and Secrecy in an Aboriginal Religion: Yolngu of North-East Arnhem Land (Oxford: Clarendon Press, 1994); John M. Roberts and Thomas Gregor, "Privacy: A Cultural View," in *Privacy,* ed. Pennock and Chapman, 199–225.

22. Roberts and Gregor, "Privacy," 219–220. See also Elizabeth A. Brandt, "On Secrecy and the Control of Knowledge: Taos Pueblo," in *Secrecy: A Cross-Cultural Perspective,* ed. Stanton K. Tefft (New York: Human Sciences Press, 1980), 123–146.

23. See Don Burgess, "Tarahumara Folklore: A Study in Cultural Secrecy," *Southwest Folklore* 5 (1981): 11–22.

24. See Erich Kolig, "Darrugu: Sacred Objects in a Changing World," in Anderson, ed., *Politics of the Secret,* 40–41.

25. Society of American Archivists, <www.archivists.org>; Christopher Anderson, "Politics of the Secret," in Anderson, ed., *Politics of the Secret,* 12.

26. The Northern Territory Supreme Court decision (29 FLR 233, 1976), from which the justice's quotations are drawn, includes a summary of the background to the case. The later case is *Pitjantjatjara Council v. Lowe and Bender* (1982). In the interests of simplicity, I have used "Pitjantjatjara," the spelling of this group's name currently used in Australia. The legal documents use varying spellings, including "Pitjantjara."

27. Public awareness about potential abuses of government databases was heightened by the revelation, in February 1999, that several states, including South Carolina and Colorado, had agreed to sell driver's license photographs to a firm that wished to use them to confirm the identities of customers presenting personal checks at retail outlets. See Anne Wells Branscomb, *Who Owns Information? From Privacy to Public Access* (New York: Basic Books, 1994).

28. George E. Marcus, "Censorship in the Heart of Difference: Cultural Property, Indigenous Peoples' Movements, and Challenges to Western Liberal Thought," in *Censorship and Silencing: Practices of Cultural Regulation,* ed. Robert C. Post (Los Angeles: Getty Research Institute for the History of Art and Humanities, 1998), 221–242.

29. One of the few legal scholars to ponder issues of cultural privacy,

Sarah Harding, concludes that "cultural secrecy" is "central to a form of sovereignty exercised through acts of cultural representation rather than political forms." Harding, "Cultural Secrecy and the Protection of Cultural Property," in *Topics in Cultural Resource Law* (Washington: Society for American Archaeology, 2000), 75. Although much of her analysis is convincing, sovereignty is a problematic concept when applied to control over information. On abuses of political sovereignty, see Fergus W. Bordewich, *Killing the White Man's Indian: Reinventing Native Americans at the End of the Twentieth Century* (New York: Doubleday, 1996), 302–344.

30. See esp. Robert C. Post, "Rereading Warren and Brandeis: Privacy, Property, and Appropriation," *Case Western Reserve Law Review* 41 (1991): 647–680.

31. David Howes argues that indigenous groups could find legal protection in the "right of publicity" derived from the commercial value of identities. But this clouds indigenous moral claims by conflating them with commercial ends. See Howes, "Cultural Appropriation and Resistance in the American Southwest: Decommodifying 'Indianness,'" in *Cross-Cultural Consumption: Global Markets, Local Realities,* ed. David Howes (London: Routledge, 1996), 138–160.

32. Edward Shils, "Privacy and Power," in *Center and Periphery: Essays in Macrosociology* (Chicago: University of Chicago Press, 1975), 344.

2. Cultures and Copyrights

1. This estimate (which I have converted to U.S. dollars) is from *NIAAA News,* Spring 2000, a publication of the National Indigenous Arts Advocacy Association, <www.niaaa.com.au/spring.html>, accessed 22 June 2000.

2. Key cases include *Bulun Bulun v. Nejlam Pty Ltd,* 1989, and *Milpurrurru v. Indofurn Pty Ltd,* 1994. A related case, *Yumbulul v. Reserve Bank of Australia and Ors,* 1991, involved the reproduction of an artist's work on Australian banknotes. See esp. two essays by Colin Golvan, "Aboriginal Art and Copyright: The Case for Johnny Bulun Bulun," *European Intellectual Property Review* 11, no. 10 (1989): 346–354, and "Ab-

original Art and the Protection of Indigenous Cultural Rights," *European Intellectual Property Review* 14, no. 7 (July 1992): 227–232. The link between art and religious duty is laid out by Bulun Bulun in an affidavit dated 16 Sept. 1997, submitted to Australian Federal Court, Northern Territory, as part of *Bulun Bulun and Milpurrurru v. R & T Textiles.* On the copyright status of Aboriginal art, see Brad Sherman, "From the Non-Original to the Ab-Original: A History," in *Of Authors and Origins: Essays on Copyright Law,* ed. Brad Sherman and Alain Strowel (Oxford: Clarendon Press, 1994), 110–130.

3. See, e.g., Richard H. Bartlett, "Native Title in Australia: Denial, Recognition, and Dispossession," in *Indigenous Peoples' Rights in Australia, Canada, and New Zealand,* ed. Paul Havemann (New York: Oxford University Press, 1999), 408–427; Frank Brennan, "Mabo and Its Ramifications for the Future of Indigenous Australians," in *Indigenous Australians and the Law,* ed. Elliott Johnston, Martin Hinton, and Daryle Rigney (Sydney: Cavendish Publishing, 1997), 167–182; Henry Reynolds, "The Mabo Judgement—Its Implications," <www.caa.org.au/publications/reports/MABO>, 1993, accessed 26 June 2000.

4. Geoffrey Bardon, "The Great Painting: Napperby Death Spirit Dreaming and Tim Leurah Tjapaltjarri," in *Mythscapes: Aboriginal Art of the Desert,* ed. Judith Ryan (Melbourne: National Gallery of Victoria, 1989), 46. See also Frank Brennan, "Land Rights—The Religious Factor," in *Religious Business: Essays on Australian Aboriginal Spirituality,* ed. Max Charlesworth (New York: Cambridge University Press, 1998), 164.

5. In his written judgment, Justice von Doussa declares: "The question however is whether those Aboriginal laws can create binding obligations on persons outside the relevant Aboriginal community, either through recognition of those laws by the common law, or by their capacity to found equitable rights in rem." *Bulun Bulun and Milpurrurru v. R & T Textiles Pty Ltd* [1998] 1082 FCA (3 Sept. 1998), 14.

6. Tony Fry and Anne-Marie Willis, "Aboriginal Art: Symptom or Success?" *Art in America,* July 1989, 116.

7. See, e.g., Fry and Willis, "Aboriginal Art"; Anne-Marie Willis, *Illusions of Identity: The Art of Nation* (Sydney: Hale and Iremonger, 1993); Jo-Anne Birnie Danzker, "Am I Authentic?" in *Dreamings—Tjukurrpa: Aboriginal Art of the Western Desert,* ed. Jo-Anne Birnie Danzker (New

York: Prester-Verlag, 1994); Philip Jones, "Perceptions of Aboriginal Art: A History," in *Dreamings: The Art of Aboriginal Australia,* ed. Peter Sutton (New York: George Braziller/Asia Society Galleries, 1988); Ian McLean, *White Aborigines: Identity Politics in Australian Art* (New York: Cambridge University Press, 1998); Eric Michaels, "Western Desert Sandpainting and Post-Modernism," in *Kuruwarri: Yuendumu Doors,* ed. Warlukurlangu Artists (Canberra: Australian Institute of Aboriginal Studies, 1987); Michael Fitzgerald, "Different Strokes: Despite a Series of Scandals over Authenticity, Australian Aboriginal Art Is More Popular—and More Valued—Than Ever," *Time International,* 26 July 1999, 72. See also Howard Morphy, *Ancestral Connections: Art and an Aboriginal System of Knowledge* (Chicago: University of Chicago Press, 1991); Fred R. Myers, "Representing Culture: The Production of Discourse(s) for Aboriginal Acrylic Paintings," in *The Traffic in Culture: Refiguring Art and Anthropology,* ed. George E. Marcus and Fred R. Myers (Berkeley: University of California Press, 1995), 81; and an exhibition catalog by Vivien Johnson, *Copyrites: Aboriginal Art in the Age of Reproductive Technologies* (Sydney: National Indigenous Arts Advocacy Program, 1996).

8. See esp. Paul Goldstein, *Copyright's Highway: The Law and Lore of Copyright from Gutenberg to the Celestial Jukebox* (New York: Hill and Wang, 1994), 3–36. My comments emphasize U.S. copyright practices rather than European ones, which give authors' rights greater weight.

9. The literature that considers innovative uses of existing intellectual property law to protect indigenous heritage, however defined, is vast. See esp. Cathryn A. Berryman, "Toward More Universal Protection of Intangible Cultural Property," *Journal of Intellectual Property Law* 1 (Spring 1994): 293–333; Michael Blakeney, "Intellectual Property in the Dreamtime: Protecting the Cultural Creativity of Indigenous Peoples," paper presented at the Oxford Intellectual Property Research Centre, 1999, available at <www.oiprc.ox.ac.uk/EJWP1199.html>, accessed 30 Dec. 2002; James Boyle, *Shamans, Software, and Spleens: Law and the Construction of the Information Society* (Cambridge, Mass.: Harvard University Press, 1996); David R. Downes, "How Intellectual Property Could Be a Tool to Protect Traditional Knowledge," *Columbia Journal of Environmental Law* 25 (2000): 253–282; Tom Greaves, ed., *Intellectual Property Rights for Indigenous Peoples: A Source Book* (Oklahoma City:

Society for Applied Anthropology, 1994); Terri Janke, *Our Culture, Our Future: Report on Australian Indigenous Cultural and Intellectual Property Rights* (Surrey Hills, N.S.W.: Michael Frankel, 1998); Amanda Pask, "Cultural Appropriation and the Law: An Analysis of the Legal Regimes Concerning Culture," *Intellectual Property Journal* 8 (1993): 57–86.

10. See Goldstein, *Copyright's Highway,* ch. 2.

11. Alain Strowel, "Droit d'Auteur and Copyright: Between History and Nature," in *Of Authors and Origins,* 235. Strowel distinguishes the European concept of *droit d'auteur* from the Anglo-American notion of copyright, a limited monopoly granted by the state. But see F. Willem Grosheide, "Paradigms in Copyright Law," in *Of Authors and Origins.* Lord Mansfield is quoted in Goldstein, *Copyright's Highway,* 50–51.

12. David Lange, "Copyright and the Constitution in the Age of Intellectual Property," *Journal of Intellectual Property Law* 1 (1993), 126; Boyle, *Shamans, Software,* xii.

13. See Goldstein, *Copyright's Highway,* 129–164, 216–217; Elisabeth Bumiller, "Battle Hymns around Campfires: ASCAP Asks Royalties from Girl Scouts, and Regrets It," *New York Times,* 17 Dec. 1996, B1.

14. Diane Conley, "Author, User, Scholar, Thief: Fair Use and Unpublished Works," *Cardozo Arts and Entertainment Law Journal* 9, no. 1 (1990): 57. On general questions of authorship, see Boyle, *Shamans, Software,* 51–60; Keith Aoki, "(Intellectual) Property and Sovereignty: Notes toward a Cultural Geography of Authorship," *Stanford Law Review* 48, no. 5 (1996): 1293–1355; Grosheide, "Paradigms"; Peter Jaszi, "On the Author Effect: Contemporary Copyright and Collective Creativity," *Cardozo Arts and Entertainment Law Journal* 10, no. 2 (1992): 293–320; Rosemary J. Coombe, *The Cultural Life of Intellectual Properties: Authorship, Appropriation, and the Law* (Durham, N.C.: Duke University Press, 1998).

15. I wish to thank David Dinwoodie for permission to share this anecdote. Months after hearing Dinwoodie's account, I was told by the chief of a different Canadian Indian band that an unnamed linguist had "copyrighted the mythology of another First Nation." Clearly variations of the story are in wide circulation in western Canada.

16. Steven Feld, "Pygmy POP: A Genealogy of Schizophonic Mimesis," in *Yearbook for Traditional Music 1996* (New York: International

Council for Traditional Music, 1996), 1–35. For promotional information about the creators of *Deep Forest*, see <www.sonymusic.fr/deep forest/>. On protecting the rights of indigenous peoples in their musical productions, see esp. Anthony Seeger, "Ethnomusicologists, Archives, Professional Organizations, and the Shifting Ethics of Intellectual Property," in *Yearbook for Traditional Music 1996*, 87–105.

17. See, e.g., Nicholas Thomas, "Kiss the Baby Goodbye: Kowhaiwhai and Aesthetics in Aotearoa New Zealand," *Critical Inquiry* 22 (1995): 90–121; Kamal Puri, "Cultural Ownership and Intellectual Property Rights Post-Mabo: Putting Ideas into Action," *Intellectual Property Journal* 9, no. 3 (1995): 316.

18. All quoted material is from Justice von Doussa's published decision, *Bulun Bulun and Milpurrurru v. R & T Textiles Pty Ltd* [1998] 1082 FCA (3 Sept. 1998).

19. Hardie's interview was broadcast on *The Law Report*, Australian Broadcasting Company, 15 Sept. 1998. In the quotations I have changed the punctuation slightly for clarity.

20. See Stephen Gray, "Black Enough? Urban and Non-Traditional Aboriginal Art and Proposed Legislative Protection for Aboriginal Art," *Culture and Policy* (Brisbane) 7, no. 3 (1996): 29–44.

21. Thomas's statement is from the decision in *Harold Joseph Thomas v. David George Brown & James Morrison Vallely Tennant* [1997] 215 FCA (9 April 1997). The *Sydney Morning Herald* article about the century's 100 most influential Australians was published on 26 Jan. 2001. For a different interpretation of the flag controversy, see Elazar Barkan, *The Guilt of Nations: Restitution and Negotiating Historical Injustices* (New York: Norton, 2000), 250–251.

3. Sign Wars

1. "Internet Poll Ranks State's Banner Best," Associated Press, 15 June 2001, accessed via Lexis-Nexis.

2. Associated Press, 16 Apr. 1994; *Arizona Republican*, 13 Feb. 1994, D4. See also *Albuquerque Journal*, 21 June 1998, B1; *Los Angeles Times*, 15 July 1999, A5; and *New York Times*, 13 Jan. 2000, F1.

3. Isidro Pino, a leader of one of the pueblo's religious societies,

testified in a public hearing in July 1999. Pino noted that knowledge of the sun symbol "is a community property . . . However, to help you understand the importance of the Zia sun symbol, our community property, I take personal risk in disclosing the following," after which he briefly described the symbol's use in four ritual contexts. "The above samplings," he concluded, "have been disclosed in hopes that you will duly consider the full protection of the Zia sun symbol as the official tribal symbol of the Pueblo of Zia." U.S. Patent and Trademark Office, *Hearing on Official Insignia of Native American Tribes,* 8 July 1999, 138–139, available at <www.uspto.gov/web/offices/com/hearings/index.html #native>.

4. Terri Janke, *Our Culture: Our Future: Report on Australian Indigenous Cultural and Intellectual Property Rights* (Surrey Hills, N.S.W.: Michael Frankel, 1998), 114–119. On authors' rights see Paul Goldstein, *Copyright's Highway: The Law and Lore of Copyright from Gutenberg to the Celestial Jukebox* (New York: Hill and Wang, 1994), 165–196.

5. See Frank H. Foster and Robert L. Shook, *Patents, Copyrights, and Trademarks* (New York: Wiley, 1989), 21–25; Thomas D. Drescher, "The Transformation and Evolution of Trademarks—from Signals to Symbols to Myth," *Trademark Reporter* 82 (May–June 1992): 301–340.

6. Rosemary J. Coombe, *The Cultural Life of Intellectual Properties: Authorship, Appropriation, and the Law* (Durham, N.C.: Duke University Press, 1998), ch. 4.

7. On the trend toward aggressive trademarking, see, e.g., "The Smell of This Magazine Is a Registered Trademark," *Forbes,* 5 May 1997, 39–40; Adam Liptak, "Legally, the Alphabet Isn't as Simple as A, B, and C," *New York Times,* 2 Sept. 2001, sec. 4, 10. "Publisher of Erotica Loses Battle to Enjoin Oprah's Magazine," *Entertainment Industry Litigation Reporter* 14, no. 4 (July 2002): 11, accessed via Lexis-Nexis. Michael B. Sapherstein, "The Trademark Registrability of the Harley-Davidson Roar: A Multimedia Analysis," Intellectual Property and Technology Forum, Boston College Law School, no. 101101 (1998), <www.bc.edu/bc_org/avp/law/st_org/iptf/articles>; "Harley-Davidson Quits Trying to Hog Sound," *Los Angeles Times,* 12 June 2000, C3. According to the *L.A. Times,* "As of 1998, only 23 of nearly 730,000 active trademarks had

been issued to protect a noise." Steve Bird, "Game, Scent and Match for Grassy Tennis Balls," *Times* (London), 25 May 2000, accessed via Lexis-Nexis.

8. On Prince, see "They're King-Sized Issues, Whatever You Call Him," *New York Times,* 21 Mar. 1999, sec. 3, 2. For a whimsical perspective on trademarking, see Felicity Barringer, "Sacred or Profane, Odd or Mundane, It Has a Trademark," *New York Times,* 5 Sept. 1999, sec. 4, 2. On the implications for free speech, see Mark A. Lemley, "The Modern Lanham Act and the Death of Common Sense," *Yale Law Journal* 108 (1999): 1687–1715.

9. The USPTO's standards for unacceptable trademarks are outlined in *Hearing on Official Insignia of Native American Tribes,* 34. For information on the Washington Redskins trademark case, see *Harjo v. Pro-Football, Inc.,* 50 USPQ2d (TTAB 1999).

10. Doug Grow, "A Time for Pride and Forgiveness," *Star Tribune* (Minneapolis), 30 Apr. 2001, 2B.

11. On the malt liquor case see Coombe, *Cultural Life of Intellectual Properties,* 199–204. The U.S. Court of Appeals decision, dated 14 Jan. 1998, is *Hornell Brewing Co. v. Rosebud Sioux Tribal Ct,* 133 F.3d 1087 (8th Cir. 1998). My source for the number of lawyers is Timothy Egan, "New Prosperity Brings New Conflict to Indian Country," *New York Times,* 8 Mar. 1998, 1.

12. Letter to the USPTO dated 29 Apr. 1999 from Donna L. Berry, a staff attorney at DaimlerChrysler, 3. See also a letter from the International Trademark Association to the USPTO, 16 Apr. 1999. Both documents were downloaded from <www.uspto.gov/web/offices/com/hearings/index.html#native>. And see Bryan Thompson, "New Zealand Pursues IP Modernization," *IP Worldwide,* July/Aug. 1998, accessed via Lexis-Nexis. According to *PATSCAN News,* a Canadian publication, official-mark laws in Canada appear to set the stage for protection of "names of native groups, native place names and native language terms," and this category of "Section 9" marks can "be very powerful since they can be asserted regardless of the wares or services involved—the only issue is that of confusing association with the institution holding the Section 9 registration." *PATSCAN News,* Spring 1998, <www.library.ubc.

ca/patscan/>. A legal summary prepared by a Canadian law firm notes that official marks are far stronger than trademarks in Canadian law. The Registrar of Trade-Marks cannot refuse to register a mark if the applicant is a public authority. Once the mark is issued, the legal power of the holder is stronger than that of a trademark holder. This has evoked complaints that existing law makes these marks invulnerable to appeal. See Sherren Hamdy, "Official Marks," <www.dww.com/articles/official _marks.htm>, accessed 25 Oct. 2001.

13. Transcript of USPTO hearing in San Francisco on 12 July 1999, 15–21.

14. Transcript of USPTO hearing in Albuquerque on 8 July 1999, 24–29.

15. *Official Insignia of Native American Tribes: Statutorily Required Study* (Washington: Patent and Trademark Office, Department of Commerce, 2000), 29.

16. Information on the Tigua service-mark (registration no. 2306017) is from a letter dated 25 July 2000 from Albert Alvidrez, Governor, Ysleta del Sur Pueblo, to Director of State Parks Division of the Texas Parks and Wildlife Department; copy in my possession. The application for registration of the mark states that it will be used in connection with "games of chance such as bingo, slot machines, card games, and dice games." Speaking Rock Casino was closed in February 2002 after the U.S. Supreme Court ruled that it had illegally begun operations without first securing permission from the state of Texas. I am grateful to Dr. Karen Harry, Director of the Cultural Resources Program at Texas Parks and Wildlife, for information about the Hueco Tanks petroglyphs.

17. See Adrienne Tanner, "Image Problem," *The Province* (Vancouver), 13 Feb. 2000, A22–23; "Petroglyph Park Offered to Nanaimo," *Newsletter of the Aboriginal Rights Coalition of BC,* 10 July 2000, <arcbc. tripod.com>, accessed 17 July 2000. In common with many other aboriginal groups, the Snuneymuxw First Nation is currently negotiating with British Columbia and the Canadian federal government for a significant expansion of its titled lands.

18. Telephone interview, 23 Oct. 2001. I am grateful to Ms. Johnnie, as well as to Kelly Bannister, for information on the Snuneymuxw petro-

glyphs case. It remains unclear how the Snuneymuxw official marks satisfy the condition that registered marks must be used in some public manner, typically on letterhead stationery or official vehicles.

19. Canadian Trade-mark Database, <strategis.ic.gc.ca/cgi-bin/sc_consu/trade-marks/search_e.pl>, applications 09099991 and 1910390 through 1919398.

20. Coombe, *Cultural Life of Intellectual Properties,* 136. The U.S. Congress has granted special protection to the marks of organizations such as the Boy Scouts of America and the Daughters of the American Revolution. Access to images of Smokey Bear, a figure created by the U.S. Forest Service in collaboration with the Advertising Council, is carefully controlled by the Forest Service. When Robert Jackall and Janice Hirota sought to reproduce a picture of the famous bear in a book on the history of advertising and public relations, the Forest Service refused to grant permission, citing what it called the "inappropriateness" of their references to Smokey Bear. See Robert Jackall and Janice Hirota, *Image Makers: Advertising, Public Relations, and the Ethos of Advocacy* (Chicago: University of Chicago Press, 2000), 216.

21. A report by Indian and Northern Affairs, Canada, states: "The Snuneymuxw have repatriated this part of their heritage." See Simon Brascoupé and Howard Mann, *A Community Guide to Protecting Indigenous Knowledge* (Ottawa: Research and Analysis Directorate, Department of Indian Affairs and Northern Development, 2001), 24. There are exceptions to the rule that the creators of rock art are nearly impossible to associate with contemporary communities. At Hueco Tanks State Historical Park in Texas, pictographs were almost certainly painted by specific Tigua and Kiowa individuals in the nineteenth century. Their descendants visit the site regularly today. See Adolph M. Greenberg and George S. Esber, "Draft General Management Plan for Hueco Tanks Park (Report Prepared for the Tigua Indian Tribe, Ysleta del Sur Pueblo)," Cultural Consultants, Inc., <www.huecotanks.com/tigua/tigua.htm>, accessed 18 Aug. 2000.

22. Candace S. Greene and Thomas D. Drescher, "The Tipi with Battle Pictures: The Kiowa Tradition of Intangible Property Rights," *Trademark Reporter* 84, no. 4 (July–Aug. 1994): 431.

23. As early as 1920 the anthropologist Robert Lowie documented many examples of copyright-like practices among tribal peoples in *Primitive Society* (New York: Boni and Liveright, 1920). William Whitman, *The Oto* (1937; New York: AMS Press, 1969), 3–4. See also, e.g., Jacob L. Simet, "Copyrighting Traditional Tolai Knowledge?" in *Protection of Intellectual, Biological, and Cultural Property in Papua New Guinea,* ed. Kathy Whimp and Mark Busse (Canberra: Asia Pacific Press, 2000), 62–80; Mark C. Suchman, "Invention and Ritual: Notes on the Interrelation of Magic and Intellectual Property in Preliterate Societies," *Columbia Law Review* 89 (1989): 1264–94; Graham Dutfield, "The Public and Private Domains: Intellectual Property Rights in Traditional Knowledge," *Science Communication* 21 (2000): 274–295.

24. Colin Golvan, "Aboriginal Art and the Protection of Indigenous Cultural Rights," *European Intellectual Property Review* 14, no. 7 (July 1992): 229.

25. See Jane M. Gaines, *Contested Culture: The Image, the Voice, and the Law* (Chapel Hill: University of North Carolina Press, 1991), 84–104; Jane M. Gaines, "Bette Midler and the Piracy of Identity," in *Music and Copyright,* ed. Simon Frith (Edinburgh: Edinburgh University Press, 1993).

26. Nicholas Thomas, *Possessions: Indigenous Art, Colonial Culture* (New York: Thames and Hudson, 1999), 144–145. But see two essays by James O. Young, "Should White Men Play the Blues?" *Journal of Value Inquiry* 28 (1994): 415–424, and "The Ethics of Cultural Appropriation," *Dalhousie Review* 80 (2000): 301–316.

27. Ben Greenman, "Dept. of Namesakes: What Do Army Aircraft and Native Americans Have in Common?" *New Yorker,* 7 June 1997, 32–33.

28. Southwest Airlines press release, 18 Sept. 2000. See also Barry Massey, "Pueblo Seeking Negotiations over Zia Compensation," Associated Press, 19 Feb. 2001, accessed via Lexis-Nexis; Michelle Pentz, "Afternoon Sunrise Lifts New Mexico's Zia to the Clouds," *Albuquerque Journal,* 21 Sept. 2000, 6. Telephone interviews with Madalena and Pino, 15 Oct. 2001 and 16 Oct. 2001.

29. The linguist Michael Krauss estimates that only about 16 percent

of the surviving indigenous languages in the United States and Canada are spoken by all generations, usually an accurate indicator of a language's survival prospects. In contrast, 67 percent are now spoken only by people in the grandparental generation or above. Michael Krauss, "The Condition of Native North American Languages: The Need for Realistic Assessment and Action," *International Journal of the Sociology of Language* 132 (1998): 12.

30. *Milpurrurru v. Indofurn Pty Ltd* (1994), cited in Ian McDonald, "Protecting Indigenous Intellectual Property: A Copyright Perspective," Discussion Paper (Redfern, N.S.W.: Australian Copyright Council, 1998), 45–46.

4. Ethnobotany Blues

1. On Schultes see E. J. Kahn Jr., "Jungle Botanist," *New Yorker*, 1 June 1992, 35–58; Wade Davis, *One River* (New York: Simon and Schuster, 1996). And see Richard I. Ford, "Ethnobotany: Historical Diversity and Synthesis," in *The Nature and Status of Ethnobotany*, ed. Richard I. Ford (Ann Arbor: Museum of Anthropology, University of Michigan, 1978), 33–49.

2. In 1989, for example, the *New York Times* published a letter from the communications director of the McDonald's Corporation that declared: "Be assured, unequivocally, that McDonald's does not now purchase, nor have we ever purchased, any beef raised on such rain-forest land . . . In Canada, McDonald's uses 100 percent Canadian beef. In this country, we use 100 percent United States beef." *New York Times*, 10 Jan. 1989, A22.

3. Mark J. Plotkin, *Tales of a Shaman's Apprentice: An Ethnobotanist Searches for New Medicines in the Amazon Rain Forest* (New York: Viking, 1993), 16. See also Leslie Roberts, "Chemical Prospecting: Hope for Vanishing Ecosystems?" *Science* 256 (22 May 1992): 1142–43; Jennie Wood Sheldon and Michael J. Balick, "Ethnobotany and the Search for Balance between Use and Conservation," in *Intellectual Property Rights and Biodiversity Conservation*, ed. Timothy Swanson (Cambridge: Cambridge University Press, 1995), 45–64; Richard Evans Schultes, "The Im-

portance of Ethnobotany in Environmental Conservation," *American Journal of Economics and Sociology* 53, no. 2 (1994): 202–205.

4. On the INBio-Merck contract see Eduardo Gudnyas, "La naturaleza ante el Doctor Fausto" (1997), <www.ambiental.net/ integracion/ApropiacionBiodv.htm.>, accessed 19 June 2001; Elissa Blum, "Making Biodiversity Conservation Profitable: A Case Study of the Merck/INBio Agreement," *Environment* 35, no. 4 (1993): 17–20, 38–45; Andy M. Sittenfeld and Annie Lovejoy, "Biodiversity Prospecting Frameworks: The INBio Experience in Costa Rica," in *Protection of Global Biodiversity: Converging Strategies,* ed. Lakshman D. Guruswamy and Jeffrey A. McNeely (Durham, N.C.: Duke University Press, 1998), 223–244. The profile of Plotkin appeared in the *New York Times,* 30 Nov. 1999, F3.

5. See Corinne P. Hayden, "A Biodiversity Sampler for the Millennium," in *Reproducing Reproduction: Kinship, Power, and Technological Innovation,* ed. Sarah Franklin and Helena Ragoné (Philadelphia: University of Pennsylvania Press, 1998), 173–206; Shayana Kadidal, "Plants, Poverty, and Pharmaceutical Patents," *Yale Law Journal* 103, no. 1 (1993): 223–258; Andrew Kimbrell, *The Human Body Shop: The Engineering and Marketing of Life* (San Francisco: HarperSanFrancisco, 1993); Mark Sagoff, "On the Uses of Biodiversity," in *Protection of Global Biodiversity,* 265–284; Vandana Shiva, *Biopiracy: The Plunder of Nature and Knowledge* (Boston: South End Press, 1997); and Seth Shulman, *Owning the Future* (Boston: Houghton Mifflin, 1999).

6. Herb Keinon, "Jews and the Genome," *Jerusalem Post,* 31 Aug. 2000, 5B. "Poet Attempts the Ultimate in Self-Invention," *Guardian,* 29 Feb. 2000, 3.

7. Stephen S. Hall, "Prescription for Profit," *New York Times Magazine,* 11 Mar. 2002, 40–45, 59–92. "Eli Lilly: Life after Prozac," *Business Week,* 23 July 2001, 80. On profit margins see Marcia Angell, "The Pharmaceutical Industry—To Whom Is It Accountable?" *New England Journal of Medicine,* 345, no. 25 (22 June 2000), 1902–04; *Rx R&D Myths: The Case against the Drug Industry's R&D "Scare Card"* (Washington: Public Citizen's Congress Watch, 2001), 11. On executive salaries see the AFL-CIO's "PayWatch," <www.aflcio.org>, accessed 31 May 2001.

8. *Rx R&D Myths,* 9.

9. See David Pearce and Seema Puroshothaman, "The Economic Value of Plant-Based Pharmaceuticals," in *Intellectual Property Rights and Biodiversity Conservation,* 127–138; Hanne Svarstad, Hans C. Bugge, and Shivcharn S. Dhillion, "From Norway to Novartis: Cyclosporin from Tolypocladium Inflatum in an Open Access Bioprospecting Regime," *Biodiversity and Conservation* 9 (2000): 1521–41. Katy Moran, Steven King, and Thomas Carlson declare in "Biodiversity Prospecting: Lessons and Prospects," *Annual Reviews in Anthropology* 30 (2001): 508, that "since the CBD [Convention on Biological Diversity] was introduced . . . no pharmaceutical bioprospecting product developed by using traditional knowledge has been commercialized; no economic profit has been realized."

10. Andrew Pollack, "The Green Revolution Yields to the Bottom Line," *New York Times,* 15 May 2001, F1. An important related issue is the potentially disastrous impact of industrial agriculture on indigenous crop varieties. Corporate breeders are now covering the world's agricultural real estate with genetically uniform (and often patented) plants that threaten the centers of diversity that have, since the late 1960s, been regarded as a kind of insurance policy against the plant plagues and pests sure to arise in the future. Immense fields of wind-pollinated crops such as maize scatter genetic material that may swamp out local varieties in a process referred to as "genetic pollution." Genetic diversity has long insulated plant populations from biological threats—animal pests, fungi, bacteria, changes in soil and climate. Industrial breeders value uniformity because it enhances productivity, at least in the short term. See E. J. Kahn Jr., *The Staffs of Life* (Boston: Little, Brown, 1984).

11. On soybeans see Shulman, *Owning the Future,* 88.

12. On the Basmati case, patent no. 5,663,484, see Rural Advancement Foundation International (RAFI), <www.rafi.org>, "Basmati Rice Update," 4 Jan. 2000, accessed 27 June 2001, and "India-U.S. Fight on Basmati Rice Is Mostly Settled," *New York Times,* 25 Aug. 2001, B1. On the contested Enola bean, patent no. 5,894,079, see Jonathan Friedland, "Litigation Sprouts Up over Claim to Invent Bean," *Wall Street Journal,* 21 Mar. 2000, C1. And on the popping bean, patent no.

6,040,503, see "Bracing for El Nuña," <www.rafi.org>, accessed 5 May 2001.

13. Glenn Wiser, "U.S. Patent and Trademark Office Reinstates Ayahuasca Patent," <www.ciel.org/Publications/PTODecisionAnalysis. pdf>, 25 June 2001, accessed 1 Feb. 2002. Stuart Luman, "Bright Ideas: Patented, Rarely Used," *Wired,* Apr. 2002, 59.

14. The case of the Enola bean is exceptional because the patent holder initiated legal action against importers of Mexican beans, sparking a firestorm of protests from Mexico. On farmers' rights, see, e.g., David A. Cleveland and Stephen C. Murray, "The World's Crop Genetic Resources and the Rights of Indigenous Farmers," *Current Anthropology* 38, no. 4 (1997): 477–515; and Stephen B. Brush, "Valuing Crop Genetic Resources," *Journal of Environment and Development* 5, no. 4 (1996): 416–433.

15. Data on patent applications and grants are from "U.S. Patent Activity, Calendar Years 1790–2000" and "Plant Patents Report, 1/1/1977– 12/31/2000," <www.uspto.gov>, accessed 31 May 2001, as well as information provided by Dominic Keating of the USPTO. And see Del Jones, "Surge in Ideas, Turnover Swamp Patent Office," *USA Today,* 11 Sept. 2000, 1A. In the agency's defense, its representatives note that information about exotic cultigens and non-Western medicinal plants is not readily available in the databases consulted by patent examiners.

16. Francesca T. Grifo, "Chemical Prospecting: An Overview of the International Cooperative Biodiversity Groups Program," in *Biodiversity, Biotechnology, and Sustainable Development in Health and Agriculture: Emerging Connections* (Washington: Pan American Health Organization, 1996), 25.

17. Corinne P. Hayden, "When Nature Goes Public: An Ethnography of Bio-Prospecting in Mexico" (Ph.D. diss., University of California, Santa Cruz, 2000), 241.

18. On costs of drug development, see *Rx R&D Myths,* 2–7; on the odds of a compound reaching the market, Pearce and Puroshothaman, "Economic Value of Plant-Based Pharmaceuticals," 133. And see Bernard Ortiz de Montellano, "Empirical Aztec Medicine," *Science* 199, no. 4185 (1975): 215–220. Ortiz de Montellano notes that the Aztecs believed the

cure for fever was to purge the body of internal heat. If an Aztec herbal medicine induced vomiting or evacuation of the bowels, it should be considered effective in Aztec terms even though it might not qualify as a fever-reducing drug from the perspective of Western medicine.

19. See GAIA/GRAIN, "Biodiversity for Sale: Dismantling the Hype about Benefit Sharing," Apr. 2000, <www.grain.org/publications/gtbc/issue4.htm>, accessed 30 Mar. 2001.

20. Shane Greene, "Intellectual Property, Resources, or Territory? Reframing the Debate over Indigenous Rights, Traditional Knowledge, and Pharmaceutical Bioprospection," in *Truth Claims: Representation and Human Rights,* ed. Mark Philip Bradley and Patrice Petro (New Brunswick, N.J.: Rutgers University Press, 2002), 229–249. I am grateful to Shane Greene for sharing a prepublication draft of his essay.

21. See Pat Roy Mooney, "Why We Call It Biopiracy," in *Responding to Bioprospecting: From Biodiversity in the South to Medicines in the North,* ed. Hanne Svarstad and Shivcharn S. Dhillion (Oslo: Spartacus Forlag AS, 2000), 37–44. In September 2001 RAFI changed its name to the ETC Group, shorthand for Action Group on Erosion, Technology and Concentration. I use the name RAFI when discussing the organization's publications that predate the reorganization and name change.

22. Interview with Sarasara, 18 July 2001, Lima, Peru.

23. Casualty figures from Neil Harvey, *The Chiapas Rebellion: The Struggle for Land and Democracy* (Durham, N.C.: Duke University Press, 1998), 229. And see Eric Herrán, "Modernity, Premodernity and the Political: The Neozapatistas of Southern Mexico," in *Ethnic Challenges to the Modern Nation State,* ed. Shlomo Ben-Ami, Yoav Peled, and Alberto Spektorowski (New York: St. Martin's, 2000), 221–235; Lynn Stephen and George A. Collier, "Reconfiguring Ethnicity, Identity, and Citizenship in the Wake of the Zapatista Rebellion," *Journal of Latin American Anthropology* 3, no. 1 (1997): 2–13; Sergio Zermeño, "State, Society, and Dependent Neoliberalism in Mexico: The Case of the Chiapas Uprising," in *Politics, Social Change, and Economic Restructuring in Latin America,* ed. William C. Smith and Roberto Patricio Korzeniewicz (Coral Gables, Fla.: North-South Center Press, University of Miami, 1997), 123–147.

24. Data from Susana Cruikshank and Mary Purcell, "Mexico: More Poor Than 15 Years Ago," <www.socwatch.org.uy/1998/english/reports/mexico.htm>, accessed 15 June 2001. See also Stephen and Collier, "Reconfiguring Ethnicity," 9.

25. Zermeño, "State, Society, and Dependent Neoliberalism," 125.

26. See Michael Hardt and Antonio Negri, *Empire* (Cambridge, Mass.: Harvard University Press, 2000), 56–59.

27. Alan Zarembo, "Magnet for Globophobes," *Newsweek,* 9 Apr. 2001, 29. See also Louis Nevaer, "Zapatistas Landing in Mexico City from Three Sides," New California Media Online, 14 Mar. 2001, <www.ncmonline.com>, accessed 16 July 2001; "Zapatista Rebels Rally in Mexico City," *New York Times,* 12 Mar. 2001, A6.

28. Quoted in RAFI, "Biopiracy Project in Chiapas, Mexico, Denounced by Mayan Indigenous Groups," 1 Dec. 1999, <www.rafi.org>, accessed 23 July 2001. Among the many online documents generated by this controversy are the following: Matilda Perez, "Saqueo de la riqueza herbolaria," 4 Feb. 2000, <www.jornada.unam.mx>, accessed 6 June 2001; and COMPITCH, "Chiapas: Genetic Pirates and Black Gold," <www.laneta.apc/org/compitch/home/english/chiapas%20biopiracy.htm>, accessed 6 June 2001. ICBG-Maya responses to these documents include "How the Maya ICBG Implements the International Society of Ethnobiology Code of Ethics," <guallart.dac.uga.edu/ethics>, accessed 18 Dec. 2000; and Elois Ann Berlin and Brent Berlin, "Knowledge? Whose Property? Whose Benefits? The Case of OMIECH, RAFI, and the Maya ICBG," 13 Dec. 1999, <guallart.dac.uga.edu/ICBGreply.html>, accessed 5 Sept. 2000.

29. Berlin and Berlin, "Knowledge? Whose Property," 2. Brent and Elois Berlin declined to be interviewed for this book, citing their determination to present the history of the ICBG-Maya project in their own words.

30. RAFI, "Call to Dialogue or Call to 911?" 2 Nov. 2000, <www.rafi.org/web/docus/pdfs/geno2000nov2.pdf>, accessed 22 Jan. 2002.

31. National Public Radio, *All Things Considered,* 1 Sept. 2000. The quotation from the Berlins is from "Knowledge? Whose Property," 2.

32. Juan Castro Soto, "Pukuj biopiratería en Chiapas," Centro de

Investigaciones Económicas y Políticas de Acción Comunitaria (CIEPAC), 2000, <www.ciepac.org>, accessed 2 Jan. 2001. Barbara Belejack, "The Professor and the Plants: Prospecting for Problems in Chiapas," *Texas Observer,* 22 June 2000. RAFI, "Message from the Chiapas 'Bioprospecting' Dispute," 22 Dec. 1999, 2. For another perspective on ICBG-Maya, see Ronald Nigh, "Maya Medicine in the Biological Gaze: Bioprospecting Research as Herbal Fetishism," *Current Anthropology* 43, no. 3 (2002): 451–477.

33. Preston Hardison, "ICBG-Maya: A Case Study in Prior Informed Consent," *Ibin.net* 16 (Nov. 2000): 1–3.

34. RAFI derides the 25 percent royalty offered to the Maya by ICBG, even though it is more than ten times the rate cited by a RAFI employee, Pat Roy Mooney, as typical for bioprospecting agreements. See Mooney, "Why We Call it Biopiracy," 41. On collecting specimens in public markets, see Hayden, "When Nature Goes Public."

35. Berlin quoted in Ron Southwick, "Maya Critics Prompt Halt of NIH Project," *Chronicle of Higher Education,* 7 Dec. 2001, A20. RAFI press release, "Mexico Biopiracy Project Cancelled," 9 Nov. 2001.

36. Shaman Pharmaceuticals press release, "Ethnobotany Accelerating Drug Discovery," Feb. 1994.

37. Joan Hamilton, "The Medicine Man Will See You Now," *Business Week,* 1 Mar. 1993, 93. See also Norman R. Farnsworth, "Screening Plants for New Medicines," in *Biodiversity,* ed. E. O. Wilson (Washington: National Academy Press, 1988), 83–97; and Paul Alan Cox, "The Ethnobotanical Approach to Drug Discovery: Strengths and Limitations," in *Ethnobotany and the Search for New Drugs,* ed. Derek J. Chadwick and Joan Marsh (Chichester, U.K.: Wiley, 1994), 25–36.

38. "Lost Tribes, Lost Knowledge," *Time,* 23 Sept. 1991; "Jungle Cures," *Newsweek,* 18 Jan. 1993; "Shaman's IPO Success Sets Example for Biotech Firms," *Wall Street Journal,* 28 Jan. 1993, B2; see also "Can a West African Plant Slow the Scourge of Diabetes?" *Life,* 15 Oct. 1998, 26. Quotation from Hamilton, "The Medicine Man Will See You Now," 93.

39. Michael J. Ybarra, "It's a Jungle out There," *San Jose Mercury News,* 29 July 1999; Chori Santiago, "The Lost and Found Cure," *Forbes*

ASAP, 29 May 2000, 88–92. See also various Internet-based financial news services.

40. Some sources estimate the cost of undertaking clinical trials for new drugs at $50 million or more. See "Treating Cancer: The Dawn of a New Era," *Business Week,* 9 July 2001, 124. "Ethnobotany: Shaman Loses Its Magic," *Economist,* 20 Feb. 1999, 77.

41. On Shaman/HFC's benefit-sharing model, see Katy Moran, "Toward Compensation: Returning Benefits from Ethnobotanical Drug Discovery to Native Peoples," in *Ethnoecology: Situated Knowledge/Located Lives,* ed. Virginia D. Nazarea (Tucson: University of Arizona Press, 1999), 249–262; and Steven R. King, "Establishing Reciprocity: Biodiversity, Conservation, and New Models for Cooperation between Forest-Dwelling Peoples and the Pharmaceutical Industry," in *Intellectual Property Rights for Indigenous Peoples: A Sourcebook,* ed. Tom Greaves (Oklahoma City: Society for Applied Anthropology, 1994), 69–82.

42. Katy Moran, "Bioprospecting: Lessons from Benefit-Sharing Experiences," *International Journal of Biotechnology* 2, no. 1/2/3 (2000): 132–144.

43. "Captain Hook Award Nominees," <twm.co.nz/CptHook.htm# anchor369142>, and RAFI, "Are Patents out of Control?" <www.rafi. org/web/action-patents.shtml>, both accessed 18 Sept. 2001.

44. For criticism of Shaman's benefit sharing, see Joan Martinez-Alier, lecture given at Harvard University, March 2000, <www.ecoethics.net/ hsev/20003text.htm>, and Viki Reyes, "The Value of Sangre de Drago," *Seedling,* Mar. 1996, <www.grain.org/publications/mar96/mar 963.htm>, both accessed 14 Aug. 2001. Figures for Shaman's total benefit-sharing expenditures were provided by Steven King.

45. Anthony Giddens, *Modernity and Self-Identity: Self and Society in the Late Modern Age* (Stanford: Stanford University Press, 1991), 18.

46. R. Ubillas et al., "SP-303, an Antiviral Oligomeric Proanthocyanidin from the Latex of *Croton lechleri* (Sangre de Drago)," *Phytomedicine* 1 (1994): 77–106.

47. Patents based on *Croton* include 5,211,944 and 5,494,661, both assigned to Shaman Pharmaceuticals, and 5,156,847 and 5,474,782, assigned to Walter H. Lewis and WoundFast Pharmaceuticals, respec-

tively. The latter two patents concern the wound-healing effects of *sangre de drago* latex. Steven King told me that Shaman had seriously considered adding the names of Amazonian herbalists and shamans to the list of inventors on its patent application related to *sangre de drago*. But the company's legal counsel argued that the healers' questionable standing as "inventors" could later provide a legal avenue for contesting the patent. My research turned up two additional U.S. patents on *sangre de drago* (3,694,557 and 3,809,749) dating to the early 1970s and now presumably expired. According to King it is theoretically possible for Shaman to use its patent protection to seek legal injunctions against the importation of *Croton* resin by natural-products firms marketing the substance for purposes similar to those of SP-303. But, King points out, such litigation would cost far more than the economic value of the patent itself unless SP-303 has a dramatic change of fortune as a pharmaceutical product.

48. Plotkin, *Tales of a Shaman's Apprentice,* 15–16. Ivan A. Ross, *Medicinal Plants of the World: Chemical Constituents, Traditional and Modern Medicinal Uses* (Totowa, N.J.: Humana Press, 1999), 109–116. Judith Sumner, *The Natural History of Medicinal Plants* (Portland, Ore.: Timber Press, 2000), 139–140.

49. Sources include Robert L. Noble, "The Discovery of the Vinca Alkaloids—Chemotherapeutic Agents against Cancer," *Biochemistry and Cell Biology* 68 (1990): 1344–51; Gordon H. Svoboda, "The Role of the Alkaloids of Catharanthus Roseus (L.) G.Don. (Vinca Rosea) and Their Derivatives in Cancer Chemotherapy," in *Plants: The Potentials for Extracting Protein, Medicines, and Other Useful Chemicals—Workshop Proceedings* (Washington: U.S. Congress, Office of Technology Assessment, 1983), 154–169; letter by Irving S. Johnson, *Science* 257 (1992): 860; and information supplied by Norman R. Farnsworth. Svoboda, Johnson, and Farnsworth worked for Eli Lilly & Co. I am grateful for Dr. Farnsworth's help in sorting out the details of this complicated history.

50. Michael A. Heller, "The Tragedy of the Anti-Commons: Property in the Transition from Marx to Markets," *Harvard Law Review* 111 (1998): 621–688; Michael A. Heller and Rebecca S. Eisenberg, "Can Patents Deter Innovation? The Anticommons in Biomedical Research,"

Science 280, no. 5364 (1998): 698–702. Heller's anticommons is an explicit reference to Garrett Hardin's essay "The Tragedy of the Commons," *Science* 162 (1968): 1243–48.

51. See Kelly Bannister and Katherine Barrett, "Challenging the Status Quo in Ethnobotany: A New Paradigm for Publication May Protect Cultural Knowledge and Traditional Resources," *Cultural Survival Quarterly* 24, no. 4 (2001): 10–13; Victor Manuel Toledo, "New Paradigms for a New Ethnobotany: Reflections on the Case of Mexico," in *Ethnobotany: Evolution of a Discipline,* ed. Richard Evans Schultes and Siri von Reis (Portland, Ore.: Dioscorides Press, 1995), 75–88. ICBG projects outside Latin America have not been completely immune to criticism. Genetic Resources Action International (GRAIN), for instance, has alleged that an ICBG project in Vietnam and Laos offers only lip service to benefit sharing; see Isabelle Delforge, "Laos at the Crossroads," <www.grain.org/publications/seed-01-6-2-en.cfm>, accessed 24 Oct. 2001. Still, the intensity of this criticism is modest in comparison to the furor over ICBG-Maya. On successful bioprospecting projects in Latin America, see Fundación Sabiduría Indígena and Brij Kothari, "Rights to the Benefits of Research: Compensating Indigenous Peoples for Their Intellectual Contribution," *Human Organization* 56, no. 2 (1997): 127–137; Jennie Wood Sheldon, Michael J. Balick, and Sarah A. Laird, *Medicinal Plants: Can Utilization and Conservation Coexist?* (New York: New York Botanical Garden, 1997). And see Russel L. Barsh et al., *The North American Pharmaceutical Industry and Research Involving Indigenous Knowledge* (Fredericksburg, Va.: First Peoples Worldwide, 2001).

52. John Madeley, "Living off the Fat of the Land," *Financial Times* (London), 1 Dec. 2001, 2. Victoria Griffith, "Samoa to Receive Percentage of AIDS Drug Profits," *Financial Times* (London), 13 Dec. 2001, 3. The U.S. patent for prostratin is 5,599,839.

53. Stephen B. Brush, "Is Common Heritage Outmoded?" in *Valuing Local Knowledge: Indigenous People and Intellectual Property Rights,* ed. Stephen B. Brush and Doreen Stabinsky (Washington: Island Press, 1996), 143–164.

54. See Bronwyn Parry, *Biocommodities: Exploring the Social and Spa-*

tial Dynamics of Trade in Genetic Materials (New York: Columbia University Press, 2003).

55. Andrew Pollack, "Drug Makers Wrestle with World's New Rules," *New York Times,* 21 Oct. 2001, sec. 3, 1. Leslie Wayne and Melody Petersen, "A Muscular Lobby Rolls Up Its Sleeves," ibid., 4 Nov. 2001, sec. 3, 1. Families USA, *Profiting from Pain: Where Prescription Drug Dollars Go,* Publication no. 02–105 (Washington: Families USA, 2002).

56. On the negative impact of the Convention on Biological Diversity on basic science in the tropics, see Andrew C. Revkin, "Biologists Sought a Treaty: Now They Fault It," *New York Times,* 7 May 2000, F1. Ironically, new research suggests that tropical rain forests may be less promising as a source of medicinal plants than are the scrubby, disturbed habitats that surround them. It seems that weeds figure far more prominently in the healing traditions of groups like the Tzeltal Maya than do plants from primary forest areas. See John R. Stepp and Daniel E. Moerman, "The Importance of Weeds in Ethnopharmacology," *Journal of Ethnopharmacology* 75 (2001): 19–23.

5. Negotiating Mutual Respect

1. S. C. Simms, "A Wheel-Shaped Stone Monument in Wyoming," *American Anthropologist* 5 (1903): 108.

2. James M. Calder, *The Majorville Cairn and Medicine Wheel Site, Alberta,* Archaeological Survey of Canada, Paper no. 62 (Ottawa: National Museums of Canada, 1977).

3. Fred Chapman, "The Bighorn Medicine Wheel, 1988–1999," *Cultural Resource Management* 22, no. 3 (1999): 5–10. I wish to thank Fred Chapman and other staff members of Wyoming SHPO for the many courtesies extended to me during my visit to their office in 1998.

4. According to the Forest Service, offerings left at the site are periodically removed by Northern Cheyenne and Crow ritual specialists. Rangers sometimes collect and remove fabric offerings that have been blown away from the immediate vicinity of the wheel by high winds. They also remove "nontraditional" offerings left by tourists, including

crystals and arrowheads purchased at local gift shops. I am grateful to Dave Myers, District Ranger, Bighorn National Forest, for this information.

5. Elder William Tall Bull and Nicole Price, "The Battle for the Bighorn Medicine Wheel," in *Kunaitupii: Coming Together on Native Sacred Sites,* ed. Brian O. K. Reeves and Margaret A. Kennedy (Calgary: Archaeological Society of Alberta, 1993), 96.

6. Chapman, "Bighorn Medicine Wheel," 7–9.

7. See R. McGreggor Cawley, *Federal Land, Western Anger: The Sagebrush Rebellion and Environmental Politics* (Lawrence: University Press of Kansas, 1993).

8. Jeffrey R. Hanson and Sally Chirinos, *Ethnographic Overview and Assessment of Devils Tower National Monument,* Wyoming, NPS D-36 (Denver: National Park Service, 1997), 31.

9. Ibid., 13–17.

10. National Park Service, *Final Climbing Management Plan,* Devils Tower National Monument, 1995, unpaginated.

11. Steven C. Moore, "Sacred Sites and Public Lands," in *Handbook of American Indian Religious Freedom,* ed. Christopher Vecsey (New York: Crossroad, 1991), 83; President William J. Clinton, Executive Order 13007, "Indian Sacred Sites," 24 May 1996, sec. 1; Patricia L. Parker and Thomas F. King, *Guidelines for Evaluating and Documenting Traditional Cultural Properties,* National Register Bulletin 38 (Washington: Government Printing Office, 1990). See also Anastasia P. Winslow, "Sacred Standards: Honoring the Establishment Clause in Protecting Native American Sacred Sites," *Arizona Law Review* 38 (1996): 1291–1343.

12. From meeting minutes, 29–30 Mar. 1996, Rapid City, S.D., National Park Service, Devils Tower National Monument; archived at the Wyoming State Historic Preservation Office, Cheyenne.

13. Quoted letters are from files of the Wyoming State Historic Preservation Office. "Cubin Bill Would Block Devils Tower Name Change," *Casper Star Tribune,* 4 Sept. 1996. The proposed naming compromise is outlined by Deborah O. Liggett, then superintendent of Devils Tower National Monument, in a briefing paper dated 11 Feb. 1997.

14. Interview with Chas Cartwright, 6 Aug. 1998.

15. See Cawley, *Federal Land, Western Anger,* 165–166.

16. This and subsequent quotations are from the defendant-intervenors' brief dated 26 Mar. 1997 for case D.C. no. 96-CV-063-D, the Federal District Court decision of Judge William Downes, 2 Apr. 1998, and the Decision of the U.S. Court of Appeals, Tenth Circuit, 26 Apr. 1999.

17. Friends of Devils Tower, "Tolerance not Segregation," <www.devils-tower.com/freedom/index.html>, accessed 7 June 1999.

18. Interview with Francis Brown, 7 Aug. 1998.

19. On Arizona, see "Tribe Says Boynton Canyon Site in Ruins," *Camp Verde Journal,* 29 May 1991; and "Forest Service Feels Impact of New Agers," *Arizona Daily Sun,* 2 Oct. 1993. I am grateful to Peter J. Pilles Jr., Forest Archaeologist, Coconino National Forest, for bringing these documents to my attention. And see Elazar Barkan, *The Guilt of Nations: Restitution and Negotiating Historical Injustices* (New York: Norton, 2000), 204–213. Quotations are from meeting minutes, 29–30 Mar. 1996, Rapid City, S.D., National Park Service, Devils Tower National Monument; archived at the Wyoming State Historic Preservation Office.

20. NPS sign quoted in an affidavit submitted by Vanessa Julliette Jimenez, a legal researcher, in support of defendants in *Bear Lodge Multiple Use Association v. Babbitt,* U.S. District Court, Wyoming, 96-CV-063-D, 21 Mar. 1997, 3.

21. "Devils Tower Closure Is Not about Religion," Mountain States Legal Foundation, June 1997, <www.mslf.net/html/june_97.htm>, accessed 5 June 1998.

22. Quoted in 485 U.S. 439, part I.

23. See Christopher A. Crain, "Free Exercise of Religion and Indian Burial Grounds," *Harvard Journal of Law and Public Policy* 12, no. 1 (1990): 246–251; Robert J. Miller, "Correcting Supreme Court 'Errors': American Indian Response to *Lyng v. Northwest Indian Cemetery Protective Association,*" *Environmental Law* 20, no. 4 (1990): 1037–62; Joshua D. Rievman, "Judicial Scrutiny of Native American Free Exercise Rights: Lyng and the Decline of the Yoder Doctrine," *Boston College Environmental Affairs Law Review* 17, no. 1 (1989): 169–199.

24. Quoted in Rievman, "Judicial Scrutiny," 195. The potential spillover effect from a case ostensibly based on the free exercise of native reli-

gion is evident in a lawsuit filed in U.S. District Court, Minnesota, in 1999 by a consortium of Minnesota logging interests. The suit alleges that the U.S. Forest Service is promoting the establishment of religion by limiting logging activities in deference to the wishes of several environmentalist groups that promote the religion of "Deep Ecology." The suit further claims that the Forest Service's restriction of logging demonstrates that it has shifted "away from multiple-use of national forests in line with the theological dictates of Deep Ecology on the sanctity of non-human nature." See *Associated Contract Loggers, Inc., and Olson Logging, Inc. v. United States Forest Service et al.*, 99–1485 JMR/RLE.

25. Meeting minutes, NPS consultation with tribal representatives, 29–30 Mar. 1996, Rapid City, S.D., 10; archived at the Wyoming State Historic Preservation Office.

26. U.S. District Court, Wyoming, 2 Apr. 1998, *Bear Lodge Multiple Use Association v. Babbitt*, 96-CV-063-D.

27. U.S. Court of Appeals, Tenth Circuit, 98–8021, 26 Apr. 1999.

28. Chapman, "Bighorn Medicine Wheel," 8.

29. Mary Ann Glendon, *Rights Talk: The Impoverishment of Political Discourse* (New York: Free Press, 1991), 171.

30. "Why the Access Fund Did Not Support the Devils Tower Lawsuit," *Access Notes* 15, <www.outdoorlink/accessfund/notes/v15/more.html>, accessed 6 June 1999.

6. At the Edge of the Indigenous

1. I have drawn largely on the following sources and on interviews I conducted in Australia in 1997: Diane Bell, *Ngarrindjeri Wurruwarrin: A World That Is, Was, and Will Be* (North Melbourne: Spinifex, 1998); Ron Brunton, "The Hindmarsh Island Bridge and the Credibility of Australian Anthropology," *Anthropology Today* 12, no. 4 (Aug. 1996): 2–7; Ron Brunton, "Hindmarsh Island and the Hoaxing of Australian Anthropology," *Quadrant* 43, no. 5 (May 1998): 11–17; Philip A. Clarke, "Response to 'Secret Women's Business: The Hindmarsh Island Affair'," *Journal of Australian Studies* 50/51 (1996): 141–149; Chris Kenny, *"It*

Would Be Nice If There Was Some Women's Business": The Story behind the Hindmarsh Island Affair (Potts Point, N.S.W.: Duffy and Snellgrove, 1996); Greg Mead, *A Royal Omission: A Critical Summary of the Evidence Given to the Hindmarsh Island Bridge Royal Commission with an Alternative Report* (Adelaide: Self-published, 1995); Robert Tonkinson, "Anthropology and Aboriginal Tradition: The Hindmarsh Island Bridge Affair and the Politics of Interpretation," *Oceania* 68, no. 1 (1997): 1–26; and three essays by James F. Weiner, "Must Our Informants Mean What They Say?" *Canberra Anthropology* 20 (1997): 82–95; "Culture in a Sealed Envelope: The Concealment of Australian Aboriginal Heritage and Tradition in the Hindmarsh Island Bridge Affair," *Journal of the Royal Anthropological Institute* (N.S.) 5 (1999): 193–210; and "Religion, Belief and Action: The Case of Ngarrindjeri 'Women's Business' on Hindmarsh Island, South Australia, 1994–1996," *Australian Journal of Anthropology* 13 (2002): 51–71.

2. Bell, *Ngarrindjeri,* 110.

3. See esp. Ken Gelder and Jane M. Jacobs, *Uncanny Australia: Sacredness and Identity in a Postcolonial Nation* (Melbourne: University of Melbourne Press, 1998).

4. Bell, *Ngarrindjeri,* 523–524, 541, 568–594; Kenny, *Women's Business,* 109.

5. Kenny, *Women's Business,* 199.

6. See Anthony Moran, "Aboriginal Reconciliation: Transformations in Settler Nationalism," *Melbourne Journal of Politics* 25, no. 1 (1998): 101–131.

7. Ben Hills, "Trouble in the Myth Business," *Sydney Morning Herald,* 3 July 1999.

8. Bell, *Ngarrindjeri,* 537.

9. Ibid., 415. Quotation from Kim Bullimore, "Australians Denounce Their Racist Government," *Women in Action,* <www.isis women.org>, no. 2, 2001, accessed 3 Feb. 2002.

10. Tonkinson, "Anthropology and Aboriginal Tradition," 6.

11. See Brian D. Haley and Larry R. Wilcoxon, "Anthropology and the Making of Chumash Tradition," *Current Anthropology* 38, no. 5 (1997): 761–794; Jon McVey Erlandson et al., "The Making of Chumash

Tradition: Replies to Haley and Wilcoxon," *Current Anthropology* 39, no. 4 (1998): 477–512.

12. The figure of 3,000 is from Haley and Wilcoxon, "Anthropology and the Making of Chumash Tradition," 762. According to the 1990 census, there are 3,208 people self-identified as Chumash; see U.S. Bureau of the Census, *1990 Census of Population, Characteristics of American Indians by Tribe and Language* (1990 CP-3-7), 7. The 1990 figure is 120 percent higher than that in 1980, suggesting that more people are choosing to emphasize their Chumash descent and, in an unknown number of cases, inventing genealogical links to Indian ancestors. I am grateful to Brian Haley for providing this information.

13. Haley and Wilcoxon, "Anthropology and the Making of Chumash Tradition," 767; see also Brian D. Haley and Larry R. Wilcoxon, "Point Conception and the Chumash Land of the Dead: Revisions from Harrington's Notes," *Journal of California and Great Basin Anthropology* 21, no. 2 (1999): 213–235.

14. Peter Matthiessen, *Indian Country* (New York: Viking, 1984), 230–231, 228; Haley and Wilcoxon, "Anthropology and the Making of Chumash Tradition," 769.

15. Haley and Wilcoxon were not the first to express doubt about the genealogical claims of Traditionalists. See, e.g., Mary I. O'Connor, "Environmental Impact Review and the Construction of Contemporary Chumash Ethnicity," in *NAPA Bulletin* 8, *Negotiating Ethnicity: The Impact of Anthropological Theory and Practice,* ed. Susan Emley Keefe (Washington: National Association for the Practice of Anthropology, 1989), 9–17; Johnny P. Flynn and Gary Laderman, "Purgatory and the Powerful Dead: A Case Study of Native American Repatriation," *Religion and American Culture* 4, no. 1 (Winter 1994): 51–75.

16. U.N. document reproduced in Tony Simpson, *Indigenous Heritage and Self-Determination: The Cultural and Intellectual Property Rights of Indigenous Peoples* (Copenhagen: International Work Group in Indigenous Affairs, 1997), 193.

17. Theo Radic', "The Chumash as Keepers of the Western Gate," *Acta Americana* 8, no. 1 (2000): 37.

18. See esp. Weiner, "Religion, Belief and Action." I am grateful to James Weiner for providing access to an early draft of this essay.

19. Hank Meshorer, "The Sacred Trail to Zuni Heaven: A Study in the Law of Prescriptive Easements," in *Zuni and the Courts: A Struggle for Sovereign Land Rights,* ed. E. Richard Hart (Lawrence: University Press of Kansas, 1995), 216. See also E. Richard Hart, "Protection of Kolhu/Wala:Wa ('Zuni Heaven'): Litigation and Legislation," ibid., 199–207.

20. Bell, *Ngarrindjeri,* 218–219.

21. Samuel D. Warren and Louis D. Brandeis, "The Right to Privacy," *Harvard Law Review* 4 (1890): 193; James L. Nolan Jr., *The Therapeutic State: Justifying Government at Century's End* (New York: New York University Press, 1998), 18–19.

22. Sources for this and the following paragraphs are Bell, *Ngarrindjeri,* 224–225, and Eugene E. Ruyle, "Comment on 'The Making of Chumash Tradition,'" *Current Anthropology* 39, no. 4 (1998): 489. See also Philip J. Deloria, *Playing Indian* (New Haven: Yale University Press, 1998).

23. David Lowenthal, *The Heritage Crusade and the Spoils of History* (Cambridge: Cambridge University Press, 1998), 121, 196, 250.

24. See Angela Gonzales, "The (Re)Articulation of American Indian Identity: Maintaining Boundaries and Regulating Access to Ethnically Tied Resources," *American Indian Culture and Research Journal* 44, no. 4 (1998): 199–225. The legal scholar L. Scott Gould notes that American Indians have the highest rate of ethnic intermarriage of any ethnic/racial group in the United States. Gould, "Mixing Bodies and Beliefs: The Predicament of Tribes," *Columbia Law Review* 101 (2001): 759. On Aboriginal Australian intermarriage and identity see Alan Gray, *The Explosion of Aboriginality: Components of Indigenous Population Growth* (Canberra: Centre for Aboriginal Economic Policy Research, 1997); see also Boyd Hunter, "Assessing the Validity of Intercensal Comparisons of Indigenous Australians, 1986–96," *Journal of the Australian Population Association* 15, no. 1 (1998): 51–67.

25. Gray, *Explosion of Aboriginality,* 14.

26. See Gould, "Mixing Bodies and Beliefs."

27. James Clifford, "Identity in Mashpee," in Clifford, *The Predicament of Culture: Twentieth-Century Ethnography, Literature, and Art* (Cambridge, Mass.: Harvard University Press, 1988), 302.

28. Quotations from Mexica Movement web pages, including <www.mexica-movement.org>, accessed 2 Aug. 2000, and <www.kal pulli.org/founding/html>, accessed 30 July 2000. See also Pauline Arrillaga, "Indigenous Mexicans Fight to Preserve Heritage," *Times-Picayune* (New Orleans), 31 Dec. 2000, 25.

29. See *Hueco Tanks State Historical Park, Public Use Plan 2000* (Austin: Texas Parks and Wildlife, 2000), 17–19. I am grateful to Margaret Howard and Karen Harry of Texas Parks and Wildlife for information about the permitting process.

30. Sources on the Washitaw Nation include a history provided by the Southern Poverty Law Center, <www.splcenter.org>, and Africa News Service, "Blacks Also Owned Miles of US Pre-Columbian Lands," 25 May 2001, accessed on Lexis-Nexis. And see Jonathan Friedman, "Indigenous Struggles and the Discreet Charm of the Bourgeoisie," *Australian Journal of Anthropology* 10 (1999): 1–14.

31. The reflections of Taiaiake Alfred, a political scientist of Mohawk descent, illustrate the complexity of this issue. Alfred sees both the "cold linearity of blood quantum" and the "tortured weakness of self-identification" as creations of the colonial state. He insists that native communities have the right to define for themselves who they are. But what of native people who aren't easily identified with a community? Discussing the Canadian situation, Alfred asserts: "Bluntly speaking, Native communities should not be expected to clean up the mess created by white society, and to further undermine their nationhood in order to accommodate people whose only connection to Native communities is a legal status ascribed to them by the state." See Taiaiake Alfred, *Peace, Power, Righteousness: An Indigenous Manifesto* (Oxford: Oxford University Press, 1999), 84–88.

32. Quotation from Justice von Doussa's ruling in *Chapman v. Luminis Pty. Ltd.* (No 5) [2001] FCA 1106 (21 Aug. 2001). See also "After the Storm: The Tiny Island Community of Goolwa Recovers from Its

Battle of the Bridge," *Time International,* 5 Mar. 2001, 12; Ron Brunton, "Secrets and Lies," *Courier Mail* (Brisbane), 1 Sept. 2001, 32; Ephraem Chifley, "Mired by Hindmarsh," *Courier Mail* (Brisbane), 3 Sept. 2001, 11.

33. Gelder and Jacobs, *Uncanny Australia,* 130, 134.

7. Native Heritage in the Iron Cage

1. Douglas J. Nakashima, "Astute Observers on the Sea Ice Edge: Inuit Knowledge as a Basis for Arctic Co-Management," in *Traditional Ecological Knowledge: Concepts and Cases,* ed. Julian T. Inglis (Ottawa: International Program on Traditional Ecological Knowledge and the International Development Research Centre, 1993), 99–110.

2. Here I use TEK in preference to alternatives that appear with equal frequency in the literature, "traditional knowledge" (TK) and "indigenous knowledge" (IK). The literature on TEK is growing at a remarkable rate, but arctic and subarctic regions still tend to be disproportionately represented. See George Wenzel, "Traditional Ecological Knowledge and Inuit: Reflections on TEK Research and Ethics," *Arctic* 52, no. 2 (1999): 113–124.

3. See Paul Nadasdy, "The Politics of TEK: Power and the 'Integration' of Knowledge," *Arctic Anthropology* 36 (1999): 1–18; Marc G. Stevenson, "Indigenous Knowledge in Environmental Assessment," *Arctic* 49 (1996): 278–291; Roy Ellen, Peter Parkes, and Alan Bicker, eds., *Indigenous Environmental Knowledge and Its Transformations: Critical Anthropological Perspectives* (Amsterdam: Harwood Academic, 2000).

4. Albert Howard and Frances Widdowson, "Traditional Knowledge Threatens Environmental Assessment," *Policy Options* (Montreal), Nov. 1997, 35; Brian Laghi, "Tempest in a Teepee: Getting into the Spirit of Things," *Globe and Mail,* 9 Aug. 1997, D1–2.

5. David J. Stephenson Jr., "A Comment on Recent Developments in the Legal Protection of Traditional Resource Rights," *High Plains Applied Anthropology* 16 (1996): 114–121; Vandana Shiva, "Reductionism and Regeneration: A Crisis in Science," in *Ecofeminism,* ed. Maria Mies and Vandana Shiva (London: Zed Books, 1993), 22; Taiaiake Alfred,

Peace, Power, Righteousness: An Indigenous Manifesto (Oxford: Oxford University Press, 1999), 147–148; Alexis A. Lury, "Official Insignia, Culture, and Native Americans," *Journal of Intellectual Property* 1, no. 2 (2000), 146, <www.kentlaw.edu/student_orgs/jip>; Joshua D. Rievman, "Judicial Scrutiny of Native American Free Exercise Rights: Lyng and the Decline of the Yoder Doctrine," *Boston College Environmental Affairs Law Review* 17, no. 1 (1989): 193–195; Gail K. Sheffield, *The Arbitrary Indian: The Indian Arts and Crafts Act of 1990* (Norman: University of Oklahoma Press, 1997), 126; Tressa Berman, "Indigenous Arts, (Un)Titled," in *Safeguarding Traditional Cultures: A Global Assessment,* ed. Peter Seitel (Washington: Center for Folklife and Cultural Heritage, Smithsonian Institution, 2001), 166–172. See also Wendy Nelson Espeland and Mitchell L. Stevens, "Commensuration as a Social Process," *Annual Reviews in Sociology* 24 (1998): 313–343.

6. Jonathan Friedman, "Indigenous Struggles and the Discreet Charm of the Bourgeoisie," *Australian Journal of Anthropology* 10 (1999): 7. See also Lawrence Rosen, "The Right to Be Different: Indigenous Peoples and the Quest for a Unified Theory," *Yale Law Journal* 107, no. 1 (Oct. 1997): 227–259.

7. Erica-Irene Daes, *Protection of the Heritage of Indigenous People,* United Nations, Office of the High Commissioner for Human Rights no. E.97.XIV.3 (Geneva, 1997), iii and 4.

8. Ibid., 21–22.

9. Ibid., 3–4.

10. Max Weber, *Political Writings,* ed. Peter Lassman and Ronald Speirs (Cambridge: Cambridge University Press, 1994), 158. See also Rogers Brubaker, *The Limits of Rationality: An Essay on the Social and Moral Thought of Max Weber* (New York: Routledge, 1984).

11. See Wendy Brown, "Freedom's Silences," in *Censorship and Silencing: Practices of Cultural Regulation,* ed. Robert C. Post (Los Angeles: Getty Research Institute for the Arts and Humanities, 1998), 313–327; Madhavi Sunder, "Intellectual Property and Identity Politics: Playing with *Fire,*" *Journal of Gender, Race, and Justice* 4, no. 1 (2000): 69–98; Sunder, "Cultural Dissent," *Stanford Law Review* 54, no. 3 (2001): 495–

567; Veena Das, "Cultural Rights and the Definition of Community," in *The Rights of Subordinated Peoples,* ed. Oliver Mendelsohn and Upendra Baxi (Delhi: Oxford University Press, 1994), 117–158.

12. Sheffield, *Arbitrary Indian,* esp. 151–158. Kay WalkingStick, "Indian Arts and Crafts Act: Counterpoint," *Akwe:Kon Journal,* Fall/ Winter 1994, 116–117. And see William J. Hapiuk Jr., "Of Kitsch and Kachinas: A Critical Analysis of the Indian Arts and Crafts Act of 1990," *Stanford Law Review* 53 (2001): 1009–75; Molly H. Mullin, *Culture in the Marketplace: Gender, Art, and Value in the American Southwest* (Durham, N.C.: Duke University Press, 2001).

13. Julie Hollowell-Zimmer, "Marked by the Silver Hand: Intellectual Property Protection and the Market in Alaska Native Arts and Crafts," in *The Protection of Indigenous Intellectual Property Rights: Facing Legal Obstacles, Developing Innovative Solutions,* ed. Mary Riley (Walnut Creek, Calif.: Altamira Press, forthcoming). I am grateful to Julie Hollowell-Zimmer for providing me with a prepublication draft of her essay.

14. See Darrell A. Posey and Graham Dutfield, *Beyond Intellectual Property: Toward Traditional Resource Rights for Indigenous Peoples and Local Communities* (Ottawa: International Development Research Centre, 1996), 150–152. Quotation from Article 16 of the Panamanian law (Act no. 20, June 2000), <www.usask.ca/nativelaw/panama.doc>, accessed 7 Feb. 2002.

15. Paul Kuruk, "Protecting Folklore under Modern Intellectual Property Regimes: A Reappraisal of the Tensions between Individual and Communal Rights in Africa and the United States," *American University Law Review* 48, no. 4 (1999): 799–806, 816, 848.

16. See John R. Bowen, "Should We Have a Universal Concept of 'Indigenous Peoples' Rights'? Ethnicity and Essentialism in the Twenty-First Century," *Anthropology Today* 16, no. 4 (Aug. 2000): 12–16. The legal scholar Martha Minow observes that when governments get into the business of assigning people to categories and assigning rights to those categories, "the use of identity groupings can injure at the same time as it can help . . . When institutions, like courts and agencies, do our

thinking for us, it is easy to forget the human authors of entrenched categories." Minow, *Not Only for Myself: Identity Politics and the Law* (New York: New Press, 1997), 64.

17. See Clifford Geertz, *Available Light: Anthropological Reflections on Philosophical Topics* (Princeton: Princeton University Press, 2000), 68–88; Jean Jackson, "Is There a Way to Talk about Making Culture without Making Enemies?" *Dialectical Anthropology* 14 (1989): 127–143; Mary Margaret Steedly, "What Is Culture? Does It Matter?" in *Field Work: Sites in Literary and Cultural Studies,* ed. Marjorie Garber, Paul B. Franklin, and Rebecca L. Walkowitz (New York: Routledge, 1996), 19–25. On boundaries and cultural rights, see Marilyn Strathern, "Potential Property: Intellectual Rights and Property in Persons," *Social Anthropology* 4, no. 1 (1996): 22–23.

18. See Brian Barry, *Culture and Equality* (Cambridge, Mass.: Harvard University Press, 2001), esp. 146–154; Monique Deveaux, *Cultural Pluralism and Dilemmas of Justice* (Ithaca, N.Y.: Cornell University Press, 2000); Will Kymlicka, ed., *The Rights of Minority Cultures* (New York: Oxford University Press, 1995); Richard H. Thompson, "Ethnic Minorities and the Case for Collective Rights," *American Anthropologist* 99, no. 4 (1997): 786–798; Simon Harrison, "Identity as a Scarce Resource," *Social Anthropology* 7, no. 3 (1999): 239–251; Stuart Kirsch, "Lost Worlds: Environmental Disaster, 'Cultural Loss,' and the Law," *Current Anthropology* 42, no. 2 (2001): 167–198.

19. Terence Dougherty, "Group Rights to Cultural Survival: Intellectual Property Rights in Native American Cultural Symbols," *Columbia Human Rights Law Review* 29 (Spring 1998): 386, 399. See also Kirsch, "Lost Worlds"; Barry, *Culture and Equality,* 44–50. A 2002 *Sports Illustrated* survey of Indian attitudes toward Native American sports names and mascots revealed that 69 percent of Indians did not find the Redskins name offensive. See S. L. Price, "The Indian Wars: The Campaign against Indian Nicknames and Mascots Presumes That They Offend Native Americans—But Do They?" *Sports Illustrated,* 4 Mar. 2002, 66–72.

20. U.S. data from Indian Health Service, <info.ihs.gov/People/

People4.pdf>, accessed 30 Oct. 2001. Canadian data from Indian and Northern Affairs Canada, <www.ainc-inac.gc.ca/gs/dem_e.html>, accessed 30 Oct. 2001. Australian and New Zealand data from Australian Bureau of Statistics, <www.abs.gov.au>, "Population: Special Article— Aboriginal and Torres Strait Islander Australians: A Statistical Profile from the 1996 Census," accessed 30 Oct. 2001.

21. See Bruce Weber, "Reggae Rhythms Speak to an Insular Tribe," *New York Times,* 19 Sept. 1999, A1; "Questions for Sherman Alexie," *New York Times Magazine,* 5 Jan. 1997, 8; the documentary film *Buried Country* (dir. Andy Nehl, Film Australia, Ltd., 2000); Toby Lester, "Oh, Gods!" *Atlantic Monthly,* Feb. 2002, 37–45.

22. Doug Munro, "Who 'Owns' Pacific History?" *Journal of Pacific History* 29, no. 2 (1994): 232–237; Haunani-Kay Trask, "Natives and Anthropologists: The Colonial Struggle," *Contemporary Pacific* 3 (1991): 159–167.

23. *Who Owns the Past?* dir. N. Jed Riffe, 2001; transcript at <www.pbs.org/wotp/film_info/transcript/index.html>, accessed 25 Nov. 2001.

24. Readers who suspect that I exaggerate the extent to which some advocates for indigenous rights demand statutory control over the representation of native cultures in public forums are advised to consult an essay by the legal scholar Rebecca Tsosie, "Reclaiming Native Stories: An Essay on Cultural Appropriation and Cultural Rights," *Arizona State Law Journal* 34 (2002): 334.

25. For a defense of cultural sovereignty, see Wallace Coffey and Rebecca Tsosie, "Rethinking the Tribal Sovereignty Doctrine: Cultural Sovereignty and the Collective Future of Indian Nations," *Stanford Law and Policy Review* 12 (2001): 191–221.

26. Erica-Irene Daes, keynote address for the conference "Protecting Knowledge: Traditional Resource Rights in the New Millennium," Vancouver, Feb. 2000; text downloaded from <www.ubcic.bc.ca/Keynote.htm>, 27 Mar. 2000. And see, e.g., Tony Simpson, *Indigenous Heritage and Self-Determination: The Cultural and Intellectual Property Rights of Indigenous Peoples* (Copenhagen: International Work Group in Indigenous Affairs, 1997), 32–40.

27. Perhaps the iron cage is the wrong metaphor for the thoroughly managed representation of indigenous life evident in a new generation of aboriginal museums. An exemplary case is the Sapmi Magic Theater, a cultural education and entertainment facility located in Karasjok, Norway. According to publicity statements issued by BRC Imagination Arts of Burbank, California, one of the firms hired to develop the facility, the Sapmi Magic Theater uses "high-tech wizardry and special effects to celebrate the long history of the Sami people, one of the few indigenous peoples of Europe." BRC Imagination Arts website, <www.brcweb.com>, accessed 14 Dec. 2001. BRC's publicists note with pride: "The Sami people are trusting us with their most precious possession: their cultural heritage. That's a big responsibility." BRC drew on its prior success at Disney's EPCOT Center to deploy visual effects guaranteed to "stand people's hair on end." One wonders whether the iron cage into which indigenous heritage is being led will eventually come to resemble a theme park. (For this observation I acknowledge my debt to Stuart Kirsch, esp. his paper "Lost Tribes, Imaginary Indians and a Cultural Jurassic Park: The Mashantucket Pequot Casino," presented at the annual meeting of the American Anthropological Association, 1997.)

28. Hugh Brody, *Maps and Dreams* (New York: Pantheon, 1982), 275–276.

8. Finding Justice in the Global Commons

1. Similar dilemmas seem to be nearing resolution at California State University, Chico, over use of the Dorothy Morehead Hill Collection. Hill, an anthropologist who died in 1998, left CSU-Chico 350 audio tapes and 4,000 photographs accumulated in a lifetime of research among the Maidu, Pomo, Wintun, and other California Indian tribes. The university has convened an oversight committee, including several Indians from the region, that will determine whether access to parts of the collection will be restricted on grounds of cultural privacy. See Taran March, "A Legacy in Trust," *Chico Statements,* Spring 2002, 8–11.

2. Mary Ann Glendon, *Rights Talk: The Impoverishment of Political Discourse* (New York: Free Press, 1991).

3. John Gray, *Two Faces of Liberalism* (New York: New Press, 2000), 7, 117.

4. Monte Williams, "This New Year in Chinatown, Mock Fireworks," *New York Times,* 13 Feb. 1999, A17.

5. Clifford Geertz, *Available Light: Anthropological Reflections on Philosophical Topics* (Princeton: Princeton University Press, 2000), 78.

6. See Elazar Barkan, *The Guilt of Nations: Restitution and Negotiating Historical Injustices* (New York: Norton, 2000), esp. 344; John Torpey, "'Making Whole What Has Been Smashed': Reflections on Reparations," *Journal of Modern History* 73 (June 2001): 333–358.

7. For doubts about the wisdom of "trying to fit the circle of Indigenous intellectual property into the square of copyright discourse," see Ian McDonald, *Protecting Indigenous Intellectual Property: A Copyright Perspective,* Discussion Paper (Redfern, N.S.W.: Australian Copyright Council, 1998), 73.

8. Gary L Reback, "Patently Absurd," *Forbes ASAP,* Summer 2002, 46.

9. For arguments in favor of liberalizing intellectual property regimes, see Lawrence Lessig, *The Future of Ideas: The Fate of the Commons in a Connected World* (New York: Random House, 2001); Jessica Litman, *Digital Copyright* (Amherst, N.Y.: Prometheus Books, 2001); Siva Vaidhyanathan, *Copyrights and Copywrongs: The Rise of Intellectual Property and How It Threatens Creativity* (New York: New York University Press, 2001). On balancing reduced intellectual property rights for industry and increased protections for folkloric knowledge, see James Boyle, *Shamans, Software, and Spleens: Law and the Construction of the Information Society* (Cambridge, Mass.: Harvard University Press, 1996); Seth Shulman, *Owning the Future* (Boston: Houghton Mifflin, 1999). On public rights in artistic works, see Joseph L. Sax, *Playing Darts with a Rembrandt: Public and Private Rights in Cultural Treasures* (Ann Arbor: University of Michigan Press, 1999).

10. The Bellagio Declaration appears in Boyle, *Shamans, Software, and Spleens,* 192–200; it can also be found on the World Wide Web. Bellagio's emphasis on the pivotal role of Western notions of authorship has not held up well; see Vaidhyanathan, *Copyrights and Copywrongs,* 8–

11. I am increasingly persuaded by Lawrence Lessig's argument (in *The Future of Ideas*) that Western intellectual property law is better seen as a regulatory regime than as a system that codifies either authorship or property.

11. Lessig, *Future of Ideas,* 240–261; Daniel Akst, "It's Time for Teamwork on New Drugs," *New York Times,* 4 Nov. 2001, sec. 3, 4.

12. Carol M. Rose, "The Several Futures of Property: Of Cyberspace and Folk Tales, Emission Trades and Ecosystems," *Minnesota Law Review* 83, no. 1 (1998): esp. 139–143. And see two works by Stephen B. Brush, *Farmers' Bounty: The Survival of Crop Diversity in the Modern World* (New Haven: Yale University Press, forthcoming), and "Bio-Cooperation and the Benefits of Crop Genetic Resources: The Case of Mexican Maize," *World Development* 26 (1998): 755–766.

13. See Lessig, *Future of Ideas,* 109–110. Another legal scholar, Gelvina Rodríguez Stevenson, has suggested that laws protecting trade secrets offer a means of protecting indigenous knowledge. This argument pays insufficient attention to the transaction costs of litigating alleged violations of cultural secrets, especially in countries with poorly developed infrastructures and byzantine legal systems. Gelvina Rodríguez Stevenson, "Trade Secrets: The Secret to Protecting Indigenous Ethnobiological (Medicinal) Knowledge," *New York University Journal of International Law and Politics* 32 (2000): 1119–74.

14. RAFI, "Call to Dialogue or Call to 911?" 2 Nov. 2000, <www.rafi.org/web/docus/pdfs/geno2000nov2.pdf>, accessed 22 Jan. 2002; Rose, "Several Futures of Property," 133. I am grateful to Carol Rose for alerting me to the anticommons aspect of the demand that every native community using a given plant be granted a right to veto commercial use of it.

15. The status of plant patents in the United States was under a legal cloud for several years, but in December 2001 the Supreme Court affirmed their validity in its ruling in *J.E.M. Ag Supply, Inc. v. Pioneer Hi-Bred International, Inc.*

16. Here my position diverges from that of Marilyn Strathern, who observes that intellectual property offers a powerful rhetorical tool "pre-

cisely because it rolls so much up into a bundle . . . and precisely because it invokes property." Strathern, *Property, Substance and Effect: Anthropological Essays on Persons and Things* (London: Athlone, 1999), 201–203. I do not question the rhetorical utility of indigenous appeals to notions of intellectual property, but I worry that what for Strathern is merely a useful metaphor may be taken all too literally by policymakers and legislators.

17. Alan Wolfe, *Whose Keeper? Social Science and Moral Obligation* (Berkeley: University of California Press, 1989), 231.

18. Glendon, *Rights Talk,* 137. And see Michael Walzer, "The Civil Society Argument," in *Dimensions of Radical Democracy: Pluralism, Citizenship, and Community,* ed. Chantal Mouffe (New York: Verso, 1992), 89–107; Robert W. Hefner, "On the History and Cross-Cultural Possibility of a Democratic Ideal," in *Democratic Civility: The History and Cross-Cultural Possibility of a Modern Political Ideal,* ed. Robert W. Hefner (New Brunswick, N.J.: Transaction, 1998), 3–49.

19. Vine Deloria Jr., "Self-Determination and the Concept of Sovereignty," in *Native American Sovereignty,* ed. John R. Wunder (New York: Garland, 1999), 123.

20. "Maoris Win Lego Battle," *Guardian,* 31 Oct. 2001, 16.

21. See, e.g., Marc Galanter, "The Legal Malaise; or Justice Observed," *Law and Society Review* 19, no. 4 (1985): 545. See also Nicola Lacey, *Unspeakable Subjects: Feminist Essays in Legal and Social Theory* (Oxford: Hart, 1998), 8–10.

22. Jonathan Fenby, *France on the Brink* (New York: Arcade, 1999), 13.

23. Someone will undoubtedly argue that this passage is an act of cultural appropriation because it includes symbols and ritual figures arising from Hopi tradition, enacted by Hopi people, and fully understood only by Hopi religious experts. To make this claim is to deny my experience as a guest of the Hopi and as a participant, however unwilling, in one of the ritual's unscripted moments. An alternative to the obsession with cultural appropriation is to see the event as a multi-layered conversation, both within Hopi society and between Hopis and outsiders. I suspect that this particular moment had little effect on Hopis who wit-

nessed it. For me, though, it was an unforgettable lesson in other ways of expressing reverence—in this instance, with forms of humor alien to my own religious upbringing. It is precisely this kind of intercultural conversation that changes minds.

24. Jill D. Sweet, *Dances of the Tewa Pueblo Indians* (Santa Fe: School of American Research Press, 1985), 35–36.

Sources on Indigenous Cultural Rights

The literature on indigenous cultural property is voluminous. The Notes point to a range of sources, from the classic to the ephemeral, the esoteric to the populist, but I make no claim to comprehensiveness. The following are useful works, some of which have figured prominently in discussions of how best to defend the cultural resources of native peoples—music, design styles, folktales, botanical knowledge, religious practices, and the like—from unwanted use by outsiders. For links to online resources keyed to each chapter of this book, as well as general information on indigenous rights and intellectual property, see <www.williams.edu/go/native>.

Russel L. Barsh et al. *The North American Pharmaceutical Industry and Research Involving Indigenous Knowledge.* Fredericksburg, Va.: First Peoples Worldwide, 2001.

James Boyle. *Shamans, Software, and Spleens: Law and the Construction of the Information Society.* Cambridge, Mass.: Harvard University Press, 1996.

Simon Brascoupé and Howard Mann. *A Community Guide to Protecting Indigenous Knowledge.* Ottawa: Research and Analysis Directorate, Department of Indian Affairs and Northern Development, 2001.

Michael F. Brown "Can Culture Be Copyrighted?" *Current Anthropology* 39 (1998): 193–222.

Wallace Coffey and Rebecca Tsosie. "Rethinking the Tribal Sovereignty Doctrine: Cultural Sovereignty and the Collective Future of Indian Nations." *Stanford Law and Policy Review* 12 (2001): 191–221.

Rosemary J. Coombe. *The Cultural Life of Intellectual Properties: Authorship, Appropriation, and the Law.* Durham, N.C.: Duke University Press, 1998.

Cultural Survival, Inc. "Intellectual Property Rights: Culture as Commodity." *Cultural Survival Quarterly,* Winter 2001.

Erica-Irene Daes. *Protection of the Heritage of Indigenous People.* United Nations, Office of the High Commissioner for Human Rights, no. E.97.XIV.3 (Geneva, 1997).

Tom Greaves, ed. *Intellectual Property Rights for Indigenous Peoples: A Source Book.* Oklahoma City: Society for Applied Anthropology, 1994.

Andrew Gulliford. *Sacred Objects and Sacred Places: Preserving Tribal Traditions.* Boulder: University Press of Colorado, 2000.

Terri Janke. *Our Culture, Our Future: Report on Australian Indigenous Cultural and Intellectual Property Rights.* Surrey Hills, N.S.W.: Michael Frankel, 1998.

Vivien Johnson. *Copyrites: Aboriginal Art in the Age of Reproductive Technologies.* Sydney: National Indigenous Arts Advocacy Program, 1996.

Ian McDonald. *Protecting Indigenous Intellectual Property: A Copyright Perspective.* Redfern, N.S.W.: Australian Copyright Council, 1998.

Darrell A. Posey and Graham Dutfield. *Beyond Intellectual Property: Toward Traditional Resource Rights for Indigenous Peoples and Local Communities.* Ottawa: International Development Research Centre, 1996.

Mary Riley, ed. *The Protection of Indigenous Intellectual Property Rights: Facing Legal Obstacles, Developing Innovative Solutions.* Walnut Creek, Calif.: Altamira Press, forthcoming.

Anthony Seeger. "Ethnomusicologists, Archives, Professional Organizations, and the Shifting Ethics of Intellectual Property." In *Year-*

Sources

book for Traditional Music 1996, 87–105. New York: International Council for Traditional Music, 1996.

Peter Seitel, ed. *Safeguarding Traditional Cultures: A Global Assessment.* Washington: Center for Folklife and Cultural Heritage, Smithsonian Institution, 2001.

Tony Simpson. *Indigenous Heritage and Self-Determination: The Cultural and Intellectual Property Rights of Indigenous Peoples.* Copenhagen: International Work Group in Indigenous Affairs, 1997.

Marilyn Strathern. *Property, Substance and Effect: Anthropological Essays on Persons and Things.* London: Athlone Press, 1999.

Bruce Ziff and Pratima V. Rao, eds. *Borrowed Power: Essays on Cultural Appropriation.* New Brunswick, N.J.: Rutgers University Press, 1997.

Acknowledgments

Winston Churchill once said that for writers a book begins as an amusement, quickly becomes a seductress, and ends as a tyrant. As I shake off the tyranny of this work, which has taken me from simple curiosity about the riddles of cultural property to months of thinking about little else, I want to thank the people and institutions who helped me along the way.

On the institutional front, I am grateful to the National Endowment for the Humanities, whose fellowship program supported my sabbatical leave in 2001–2002, and to the Institute for Advanced Study, which provided me and my family with a congenial place to live and work during that year. Above all I wish to thank my home institution, Williams College, for offering an ideal setting for scholarship and teaching. My long-time colleagues in the Department of Anthropology and Sociology at Williams—David B. Edwards, Peter Just, Robert Jackall, Antonia Foias, and James L. Nolan Jr.—have been a constant source of encouragement. Beyond my own department, I benefited greatly from Gary J. Jacobsohn's knowledge of constitutional law and Mark C. Taylor's thoughts on everything else. I also wish to thank former president Harry C. Payne, whose financial support put this project in motion in 1997.

In Australia, the project drew on the hospitality and logistical help of Christopher Anderson, Julie Finlayson, James Fox, Colin Golvan and family, Martin Hardie, Terri Janke, Margaret Jolly, Francesca Merlan, James Weiner, Margie West, and Susan Woenne-Green. Justice John von Doussa of the Federal Court of Australia kindly granted me access to court records. Research in Wyoming was facilitated by Fred Chapman and other employees of the Wyoming State Historic Preservation Office, and by Chas Cartwright, then superintendent of Devils Tower National Monument. Lin Poyer and Robert Kelly were superb hosts during my visit to Laramie. In Arizona, the staff of the Hopi Cultural Preservation Office was very helpful, and I am grateful to have been invited by Peter Pilles Jr., archaeologist of the Coconino National Forest, on a memorable walking tour of petroglyphs not far from Flagstaff, during which he briefed me on the problem of New Age vandalism of archaeological sites. Where museum and archival practice is concerned, my tutors included Duane Anderson, Sylvia Kennick Brown, William L. Merrill, Willow Powers, Karen Underhill, and Diane Vogt-O'Connor. In matters legal, especially relating to intellectual property, I benefited from the expertise of Eleanor Meltzer and Dominic Keating of the United States Patent and Trademark Office in Washington.

Colleagues who responded to my bothersome questions about their areas of expertise included Kelly Bannister, Patricia Crown, Richard I. Ford, Brian Haley, James Howe, Steven King, Fred Myers, Robin Ridington, and Peter Whiteley. When conducting photo research, I received help from Duane Anderson, Diane Bird, Wade Davis, Sarah Demb, Laura Holt, Lee Hyeoma, Vivien Johnson, Lou Stancari, John Thiessen, James Weiner, and Wilma Wetterstrom. For other kinds of logistical support I owe thanks to Donna Chenail, the administrative secretary of my department at Williams, and Christine Ménard, whose gifts as a research librarian saved the day on innumerable occasions.

The following people were kind enough to read and comment on individual chapters: Kelly Bannister, Barbara Belejack, David Elpern, Richard I. Ford, L. Shane Greene, Brian Haley, Julie Hollowell-Zimmer, Courtney Jung, Steven King, Eleanor Meltzer, Molly Mullin, and Benjamin Orlove. Drafts of the entire book were evaluated critically by Sylvia Kennick Brown, Clifford Geertz, Robert Jackall, Stuart Kirsch, and William L. Merrill, as well as three anonymous readers for Harvard University Press. Special thanks are due Stuart Kirsch, who constantly prodded me with challenging questions. My gratitude does not implicate any of these friends and colleagues in the book's failings. Some of them, in fact, disagree vigorously with my approach to cultural and intellectual property. It is not their fault if I sometimes failed to heed their good advice.

My literary agent, Gerry McCauley, waited patiently for this project to unfold, and I greatly appreciate his expertise and wise counsel.

As always, it was a special pleasure to work with Joyce Seltzer, my editor at Harvard University Press, and with her able assistant David Lobenstine. I also owe thanks to Camille Smith, my HUP manuscript editor, for unsnarling tangled sentences, calming the turbulent waters of overwrought prose, and exiling mixed metaphors to their semantic Elbas.

Index

Index

Index

Index

Index

International Cooperative Biodiversity
Groups. *See* ICBG
Internet, 6, 35–36
Inuit, 205–206
Ishi (Yahi Indian), 18

Jackall, Robert, 269n20
Jacobs, Jane M., 204
Johnnie, Kathleen, 84, 85, 86–87

Kachinas, 19, 257n8
Kangaroo, as intellectual property, 2
Kartinyeri, Doreen, 175, 180
Kennewick Man, 223
Kenny, Chris, 180
King, Steven, 125–126, 127, 129–130, 131
Kiowa, 87–89, 151, 152, 163; pictographs,
201, 269n21
Know-how licenses, 241
Krauss, Michael, 270n29
Kuruk, Paul, 217

Lakota, 151–152, 153, 167, 179
Lame Deer, Archie Fire, 188, 189, 192
Land titles, 46–48, 49
Lange, David, 56
Language, 91; loss of native, 93, 248,
270n29
Latter-Day Saints, Church of Jesus Christ
of, 12, 244
Law, 7, 53–54, 197, 243, 246–247, 248–249;
and regulation of culture, 196, 226–227,
248; unintended consequences of, 213–
216, 217–218; customary, 217, 224, 225;
shadow of, 246–247. *See also Lex loci;*
Total Heritage Protection
Leary, Timothy, 96
Lego, 3, 246
Lessig, Lawrence, 5, 238, 296n10
Leura, Tim, 48
Lex loci, 225–226
Liberalism, 8–9, 30, 197, 219
Life-forms, patents on, 101–102, 241
Liggett, Deborah, 152
Limited Common Property (LCP), 239–
240

Little Bluff, 87–88
Lomayestewa, Lee Wayne, 18
Lomayesva, Casper, 223
Lowenthal, David, 15, 197
Lowie, Robert, 270n23
Lyng v. Northwest Indian Cemetery Protec-
tive Association, 164–167, 168

Mabo, Eddie, 46–47
Mabo decision (*Mabo and Others v.*
Queensland, No. 2), 46–47, 50, 177, 209
Maca (*Lepidium meyenii*), 2
MacLean, Donna Rawlinson, 102
Madagascar, 136–137
Madalena, James Roger, 92
Madonna (pop singer), 62
Magpie Geese and Waterlilies at the Water-
hole, 45, 49, 51, 54, 64
Mails, Thomas, 22
Mann, Charles C., 6
Mansfield, Lord, 56
Maori, 3, 246, 248
Marcus, George E., 36
Markham, Sir Clements, 105–106
Masayesva, Marilyn, 23
Masayesva, Vernon, 14–15
Mashpee, Mass., 199–200
Mass societies, 10
Mathias, Fern, 80
Mato Tipila. *See* Devils Tower National
Monument
Matthiessen, Peter, 188, 192
Maya, 116–117; rights to local knowledge,
121; romantic views of, 125
McDonald's Corporation, 99, 271n2
Medicine Wheel Coalition, 148, 159
Medicine wheels, 145. *See also* Bighorn
Medicine Wheel
Mennonite Library and Archives, 15
Mennonites, 11–12
Mera, Dr. Harry P., 69, 72
Merck, 128
Meshorer, Hank, 193–194
Mexica Movement, 200–201, 244
Mexico, 116–117, 246; bioprospecting in,
110

Index

Index

Personality, rights in, 38, 90
Peru, 97, 241, 246
Petroglyphs, 82, 84–87. *See also*
    Pictographs
Pharmaceutical industry, 4, 103–105, 142–
    143; and bioprospecting, 110–112
Pictographs, 83, 201, 269n21
Pino, Peter, 71, 91–92, 94
Pitjantjatjara, 33–34, 180, 260n26
Plant patents, 106–108
Plotkin, Mark, 97, 100
Plowman, Timothy, 97
Pluralism, 8, 212, 218, 231–232, 244, 251
Point Conception, Cal., 185, 188–190, 191–
    192, 195
Practice, as legal evidence, 191–194, 243–
    244
Prince (pop musician), 76
Privacy, 27–42, 59
Property, 3, 7, 38, 55. *See also* Limited
    Common Property
Prostratin, 141
*Protection of the Heritage of Indigenous Peo-
    ple. See* Daes Report
Public domain, 5, 7, 23, 24, 85, 108, 236,
    237, 239, 246
Publicity, right of, 38, 78, 261n31
Pueblo Indians, 30, 250–251. *See also* Hopi;
    Tewa; Zia Pueblo; Zuni
Pygmies, 61–62

Qotswisiuma, Clyde, 18–19, 20–21
Quinine *(Cinchona),* 106

Radical alterity, 185, 190
RAFI (Rural Advancement Foundation
    International), 113–114, 120–125, 132–133,
    134, 240, 275n21, 277n34
Rain forests, 97–100, 127, 143, 281n56
Rational drug design, 110, 141–142
Rationalism, 195, 212–213. *See also* Bureau-
    cracy; Law; Weber, Max
Reagan, Ronald, 149, 150
Reconciliation movement (Australia), 176,
    182
Reggae, 221, 223

Religion, 4–6, 40, 222; free exercise of,
    165–166, 175, 193
Rendon, Marcie, 25
Reparations, 7, 141, 234
Repatriation, 3, 15, 18, 86. *See also*
    NAGPRA
Rice, golden, 105
Right of integrity, 62
Rights, discourse of, 226, 231–232
*Rights of Indigenous Peoples, Draft U.N.
    Declaration of,* 16
Rockefeller Foundation, 3, 237
Root, Deborah, 3–4
Rose, Carol, 239, 240
Rosebud Sioux Tribal Court, 77–78
Rubber *(Hevea brasiliensis),* 106
Rural Advancement Foundation Interna-
    tional. *See* RAFI

Sacred sites, 9, 167; legal status of, 155,
    164–165, 190; Australian, 177
Sagebrush Rebellion, 149–150
Sami, 294n27
Samoa, 141
San, 141
Sangre de drago (Croton lechleri), 128, 132–
    135, 278n47
Santa Ynez, 186
Sapmi Magic Theater, 294n27
Sarasara, César, 114
Schultes, Richard Evans, 96–97, 98, 100,
    107, 143
Science, 206, 208
Secrecy, 13–14, 20, 30–34, 146, 175–176,
    179–180, 182, 296n13. *See also* Privacy
Secwepemc First Nation, 140
Serrano, Andres, 24
Shaman Pharmaceuticals, 125–135; benefit-
    sharing, 130–133; patents, 135, 287n47.
    See also Healing Forest Conservancy
Shamans, 96, 126, 133, 279n47. *See also*
    Traditional healers
Shije, Amadeo, 81–82
Shils, Edward, 42
Shiva, Vandana, 208
Shoshone, 145, 149, 152

Index

Index